THE FUTURE
OF
MERIT

THE FUTURE

OF

MERIT

TWENTY YEARS AFTER THE CIVIL SERVICE REFORM ACT

EDITED BY
JAMES P. PFIFFNER
AND
DOUGLAS A. BROOK

THE WOODROW WILSON CENTER PRESS
WASHINGTON, D.C.

THE JOHNS HOPKINS UNIVERSITY PRESS
BALTIMORE AND LONDON

EDITORIAL OFFICES

The Woodrow Wilson Center Press
One Woodrow Wilson Plaza
1300 Pennsylvania Avenue, N.W.
Washington, D.C. 20004-3027
Telephone 202-691-4010
wwics.si.edu

ORDER FROM

The Johns Hopkins University Press
P.O. Box 50370
Baltimore, Maryland 21211
Telephone 1-800-537-5487
www.press.jhu.edu

2 4 6 8 9 7 5 3 1

Library of Congress Cataloging-in-Publication Data

The future of merit : twenty years after the Civil Service Reform Act/edited by James P. Pfiffner and
   Douglas A. Brook.
      p.   cm.
Includes bibliographical references and index.
   ISBN 0-8018-6465-8 (paper : acid-free paper)
   1. Civil service reform—United States.   2. Civil service—United States.   I. Pfiffner, James P.
II. Brook, Douglas Alan, 1944–
   JK692 F87 2000
   352.6'3228'0973—dc21

                                                                                            00-009187

ABOUT THE CENTER

The Center is the living memorial of the United States of America to the nation's twenty-eighth president, Woodrow Wilson. Congress established the Woodrow Wilson Center in 1968 as an international institute for advanced study, "symbolizing and strengthening the fruitful relationship between the world of learning and the world of public affairs." The Center opened in 1970 under its own board of trustees.

In all its activities the Woodrow Wilson Center is a nonprofit, nonpartisan organization, supported financially by annual appropriations from the Congress, and by the contributions of foundations, corporations, and individuals. Conclusions or opinions expressed in Center publications and programs are those of the authors and speakers and do not necessarily reflect the views of the Center staff, fellows, trustees, advisory groups, or any individuals or organizations that provide financial support to the Center.

CONTENTS

FOREWORD

Woodrow Wilson was one of the founders of American public administration as a field of thought and practice. He understood as well as anyone that politics and administration are closely bound up with one another, necessarily so, at the top levels of government, and yet he knew that they must be kept distinct for analytical purposes. He understood thoroughly the need in the nation's civil service for competence of the highest order and of a peculiar kind, qualitatively different from other professions—an ability to transcend partisanship without slighting the values that are at stake in partisan controversy, a willingness to work loyally for for the government of the day, knowing that there will be other governments and other days, and most importantly the gift of critical intelligence ready to speak to the special problems of institutional integrity and capacity that are so often overlooked in the constant motion and changefulness of politics. He would have been deeply interested in the topics taken up in these essays, so hard to foresee from the vantage point of his life and times, and yet so close to its central preoccupations.

As the nation's official memorial to Wilson as a scholar and statesman, the Center is concerned mainly with research in the fields of history, government and public affairs. Its American program is devoted to furthering critical reflection on the relations between ideas and institutions in modern America, particularly the institutions of government. It aims to provide a forum in

Washington, D.C., for the presentation and assessment of new scholarly perspectives on the American experience, and to do what it can—through its fellowships, scholarly working groups, conferences and publications—to develop our knowledge of those long term, fundamental, underlying issues and conflicts that have shaped our understanding of the public and its problems.

Surely everyone would agree that the problems and prospects of the civil service system, here carefully examined twenty years after the passage of the Civil Service Reform Act of 1978, which carried such high hopes of so many in government, have a place in the list of fundamentals. A special word of thanks is due to all the authors whose work appears in this volume, but especially to James Pfiffner and Douglas Brooks, whose energy and leadership made the book possible.

Michael J. Lacey
Director, American Program
Woodrow Wilson International Center for Scholars

PREFACE

This book had its origins in a conference held at the Woodrow Wilson International Center for Scholars in November 1998 that brought together scholars and practitioners concerned with the Civil Service Reform Act of 1978. There have been only two major civil service laws enacted in the history of the United States. The Pendleton Act of 1883 created the merit system by providing for selection and promotion by merit and partisan neutrality of the civil service. It established the Civil Service Commission to administer the merit system. The Civil Service Reform Act of 1978 (CSRA) set out to improve on the Pendleton Act by creating new institutions, instituting performance appraisal and merit pay, and creating the Senior Executive Service, among other things.

The editors felt that the twentieth anniversary of the passage of the CSRA would be an appropriate time to consider its successes and failures. But an evaluation of the CSRA would not be complete without an exploration of crucial issues that must be faced in the near future. Given the vast changes in the nature of governance over the past several decades—political attacks on the legitimacy of the career civil service, increasing privatization and contracting out, battles between the president and Congress over the role of government—we felt that an examination of the future of the merit system was in order.

Thus we solicited contributions from a number of scholars who had followed the development of CSRA from its inception. Some of them had participated in the implementation of the Act itself, and some had devoted a portion of their scholarly careers to evaluating its effects. Those who accepted our invitation wrote high-quality analyses that they presented at the symposium at the Woodrow Wilson Center.

The final papers included in this book have the added advantage of benefitting from the insights of those who arguably know the most about the implementation of the CSRA—the former directors of the Office of Personnel Management: Jule Sugarman (Carter administration), Donald Devine and Constance Horner (Reagan administration), Constance Berry Newman and Douglas A. Brook (Bush administration), and James B. King (Clinton administration). Each of the former directors attended the symposium and commented on the papers and presentations by the scholars. The authors then incorporated their comments along with comments from the many others who attended the conference when they rewrote their papers for publication.

The structure of the book reflects the purpose of the symposium and this collection. In the introduction Douglas Brook presents background on the CSRA, the issue of political responsiveness, and the context for reform. Part one begins with an analysis of the changing role of the public service (Pfiffner) and an examination of the intentions of the framers of the 1978 CSRA (Ink, who was executive director of President Carter's taskforce that designed the CSRA). These chapters are followed by a comparison of CSRA with the National Performance Review (Ban) and an analysis of the current state of the Senior Executive Service (Aberbach and Rockman).

Part two takes up the issues of performance (Ingraham and Moynihan), incentives (Rainey and Kellough), and accountability (Romzek) in the implementation of the CSRA as well as the implications of these issues for future reforms. Part three presents contrasting scenarios of the future of governance in the United States. Two contrasting visions are projected from current trends, one somewhat bleak (Huddleston) and one guardedly optimistic (Newland). In the conclusion Hugh Heclo states that the higher civil service is inextricably bound up in the struggle for political power in the United States. But what is lacking in this struggle for power, he argues, is a strong voice for the long-term institutional interests of the civil service and thus the nation. Each of the authors in the volume focuses on different dimensions of public personnel management and the pressing issues confronting the United States as we create a new public service to face the challenges of governance in the next century.

ACKNOWLEDGMENTS

The editors would like to acknowledge the crucial roles played in the creation of this book by the hard work of our colleagues. Michael Lacey of the Woodrow Wilson Center included our project in his agenda in the United States Studies Division of the Woodrow Wilson Center, which sponsored the scholarly portion of the symposium and provided a beautiful venue for the conference. Professor Tom Hennessey of George Mason University and director of the Congressional Institute of the Future provided valuable advice and arranged many of the administrative aspects of the conference. Susan Nugent of the Woodrow Wilson Center worked overtime with graciousness and efficiency to assure that all of the arrangements were effectively completed and coordinated. Mark Abramson was generous in arranging for support for the conference, and he also moderated one of the panels. Megan Berkey and Amy Batson, graduate students in George Mason's Master's of Public Administration program, provided professional assistance in conference arrangements. Finally, we would like to thank Philip Morris, the Endowment for the Business of Government at Price Waterhouse Coopers, and EDS for generous financial support for the conference upon which this volume is based.

James P. Pfiffner
Douglas A. Brook

THE FUTURE
OF
MERIT

MERIT AND THE CIVIL SERVICE REFORM ACT

DOUGLAS A. BROOK

Merit is fundamental to the concept of a *civil service*. It has been the foundation for the institutions and personnel systems that constitute the civil service since the term was first codified. The term "civil service" itself derives from the British East India Company. As this trading company evolved, "its employees became administrators instead of traders and were referred to as its 'civil servants' to distinguish them from its army, navy, and ecclesiastical employees."[1] The first codified civil service, with merit at its core, dates from the British 1854 *Report on the Organization of the Permanent Civil Service* (the *Northcote-Trevelyan Report*).

The objectives of the *Northcote-Trevelyan Report* were to replace an uncoordinated, inefficient, and patronage-ridden public employment system with one, which would:

1. Provide by a proper system of examination, for the supply of the public with a thoroughly efficient class of men.
2. Encourage industry and foster merit.
3. Mitigate the evils, which result from the fragmentary nature of the service and to introduce into it some elements of unity.[2]

This report was a "charter for meritocracy—the determined recruitment of talent, its promotion on the basis of demonstrable merit, and its efficient distribution throughout the public service to rid Whitehall of patronage, inefficiency, and narrow departmentalism.[3] The three enduring principles of *Northcote-Trevelyan*—entrance by examination, promotion by merit, and a unitary system—were also to become central to the U.S. civil service, and none was more important than merit.

The U.S. civil service also has its origins in a reaction to the corruption and inefficiency of a patronage system. The Pendleton Act of 1883 established the bipartisan Civil Service Commission and introduced the concepts of nonpartisan merit and protection from political influence in the recruitment, promotion, and retention of federal government workers. It established that federal civilian employees are "hired on the basis of merit, promoted within the framework of civil service rules, are not to be explicitly involved in political campaigns, and . . . once beyond a probationary period, essentially have job tenure."[4] At first, the Act covered only about 10 percent of the federal workforce, but the coverage steadily expanded.

THE CIVIL SERVICE REFORM ACT OF 1978

The Civil Service Reform Act of 1978 (CSRA) was the first major reform of the federal public service personnel system since the Pendleton Act. It was the product of President Carter's Personnel Management Project, itself a component of Carter's Reorganization Project. The mandate for the personnel project was to develop a civil service reform proposal that would make government more efficient and businesslike. Dwight Ink was the executive director of the Personnel Management Project. His chapter in this book outlines the objectives of the project, which sought to modernize human resource management by streamlining the system through simplification and decentralization, to restructure for better management by replacing the Civil Service Commission, creating the Senior Executive Service, and to address such issues as productivity, job quality, workforce planning, recruiting, training, development, compensation, and performance evaluation. Ink also explains that the administration sought to enhance the safeguards against political abuse through creation of the Merit Systems Protection Board, specifying merit principles and prohibiting practices.

The resulting proposal for the Civil Service Reform Act of 1978 had these elements: 1. abolition of the Civil Service Commission, and creation of the Office of Personnel Management and the Merit Systems Protection Board (Congress later added the Federal Labor Relations Authority); 2. a performance evaluation system to increase productivity and establish a link between pay and performance; 3. a merit pay system for mid-level managers; 4. creation of the Senior Executive Service; 5. greater protection for whistleblowers; 6. limitations on veterans' preference (later rejected by Congress); 7. new authority for personnel administration research and development; and 8. a commitment to equal employment opportunity and a socially representative bureaucracy.[5] As noted, some of these were altered in the legislative process, but the essential elements of the reform package—linking performance and pay, a new federal personnel management organizational structure, and the Senior Executive Service—were enacted. Each was endowed with some aspect of the concept of merit.

Merit pay for mid-level federal managers represented a significant departure from the traditional civil service pay structure. It was based on what were perceived at the time to be private-sector models of performance-based compensation. The goal was to create incentives for better performance by rewarding merit on an individual basis. Prior to CSRA, pay raises were achieved through within-grade step increases generally related to tenure. They were all but automatic without any clear relationship between performance and scheduled pay increases. In fact, this rigid system was seen as protecting the civil servant from abuse. Under CSRA, only half of the pay increase was to be automatic. The remainder was to be placed in a pool and awarded to employees according to their performance rating. Ingraham and Moynihan observe in chapter 5 that this shift in emphasis from protection to performance was one of CSRA's boldest and most important steps.

The institutional reforms of CSRA centered on preserving the principle of merit while improving the management of the federal personnel system. It separated the inherently conflicting functions of the old Civil Service Commission—protecting civil servants from political abuse, while advising the president on personnel matters, and administering a personnel management system. In its place, CSRA created the Office of Personnel Management (OPM), the Merit Systems Protection Board (MSPB), and the Federal Labor Relations Authority (FLRA). The latter two were to be essentially adjudicatory, investigatory, and regulatory bodies; OPM was to be the federal government's central management agency for personnel. As described by its first director, Alan K. (Scotty) Campbell, OPM was "to serve as the President's principal agent for managing the federal workforce . . . performing for the President the same role relative to personnel management that OMB does for financial management."[6]

For some, the Senior Executive Service (SES) was the centerpiece of the CSRA. Its aim was to create a higher civil service: an elite cadre of top-ranking managers selected, promoted, and rewarded on merit. The SES was to have its own personnel management system. It provided for a rank-in-person mobility system, wherein senior executives, much like military officers, would personally retain the rank, pay, and privileges of the SES as they moved from assignment to assignment. For those below the SES, civil service ranks would continue to be determined by the grade of the position they held—a rank-in-position system. The SES also included pay-linked performance systems with performance-based cash bonuses, eligibility for large cash awards, executive development programs, and sabbatical leaves. Noncareer political appointees were permitted to occupy a limited number of SES positions and career SES members were to be eligible for political appointments without sacrificing their career status.

EVALUATIONS OF CSRA

Scholarly evaluations of the CSRA have generally appeared in three distinct periods: a five year review,[7] a symposium at the ten-year point,[8] and contemporary looks at the condition of the public service focused less on further evaluation and more on future reforms. Assessments at the five-year point were markedly unfavorable as important aspects of CSRA ran up against pay problems and the changing political priorities of a new administration. By the tenth year, the general conclusion was that CSRA had fallen short of its loftiest objectives. Though CSRA had been successfully implemented as a personnel management system, achievement of its higher goals of greater efficiency and effectiveness, and improved government performance had been less successful.

Performance appraisals and merit pay were standardized and procedurally sound but lacking in higher productivity outcomes. The performance-linked pay system showed little evidence of success in achieving the overall objective of improved performance. The original merit pay system was eventually replaced in 1984 by the Performance Management and Recognition System (PMRS), which remained in operation until merit pay was effectively abandoned in 1993. One report of twelve academic and government empirical studies of the merit pay system and the subsequent PMRS found mixed results in achieving intermediate objectives—relating pay to performance, recognizing good performance with cash awards, and motivating employees. On the ultimate objectives of improving productivity, timeliness, and quality of work, none of the studies reported a positive outcome. "Federal managers and policy makers have learned how to operate merit pay to minimize the pain, but they have not necessarily achieved their strategic goals: improved productivity and effectiveness."[9]

Carolyn Ban, in her analysis of the National Performance Review (NPR) in chapter 3 observes that NPR shifted the focus away from CSRA's emphasis on individual performance appraisal and rewards, and toward agency or organizational goals instead. Patricia Ingraham and Donald Moynihan also point out, in chapter 5, that over the last twenty years there have been major shifts toward the linkage of individually based performance to broader organizational and policy goals. There has been a shift from individual to organizational performance, replacing standardized systems with more flexible arrangements, and changing confidential individual accountability to a more public sense of organizational accountability. The matter of accountability itself is complex, as Barbara Romzek explains in chapter 7. She identifies four major types of accountability—hierarchical, legal, professional, and political—and argues that those who demand more accountability often really mean that they want a different kind of accountability. CSRA, agencies, and NPR may each have been emphasizing different types of accountability.

A key issue in any personnel system is the question of incentives. Hal Rainey and J. Edward Kellough argue in chapter 6 that performance-based incentives programs require preconditions of a trusting organizational culture, adequate funding, and an accepted process for evaluating and measuring performance. Each of these can be difficult in a large governmental setting. Moreover, Rainey and Kellough suggest that incentives other than pay or discipline are often more effective as motivating factors in the public service, including political and agency leadership, and the intrinsic value of work in the public service.

OPM never achieved the status that its framers sought. Rather than becoming an equal of OMB, it has more often contested with OMB for supremacy in personnel management and advice to the president. Additionally, the question of centralized versus decentralized personnel management has hovered over OPM. Though CSRA intended to create an essentially decentralized personnel management structure in the federal government, OPM often evolved into a centralized maker and keeper of the rules despite efforts to decentralize. Again looking at NPR as an evaluation of CSRA, Carolyn Ban reports in chapter 3 that NPR called for further decentralization of the personnel process to provide greater flexibility in agency personnel management and much of that has been implemented.

OPM's history also shows that it has been highly identified with its political leadership. Its priorities and performance have been very much a function of the OPM directors and of the presidents they served. Scotty Campbell and Jule Sugarman began the implementation of CSRA; they oversaw the establishment and early operations of OPM. Donald Devine brought a new emphasis on political management of federal personnel as he and President Reagan strove to gain political and policy control over the federal bureaucracy. Constance Horner, equally politically attuned, was aware also of tremendous managerial challenges that faced OPM, and she concentrated great attention on issues of OPM's professionalism and competence. Constance Newman, reflecting President Bush's respect for the civil servant, shepherded a major pay raise through Congress and served as an advocate for the civil service. James King made OPM the focus for his administration's reinvention of government management. He eliminated the *Federal Personnel Manual* and drove a major downsizing and reorganization of OPM. Whether manager, advocate, politician, or reformer, OPM's directors put a very personal mark on their tenure with the agency, as they followed their own instincts and the policy preferences of their presidents.

Finally, the SES had not become the higher civil service that its framers had envisioned. Once the centerpiece of CSRA reform, the SES may now be its greatest disappointment. Beset by early problems in the areas of pay and performance bonuses, conflicting images and objectives, and the political turmoil of a change in administration, the SES did not have a successful launch. The study by Joel Aberbach and Bert Rockman in chapter 4 presents more recent data on evaluations of the SES that indicate that pay raises in the early 1990s have helped to mitigate some of the disappointment among SES members. Yet the SES continues to be dominated more by technical experts than generalist managers, and the anticipated mobility between agencies and departments of high-level career managers has failed to materialize. Political leaders from both parties have nearly filled their total quota of noncareer SES positions, and some career SES members have occupied political appointments, but the distinctions between career and political managers have not been eliminated. Nevertheless, the SES does provide some measure of prestige for the very senior career civil servants, and it provides a focus for leadership and career development. Moreover, its rank-in-person system and mobility rules give any administration the tools it needs for aligning senior career and political leadership if, as Aberbach and Rockman conclude, it chooses to use them.

POLITICAL INFLUENCE AND CONTROL

U.S. civil service and the concept of nonpartisan merit in the public service have been profoundly affected by the notion of the politics-administration dichotomy, put forth by Woodrow Wilson in his famous essay, "The Study of Administration." He argues that "policy making and administration would be distinguished so that politics would not be an issue in the bureaucracy."[10] For much of the history of administration in the United States, the implication has been clear: politics and policy are the provinces of the elected or politically appointed official; neutrally competent nonpolitical administration is the job of the civil servant. Certainly this view is consistent with the concept of a merit-based civil service.

A key objective of the CSRA, however, was to break down the barriers to responsiveness, cooperation, and coordination between career managers and political appointees that had resulted in a "government of strangers."[11] The aim was to reduce the distinctions between career and noncareer executives at the highest levels of the bureaucracy, and to allow for the free flow of political direction and professional advice, while preserving a merit system and protecting against political abuse. Despite such efforts to blur this distinction, the norms of the politics-administration dichotomy still dominate much of the practice of public administration in the United States. In fact, there remain some serious impediments to improving the relationships between career managers and political leaders. The structure of government in the United States affects the ability to give clear political direction to the career bureaucracy, and distrust of civil servants by political leaders persists.

Separation of powers encourages multiple centers of power and policy direction. Divided government is common. Different parties can hold Congress and the presidency and governing majorities are not always attainable on particular votes or policies by either the president or the leadership of the majority party in Congress. Policy direction can come from the president, the Congress, or even from smaller committees and subcommittees within the Congress. For the bureaucracy, who rules is often neither clear nor consistent. "[P]ublic managers may receive opposing signals or policy directives from their legitimate bosses in Congress and the executive branch."[12] Policy precedence does not rest solely with either branch. "What we find in domestic and much of foreign affairs is neither presidential nor congressional dominance but a mixed picture, depending on time and circumstances."[13] Under such conditions, the loyalty of civil servants might understandably be more devoted to their agencies, programs, or careers than to their temporary political leaders.

Presidents have often been suspicious that the career leaders they inherit from their predecessors can be relied upon for neutral and responsive service. "Such lack of trust in civil servants has been particularly evident when presidents come to office after their political party has endured a long period . . . [out of] the White House."[14] Though this distrust appears to dissipate over time, this perceived problem is often addressed early in an administration by the placement of even more political appointees into the bureaucracy. This was clearly the case in 1981. The Reagan administration "sought to politicize the upper echelons of the federal bureaucracy through formal and informal means."[15] The 1978 Civil Service Reform Act gave Reagan the tools that he needed. Through its application, and "the management of the Senior Executive Service, Reagan sympathizers were infiltrated into the permanent bureaucracy."[16] In some ways, Reagan's distrust of the career ranks reinforced the politics-administration dichotomy and led to the widespread appointment of political operatives into the bureaucracy. There has been every indication that the Clinton administration has continued this practice. This increase in the number of political appointees[17] has raised its own set of issues. Political appointees tend not to stay in one position for very long, and many of them lack minimal technical qualifications or understanding of how to work with the career civil service.[18] Their increased number creates an extra political and management burden for the White House. And it is not always clear that all political appointees understand the nature and requirements of a merit system.

Indeed, questions about politics and the CSRA have persisted. Was CSRA intended to increase the political responsiveness of senior civil servants? Ban contends that the framers of CSRA intended such political responsiveness. Ink, on the other hand, seems to argue that it was not. Intent is sometimes a difficult concept when explaining legislation. Different people with different intentions often agree on the same policy choices. In this instance, as Aberbach and Rockman point out, CSRA gave potent partisan powers to the party that controls the presidency. The irony is that a Democratic Congress enacted CSRA, giving a powerful tool for political leadership to a subsequent Republican administration that used it vigorously.

Did CSRA open the door for politicization of the bureaucracy and political abuse of the merit system? Ban argues that claims of reduced political abuse have been greatly exaggerated, and she asserts that a culture of abuse is rampant in some agencies. Ink seems to share this view. On the other hand, Newland, while acknowledging the abuses, is critical of the administrative state's attempts to insulate the bureaucracy from politics. Instead, he argues for the essential connectedness of bureaucracy, politics, and civic culture. In a detached bureaucracy, he suggests, the orientation is more toward serving the organization rather than toward serving the people. Newland seems almost to return to Ink's objective of creating a civil service system that better served the people, but he sees a political element to that objective that Ink eschews.

THE FUTURE OF MERIT AND THE CONTEXT OF REFORM

Initial civil service reforms in Britain and the United States grew out of a larger context of governance—in these instances, a reaction to patronage, corruption, and inefficiency. The context in which CSRA was addressed was different. After decades of an enlarging governmental role and a corresponding growth in government administration, there was widespread dissatisfaction with bureaucracy and public management from a variety of perspectives. For some, the career ranks had been politically abused. For others, the personnel system was too rigid. Many saw a civil service system that protected incompetents, encouraged mediocrity, and had no dedication to quality, productivity, or performance.

The context of reform for the future will be important going forward, as well. Some have argued that a greater concern for politics is required and that an inadequate understanding of political considerations had an important effect on the design and implementation of CSRA.[19] In the first chapter of this volume, James Pfiffner's historical overview of the context of politics and governance in which debates over public management take place explains that changes in opinions about the legitimacy of government also affect public opinions about public management. The current changing nature of governance, wherein many governmental functions may be performed by nongovernmental entities or by people outside the civil service system, raises important questions for the future of merit and the preservation of the concept of public service. There is also the question of whether public management is in crisis and whether merit system reform is needed to deal with a radically different future. Rainey and Kellough argue that there is no crisis in administration of government in the United States and that the resulting lack of urgency militates against comprehensive reform. On the other hand, Mark Huddleston's vision is of a globalized future that induces crises in accountability, competence, and legitimacy for public administration. In the concluding chapter Hugh Heclo draws from the rest of the book in addressing the issue of merit, but from a broader perspective. He identifies two kinds of merit—substantive and institutional—and he argues that it is often substantive merit that reformers seek, but institutional merit that reforms address.

Whatever the view of the context for the future of public management, or the models used to craft civil service reforms, the issue of merit will remain a question that is fundamental to the very idea of public service. Can it be preserved if nongovernmental organizations perform governmental functions? Can a differently structured merit system stimulate better efficiency, effectiveness, and improved governmental performance? Should reforms address structure and organization or people and leadership? What is the future for a distinct national meritocratic career civil service in a globalized and privatized economy? If there is to be another major civil service reform in the United States, it is hoped that the questions and insights offered in this volume will help to inform the discussion and debate.

NOTES

1. Richard A. Chapman, *The Higher Civil Service in Britain* (London: Constable, 1970), 9.

2. Quoted in ibid., 26.

3. Peter Hennessy, *Whitehall* (New York: The Free Press, 1989), 42.

4. Ronald L. Johnson, "Patronage to Merit and Control of the Federal Government Labor Force," *Explorations in Economic History* 31 (1994): 91–2.

5. Patricia W. Ingraham and David Rosenbloom, eds., "Symposium on the Civil Service Reform Act of 1978: An Evaluation," *Policy Studies Journal* 17 (Winter 1988–9): 311–12.

6. Larry M. Lane, "The Office of Personnel Management: Values, Policies, and Consequences," in Ingraham and Rosenbloom, eds., "Symposium on the Civil Service Reform Act of 1978," 104.

7. Patricia W. Ingraham and Carolyn Ban, eds., *Legislating Bureaucratic Change: The Civil Service Reform Act of 1978* (Albany: State University of New York Press, 1984).

8. Ingraham and Rosenbloom, eds., "Symposium on the Civil Service Reform Act of 1978," 311–69.

9. James L. Perry, "Making Policy by Trial and Error: Merit Pay in the Federal Service," *Public Administration Review* 17 (Winter 1988–9): 399.

10. Robert Maranto and David Schultz, *A Short History of the United States Civil Service* (Lanham, Md.: University Press of America, 1991), 56.

11. Hugh Heclo, *A Government of Strangers: Executive Politics in Washington* (Washington, D.C.: Brookings Institution Press, 1977), 1.

12. James P. Pfiffner, "The American Tradition of Administrative Reform," in Yong Hyo Cho and H. George Fredrickson, eds., *The White House and the Blue House* (New York: University Press of America, 1997).

13. Hugh Heclo, "What Has Happened to the Separation of Powers," in James P. Pfiffner, ed., *Governance and American Politics* (Fort Worth: Harcourt Brace, 1995): 312.

14. Francis E. Rourke, "Responsiveness and Neutral Competence in American Bureaucracy," *Public Administration Review* 52 (November–December, 1992): 540.

15. Donald Savoie, *Thatcher, Reagan, Mulroney: In Search of a New Bureaucracy* (Pittsburgh: University of Pittsburgh Press, 1994), 219.

16. Ibid., 237.

17. See Paul C. Light, *Thickening Government* (Washington, D.C.: Brookings Institution Press, 1995).

18. See Carolyn Ban and Patricia W. Ingraham, "Short-Timers: Political Appointee Mobility and Its Impact on Political Career Relations in the Reagan Administration," *Administration and Society* 22 (May 1990): 106–24.

19. See, for instance, Ban in this volume, and Patricia W. Ingraham and John White, "The Design of Civil Service Reform: Lessons in Politics and Rationality," in Ingraham and Rosenbloom, eds., "Symposium on the Civil Service Reform Act of 1978," 329.

PART ONE

THE CHANGING ROLE OF THE CIVIL SERVICE

CHAPTER ONE

GOVERNMENT LEGITIMACY AND THE ROLE OF THE CIVIL SERVICE

JAMES P. PFIFFNER

As the scope and roles of the U.S. government changed in the twentieth century, so did the role and legitimacy of the public service. This essay examines the changing relationship between government and the public service from the Progressive Era to the end of the century with an emphasis on the decline of the legitimacy of the state in recent decades. It then looks at the effects of that change in legitimacy on the role of the public service, specifically contracting out, privatization, and the fragmenting of the civil service. Finally, it takes up the implications of the disintegration of the national civil service system for the future of merit, the public service ethic, and accountability in the opening years of the twenty-first century.

I. GOVERNMENT LEGITIMACY AND THE ROLE OF THE CIVIL SERVICE

The civil service has always been caught between U.S. citizens' skeptical attitudes toward government and the role of the national government. In the early twentieth century, the civil service was just emerging from the era of the spoils system. From the presidency of Andrew Jackson until the Pendleton Act of 1883 the staffing of the federal government was largely conducted by presidential administrations on the basis of political loyalty. Based on the premises that government work was basically simple, the political parties needed government jobs as incentives for their membership, and politically loyal implementors were needed for faithful execution of the laws, the spoils system flourished. Governmental reform groups sprang up to criticize the inefficiencies of the constant turnover of government workers and the corruption the system spawned in the quadrennial fight over government jobs.

The 1883 Pendleton Act initiated the replacement of spoils with merit, but only at a gradual pace. Initially, the intent of the merit system was that recruitment and promotion would be based on ability rather than partisan affiliation and that there would no partisan interference with merit system personnel decisions. These protections for civil service workers were premised on the assumption that the civil service would work with equal enthusiasm for whichever political party was in power. That is, government workers would be neutral with respect to party and competent with respect to their jobs. This ideal of neutral competence would become the hallmark of the civil service. In the 1980s, however, it would be attacked as leading to insufficient enthusiasm for the policies of the administration currently in power, and in the 1990s it would be criticized as not sufficiently flexible for the information age.

A. From the Progressive Era to the "Golden Age" of Merit

In the early twentieth century the Progressives sought a new, more active role for the government in the U.S. economy. President Theodore Roosevelt led the national government to a more active role in conservation of natural resources and curbing the excesses of big business. Independent regulatory commissions were created to monitor and regulate business activity. World War I brought further governmental interventions in the economy and the expansion of the merit system. By 1933, 80 percent of federal government workers were within the classified civil service.[1]

The experience with the Great Depression and the coming of the New Deal brought drastic changes in attitudes toward government. Panic over the state of the economy led to experimentation with government policy toward the economy and the profusion of government agencies to deal with various aspects of the Depression. Despite conservative opposition to government growth and intervention in the economy, public programs were welcomed by many, and the government was seen as an engine of change. With unemployment approaching 25 percent, welfare programs were accepted by many as legitimate assistance for those who could not find work. Scholars and business leaders came to Washington to help lead the nation out of the Depression, some as "dollar-a-year" executives who were rich enough not to need a salary but who wanted to contribute to the common good.

World War II brought increased legitimacy to big government. The whole economy was harnessed and guided by the national government so that the United States became the "arsenal of democracy" that contributed as much as American soldiers to the defeat of the Axis powers. Most of society was involved, in one way or another, in the national government's fight for victory over Germany and Japan. The patriotism that marked World War II carried over to the following Cold War era. As the Soviet Union came to be seen as the major threat to world peace and the Korean War was slowly brought to a truce, the role of a large federal government was further legitimized. The 1950s saw the broad college education of veterans through the GI Bill, the creation of the interstate highway system, the support for science to counter the Sputnik threat, and the National Defense Education Act. All brought the federal government further into areas of society than it had been before.

The huge growth of the civil service between the 1930s and the 1960s, from 800,000 in 1938 to 2.6 million in 1952, reflected the much larger role of the federal government. With this growth, the merit system was also expanded, covering 66 percent of the civil service in 1938 and 86 percent in 1952.[2] The national government became much more professionalized and much more institutionalized. The Brownlow Committee Report in 1937 recommended the expansion of the civil service, and the Hoover Commission Report in 1949 led to its increased regularization and professionalization.

The 1950s Cold War consensus on a large military establishment and a temporary consensus on a relatively small social welfare establishment, brought with it a "golden era" of the civil service.[3] Agreement on the relative size of the government and its purposes was accompanied by an acceptance of the legitimacy of the civil service, with its professionalism and competence. But the legitimacy enjoyed by the civil service and its increased size also led to the rigidification of processes and procedures. The Civil Service Commission became the central policy maker for personnel administration and the central clearing house for recruitment for government workers. Thus the consensus on the role of the government and success of the CSC in institutionalizing the public service contained the seeds of disintegration as the role of government was expanded in the 1960s and questioned in the 1970s.

The surface consensus and relative calm of the 1950s hid the simmering racial inequality that was slowly undermined after *Brown v. Board of Education* in 1954 and exploded in racial strife in the 1960s. The response of the political system to racism, inequality, and environmental degradation was a flurry of activist public policy innovation and social legislation. A booming economy and an activist optimism engendered a plethora of governmental programs to attack areas of neglect and to pioneer new initiatives, from literacy, to health, to environmental clean-up, to social welfare. The burst of governmental optimism and activism led to legislative activism by Lyndon Johnson that rivaled the famous "100 Days" of Franklin Roosevelt in 1933. But the flurry of activity also included some poorly thought out programs that would lead to a backlash in the future. The civil servants who helped design the programs would later be blamed when the programs were not as successful as promised.

President Johnson's political skills and the optimism (or hubris) of the 1960s also led to the increasing involvement of the U.S. military in Vietnam and the secret escalation of the war in 1965. The 1960s were years of upheaval, with racial unrest in the South and large cities of the North and growing opposition to the war in Vietnam. The public service was in the middle of both and embodied both the idealism of programs that attacked injustice and the military effort that wanted to save South Vietnam from communism. But the large governmental activism also mirrored the idealism of America's domestic and foreign policies with the arrogance of imposing solutions on Vietnam and thinking that all of society's ills could be cured by large governmental programs. The seeds of the 1970s reaction to the optimism and arrogance of governmental activism were planted in the 1960s.

B. The 1970s and 1980s: Deficit Politics and Delegitimizing Government

The narrow victory of Richard Nixon over Hubert Humphrey in 1968 accurately reflected the changing attitude toward government in the American public. Nixon presided over a portion of the liberal legislation at the end of the 1960s era, but his political instincts were leading him toward a reining in of the activist impulse and toward a conservative reaction against governmental activism in social policy. Nixon's landslide victory in 1972 reflected public rejection of further liberal experiments in public policy, but the Watergate "horrors" engendered further public cynicism about big government. In addition, the economy suffered from "stagflation"—simultaneous inflation and stagnation. The inflation was set off by Lyndon Johnson's policies of guns and butter and the creation of OPEC that led to the drastic increase in oil prices in 1973. Inflation and a stagnant economy further eroded public confidence in governmental policy.

These far-reaching changes were reflected in attitudes toward the public service. Kennedy and Johnson saw the public service they inherited from the 1950s to be too stodgy and bureaucratic to create bold, new policy options. Richard Nixon, however, held a deep distrust toward the career services, seeing them as "dug-in establishmentarians fighting for the status quo."[4] Nixon also came to distrust his own political appointees and felt that they had been coopted by the career bureaucracy. The civil service came to be identified with the policies of the federal government and thus blamed for them in a parallel to the way some antiwar activists blamed soldiers for U.S. policies in Vietnam. Thus, the reaction of the public to the domestic, political, and foreign policy excesses of the 1960s led to a distrust of the federal government. The opportunism of politicians then led to gradual delegitimization of government and political attacks on the public service.

In his quest for the presidency, Jimmy Carter ran against Watergate and the excesses of Richard Nixon, but he combined his partisan attack with an assault on the federal government ("Our government in Washington now is a horrible bureaucratic·mess.")[5] and its employees ("There is no merit in the merit system.").[6] Reflecting the changing political landscape, Carter was not a traditional Democrat but was a fiscal conservative. He was also skeptical of federal government intervention in state policy. Carter's skeptical approach to government provided a transition to the much more conservative and antigovernment administration of Ronald Reagan. Carter's Civil Service Reform Act gave future administrations tools to elicit greater responsiveness from the career bureaucracies.

Reagan's antigovernment rhetoric was honed over decades of political activity and his governorship of California. Reagan was able to capitalize on public disillusionment with the optimism of the 1960s and the cynicism born of Vietnam and Watergate. He argued that government was the problem, not the solution to social ills. His antigovernment conservativism was rationalized by public choice economics that argued that government workers were primarily self-interested and would protect their programs, thus melding disagreement with past public policy with hostility toward the government and its workers.[7] The political appeal of this approach was attractive to conservative politicians, and Republicans made significant gains in the 1980s with this antigovernment theme.

Despite Reagan's campaign promises to balance the budget, his unwillingness to sacrifice his priorities in defense spending and tax cuts along with a severe recession combined to produce historically huge deficits in his early years in office. The failure of the government to reduce defense or entitlement spending or to increase taxes to reduce enormous deficits resulted in continued shortfalls of hundreds of billions of dollars. The national debt increased from about one trillion dollars in 1981 to two trillion in 1984 to three trillion in 1988. The trend continued, with the total debt reaching four trillion during the Bush administration and passing five trillion in the Clinton administration. This fiscal overhang increased pressure on governmental programs, particularly on the "controllable" part of spending (excluding entitlements, contracts, and interest on the debt). Budget agreements to reduce the deficit, particularly in 1990 and 1993, restricted spending on programs and contributed to a balanced budget in FY 1998.

C. The Clinton Administration, the NPR, and the 104th Congress

The Clinton administration had two major effects on the state of government management and the civil service. The National Performance Review was the broadest attempt to change federal management in U.S. history, but perhaps more far reaching were the policy battles that Clinton fought with the Republican 104th Congress.

1. The NPR

Vice President Gore took leadership of the administration's push to reform the way the government does business. The NPR leadership argued that the prevailing paradigm of government management was formed during the Progressive Era and was designed to counter the evils of the spoils system and corruption. In trying to prevent corruption and political interference with administration, the merit system became gradually encrusted with a plethora of rules and regulations to prevent government managers from using their discretion. The system was designed during the industrial revolution and modeled on large-scale bureaucracy with hierarchical control from the top to ensure responsiveness to law and adherence to policy. But this system was now cumbersome and outmoded and should be replaced with a management structure appropriate for the information age.

The information age at the end of the twentieth century, argued the NPR, needs more flexible organizations with flatter structures that can respond creatively to the challenges of changing technology and global competition. The proponents of the NPR argued that government should "steer rather than row." That is, government should not produce goods and services directly, but rather set up incentive systems that encourage citizens to do things themselves, use contracting to take advantage of market incentives, and encourage competition between government agencies and with the private sector. The approach envisions government as catalyzing, enterprising, decentralized, community owned, competitive, mission driven, customer friendly, market-oriented, and results oriented. The further implication was that government employment could be much smaller than it was.[8]

The NPR encompassed a wide range of management reforms and had broad effects on the public service. While the intention was to change the culture of government organizations and transform them into entrepreneurial, creative, and customer driven organizations, the success of moving in these directions was mitigated by the budget-driven mandate to reduce significantly the number of employees of the federal government. The Clinton administration cuts of more than 300,000 positions brought the size of the civilian component of the federal government down to the smallest it had been since the Kennedy administration.

2. President Clinton and the 104th Congress

Perhaps more far reaching than the management changes brought on by the National Performance Review were the battles between the Clinton administration and the Republican 104th Congress over the role of the federal government. President Clinton came to office as a "new Democrat" who supported fiscal discipline and a limited, though positive role for the federal government. He had absorbed the political lessons of the 1980s and promised to "end welfare as we know it" and to produce an efficient federal government. But the policy centerpiece of his first year in office, his health care reform proposal, seemed to belie his "new Democrat" intentions. His health care reform plan, while based on private-sector insurance and care provision, was premised on complex and far-reaching government regulation of the industry. The Republicans' defeat of health care reform in 1994 was one of the major factors in their recapture of control of Congress for the first time since 1952.

The House Republicans, led by Newt Gingrich, set out to accomplish what Ronald Reagan had failed to finish: to move the country much further in a conservative direction by dismantling many of the programs of the welfare state that had been enacted during the Roosevelt and Johnson administrations. The Republicans had run on a "Contract with America," a list of mostly conservative policy initiatives that included balancing the budget, welfare reform, tax cuts, tort reform, congressional reform, and several other issues.[9] Some of the contract items were enacted, but most foundered in the Senate, which, though Republican, was not as conservative as the House.

But the most controversial policy changes sought by the House Republicans were not in the contract but were put into appropriations measures and included in a massive reconciliation bill that they passed in the fall of 1995. The proposed policy changes included severe cuts in Medicare, Medicaid, welfare, environmental programs, and other domestic programs. They also proposed abolishing of several cabinet departments (Education, Energy, and Commerce) and severe cuts in the Environmental Protection Agency. When President Clinton vetoed the bills, including these cuts, the Republicans refused to modify their proposals, and much of the government was shut down for lack of appropriated funds. After two prolonged shutdowns it became clear that the public was blaming the Republicans in Congress for disruptions, and GOP leaders reached an agreement with President Clinton on a plan to balance the budget. Though the Republicans lost the political battle over blame for the shutdowns and Clinton was on the way to reelection, the Republicans won many cutbacks in domestic programs and agreement on a plan to move the budget toward balance.

The significance of this pitched political battle in 1995 was that the irresistible force of the Republicans in Congress had met the immovable object of Clinton in the White House, and they had fought each other to a forced accommodation. Clinton, a moderate Democrat much closer to Carter than Johnson in policy terms, had been forced to move his policy preferences significantly to the right. He also had to accept a plan to balance the budget that precluded many policy initiatives (in workforce retraining, education, and environmental policy) that he favored. The congressional Republicans, on the other hand, had to accept the fact that most Americans had come to expect the benefits provided by the major programs of the New Deal and the Great Society and would support Medicaid, Medicare, Social Security, environmental protection, and other domestic governmental programs.

Emblematic of the new "consensus" on the role of government was the statement by President Clinton in his 1996 State of the Union message that "The era of big government is over." While this rhetoric appealed to the symbolic preferences of most Americans, it assumed that most of the programs of the federal government, over which there had just been a major pitched battle, would remain basically the same. In saying this, Clinton clearly did not embrace the attitude toward government of Ronald Reagan in 1981 or of Newt Gingrich and the freshmen Republicans of the 104th Congress.[10] What Clinton did accept was the political reality that the public was not ready for further large-scale government programs.

This major battle over budget, policies, and programs may very well signify a broad agreement (but not consensus) in the American electorate on the role of the national government and may define the range within which future policy battles may take place. To be sure, significant battles will continue over particular programs (e.g., how to limit Medicare and Medicaid spending, how to pay for Social Security, how to administer welfare programs, etc.), but the broad boundaries of political agreement over the scope of government may have been established for the time being. This agreement may be on the part of the public rather than politicians in Congress, but the political reality of what the electorate will support may lead to a standoff in Congress. This possible agreement bodes well for the public service. It may allow a focus on how best to manage the provision of goods and services rather than the blaming of government workers for the existence of the programs they implement (bureaucrat bashing).

General agreement on the role of government may narrow the scope of conflict, but it does not mean that the public service will not be subject to disagreements about how to organize public programs or who should carry them out.

II. THE ILLUSION OF SMALLER GOVERNMENT AND ITS EFFECTS ON THE PUBLIC SERVICE

Despite the delegitimizing of the federal government from the 1970s to the 1990s, the reality is that the American public wants and demands the benefits of big government at the same time that it rewards politicians for railing against it. But the consensus among Americans in favor of the benefits of big government and the rhetoric of small government has had important effects. Politicians want to limit government without having to cut programs that have popular support. The solution is to deliver the appearance of a shrinking government but at the same time maintain the ability to provide the goods and services that the public demands. This solution has, in turn, led to the fragmenting of the public service.

A. The Tools of Contracting, Grants, and Mandates

Since the most visible and easily understandable sign of big government is the number of public employees, the easiest way to reduce the visibility of big government and to claim credit for shrinking the government is to reduce the number of public employees. There are a number of ways to accomplish this. The federal government (as well as state and local governments) can accomplish public purposes and deliver services through a number of different "tools" that minimize the number of government employees. Tax breaks can be provided to encourage certain activities; mandates can compel businesses or governments to take certain actions; grants can be provided for the accomplishment of certain tasks; and contracts can be made for the provision of goods and services. The delegitimizing of government over the past few decades has made these options for the provision of government services much more attractive and has increased their use.

To put the activities of the federal government into perspective, only about 4 percent of the federal outlays is spent on public workers directly providing goods and services. The majority of spending goes to payments to individuals (58 percent), interest on the debt (15 percent), contracts with private companies for goods and services (13 percent), grants to state and local governments (5 percent), and the armed forces (5 percent).[11]

Many reasons exist for contracting out for goods and services, but in the past several decades other incentives have been added to use contracting.[12] One is the assumption, encouraged by the business sector and many politicians, that businesses are inherently more efficient and better managed than governments, and that money is much better spent if it goes to the private sector.[13] Another driving force in the move to contract out is the delegitimizing of the government; it is much easier for politicians to say that money is being spent efficiently in the private sector. A third driver is the political need to make the government look smaller. These three factors have been constants in the Republican Party, particularly with the conservative turn of the country since the 1970s. But the political appeal of such moves also affected the Democrats, especially the "New Democrats" of the Clinton administration.

The NPR under Gore and Clinton argued for a government that is smaller and costs less. They "delivered" on their promise by cutting the size of the federal civil service by more than 330,000 between 1993 and 1998. This reduction in the federal civilian workforce (excluding the Postal Service) of 15.4 percent brought the number of federal government employees to the lowest level since the Kennedy administration.[14] But the reality may be that these cuts have contributed to a government that appears smaller but continues to deliver the level of services that Americans demand.

Paul Light has challenged the claim that the government is smaller in the 1990s than it has been since the 1960s by calculating what he calls the "shadow government" of those whose jobs are based on grants, contracts, and mandates. He calculates that the $200 billion that the federal government spends on contracts each year creates 5.6 million jobs and that the $55 billion in grants creates 2.4 million jobs. He also argues that federal mandates entail another 4.7 million jobs in state and local governments. Whether or not his methods for counting workers is airtight, his main point stands. Millions of workers not on the federal government payroll are needed to deliver the goods and services that the federal government provides.

The cuts in numbers of employees without significant cuts in the programs of the government imply that the contracting out trend has increased during the Clinton administration (in line with NPR objectives and administration policy). Light's data also make the interesting point that the purposes of contracting have been shifting from the production of goods and products to the provision of services. According to Light, in 1984 one half of contract jobs produced products, whereas in 1996 only one fifth of them were for goods and 80 percent were for services.[15]

B. The Fragmentation of the Civil Service

At the same time that the government has been contracting out more of its functions, the traditional civil service has been fragmenting. The traditional standard for the merit system in the federal government has been the inclusion of employees in the "competitive service" who are subject to appointment under Chapter 33 of Title 5 of the U.S. Code.[16] After the passage of the Pendleton Act of 1883 only 10 percent of federal employees were included in the competitive service, and the law provided that more could be added by presidents "blanketing in" through executive order those not covered. Thus the coverage of the merit system increased to more than 40 percent by 1900 and to 80 percent by 1933 (cut to 66 percent during the New Deal). The high point of the merit system was reached during the 1950s when more than 86 percent of employees were covered.[17]

Since the 1950s the traditional merit system (i.e. the competitive service) has been increasingly fragmented, with coverage dropping to 52 percent in 1996.[18] The rest of federal government employees are in "excepted service," excepted meaning not covered by the hiring authority of Title 5. For instance, the U.S. Postal Service has established its own personnel system since it left the competitive service in 1970. The Foreign Service has its own system, as do the intelligence gathering agencies. In all, 123 organizations of the federal government employ people in excepted services.[19] The fragmenting trend is continuing with the Federal Aviation Administration receiving authority to set up its own system in 1995 and the proposals of the Clinton administration to create separate performance-based organizations (PBOs) with their own hiring authorities outside Title 5.

In 1977 the president's Personnel Management Project, which laid the groundwork for the CSRA, described the excepted service as "a tangled, confusing web of laws, regulations, authorities, and exceptions."[20] The thrust of the CSRA was not to consolidate personnel practice into one plan, however, but to delegate personnel authority to agencies and reserve for OPM oversight and advisory capacity. In recent years, many new members of the civil service entered through excepted authorities rather than through traditional, standardized examinations.[21] In the 1990s OPM has continued to delegate authority to agencies, and by 1998 virtually all hiring has been decentralized and the central registers of OPM no longer exist.[22] The recommendations of the NPR have favored this decentralization and have argued that the old model of centralized authority and uniform rules were based on the manufacturing age of large bureaucracies and no longer appropriate to the information age of small organizations and flat hierarchies.

In another manifestation of this fragmentation, the Department of Defense, which employs about half the government's civilian workforce, was exploring in 1998 possible changes to rationalize its civilian workforce for the future. The assumption was that the workload of the department would fluctuate in the future as it had in the past and that its workforce should be structured so as to be able to gear up for periods of high activity but also be able to gear down for slacker periods without going through disruptive reductions in force. According to its planning proposals, the DOD would contain a core of permanent employees that would be sized to perform a minimum or constant workload that is not appropriate for outsourcing. In the next concentric circle would be a tier of temporary employees who could be hired for periods up to five years. Finally, the third circle would be a large pool of employees who could be hired under contract for specific periods of time.[23]

The National Academy of Public Administration (NAPA) has also made a number of proposals for consideration by the federal government as it adapts to the changing realities of the labor market. The academy proposes that not all federal government workers necessarily be "full-time permanent" employees but that differing relationships between government and employees may create a more flexible workforce. NAPA proposes that the number of competitive federal hiring methods be reduced to three: permanent workers, temporary workers who could be hired without time limits and who would have full benefits, and temporary workers with limited benefits and limited time periods.[24] NAPA argues that inherently governmental or "core" work would be done by employees who have an expectation of continuous work and that noncore work could be done by supplemental workers who do not have the expectation of continuous work.[25]

III. MERIT, THE PUBLIC SERVICE ETHIC, AND ACCOUNTABILITY

The thrust of the above analysis is that recent decades have brought about profound changes in the nature of governance in the United States, the relationship between the role of government and the public service, and the relationship between people who do the public's work and the government. This section takes up three issues that demand consideration. First, how can the ideals of merit be preserved in an environment in which the traditional merit *system* has been coming apart? Second, how can a public service ethic be engendered when most people doing the government's work do not work for the government? Third, how can accountability for public programs be enforced when the workers managing programs are one or several times removed from those responsible for accomplishment of the mission?

A. Merit in Contracting and Political Appointments

Two issues of merit are basic: how to apply it in a new environment and how it relates to political appointees.

1. Merit in Contracting
The merit system, as established by the Pendleton Act of 1883, was based on the foundation of three principles: entry to the system by way of competitive examination, promotion and penalty based on performance, and pro-

tection from actions based on partisan political pressure.[26] In the years since its establishment, many refinements and additions have been overlaid on the merit system.[27]

- Equal opportunity and affirmative action regulations have been included to ensure that entry and promotion are based on merit rather than prejudice.
- Hatch Act (1939 and 1993) regulations have been added to ensure that partisan political activity cannot be coerced.
- Classification systems have been added to facilitate equal pay for similar work across the government.
- Veterans' preferences have been added by law as reward for previous service.
- Agreements have been made with unions in collective bargaining agreements.

The carrying out of merit principles has also come to mean that, after a worker has passed successfully the probationary period, the employee has in effect a guarantee of career-long employment with the government during reasonable performance. The only exceptions are a difficult separation action or a reduction in force.

But the essence of merit is the evaluation of individuals based on their qualifications and performance and the protection from partisan political abuse, that is nonpartisan (or neutral) competence.[28]

In protecting the principle of nonpartisan competence in the traditional merit system the civil service developed a host of rules, regulations, and laws that did a good, though imperfect, job of protecting merit. But the complex system of regulations also tended to bog down the system in procedural detail that impeded managers from managing. It is these negative effects that have led in part to the reaction against the system and to its fragmentation. Managers could not hire or promote without heavy-handed oversight and second guessing from agency personnel shops or the central personnel authority. Neither could managers discipline or fire poor workers without burdensome and elaborate record-keeping and the threat of long, drawn out legal proceedings.[29]

Given the new reality of administrative arrangements (in part created to get around the barnacles of the merit system), how can law assure that the essence of merit—nonpartisan competence—will be preserved? Many public purposes are now being accomplished through indirect administrative linkages in which the government does not have the personnel authority to enforce the traditional trappings of merit. Of course it might try to ensure merit by imposing requirements in contracts that private and nonprofit organizations comply with all of the traditional requirements of the merit system. But that would defeat the purpose of the creation of many of these arrangements in the first place.

What is really needed is the accomplishment of governmental goals, that is, the faithful execution of the law, in an economical, efficient, and effective manner. New institutional arrangements, such as contracts written with private or nonprofit organizations, do not alter these basic goals. What is needed as the minimum, but sufficient, requirement is that these goals be accomplished without discrimination or partisanship. Thus private contracting organizations need to comply with the broadly accepted nondiscrimination principles with which all businesses in the country must comply.

But what should be the concerns with competence beyond nondiscrimination? If a business fulfills the requirements of the contract, should the government care about the internal determination of who is hired or how they are promoted? Imposing intrusive procedural requirements on internal hiring and promotion decisions on private-sector contractors would be unduly intrusive and self defeating. It would bureaucratize and governmentalize the private-sector contractor. Thus, beyond the ensuring of nondiscriminatory policies, it does not make sense for the government to impose the requirements of the traditional merit system on governmental contractors.

On the other hand, this does not imply that contractors should feel free to make hiring and promotional decisions based on nepotism, cronyism, or arbitrary managerial decisions. These practices, apart from their ethical improprieties, impose heavy costs on any organization. Employees are acutely sensitive to these types of maladministration, and any company or nonprofit organization that practices them may suffer negative consequences. But this hands-off approach implies a willingness to put up with some bad managerial judgments in order to provide the necessary flexibility for managers to exercise informed managerial decision making in contracting organizations.

With respect to the merit principle of protection from partisan political interference, either to hire or fire government workers, how can this principle be applied to contractors? Partisan pressure on contractors with respect to personnel decisions, from the executive branch or Congress or political parties, is inappropriate and unlawful. But vigilance is also needed that the awarding of contracts for goods and services not be made on partisan grounds. Thus the oversight of inspectors general in the contract granting departments and agencies is essential to the integrity of the contract process. At the same time, the new flexibilities in contracting achieved in the Clinton administration ought not to be nullified.[30]

In sum, enforcement of the principles of merit in the new world of contracting out much of the government's business ought to focus on essentials and not reimpose all of the burdensome regulations of the traditional merit system. Individuals must be protected from overt discrimination through normal legal processes, and personnel and contracting decisions must not be made on the basis of partisan politics. Beyond that, care is needed that added requirements do not replicate the regulations of the traditional merit system that the new forms of administrative arrangements were designed to escape.

2. Merit and Political Appointments

The antigovernment rhetoric that began in the 1970s and the bureaucrat bashing that it entailed led to a desire for more control by politicians to circumvent what some believed to be iron triangles of linkages among bureaucrats, interest groups, and congressional staffers. One of the results of this felt need for more control was an increase in the number of political appointees in the executive branch. While Germany, France, and Britain each have one or two hundred political appointees who change when partisan control of the government changes, the United States has significantly more. The president can make about five thousand political appointments upon taking office, and about three thousand of these are full-time members of the executive branch.[31]

In 1989 the Volcker Commission recommended that the number of executive branch appointees had been increasing over the past several decades and that the total number of political appointees should be reduced from about 3,000 to about 2,000.[32] According to Paul Light's calculations, the total number of senior executives and presidential appointees increased from 451 in 1960 to 2,393 in 1992.[33] The reasoning behind the Volcker Commission's recommendations was that the increasing numbers of appointees, rather than giving the president more control, actually attenuated responsiveness to the president. That is, appointees often come with political loyalties to sponsors (patrons) other than the president, and the increasing numbers necessarily lead to increasing layers of authority, distancing the appointee responsible for mission accomplishment from the career civil servants actually doing the job.

Light calculates that in 1960 there were up to 17 layers of management at the top of the federal government, and by 1992 there were up to 32.[34] In addition to the management problems brought on by layering and the frequent turnover of appointees, the deeper penetration of the bureaucracy cuts short the careers of the most able civil service executives. Thus a cut in the number of political appointees would lead to an increase of expertise and professionalism near the top of agencies while still allowing for appropriate control of administration policy by presidential appointees.[35] In addition, the large numbers of appointees and their control by the White House have led to a significant slowing of the ability of a new administration to get its appointees in place.[36]

The conditions that led to the recommendations of the Volcker Commission in 1989 have not changed in the ensuing years of the twentieth century. In fact, two of the major changes in the federal civil service reinforce the argument the government has more political appointees than needed. First, the federal civilian workforce has been cut by 330,000, although the reductions were only in the career ranks; the number of political appointees was not reduced. Second, since much of the work of the government has shifted from actually producing goods and services to the oversight of contracts of those who provide the services, the need for political direction of government management should be less. What is needed in the negotiation and oversight of contracts is expertise; the government does not need more political influence in the awarding of contracts.

As Chester Newland has argued (in this volume), merit in the career ranks must be accompanied by merit in the political and executive ranks. Without dedicated and competent political appointees, it will be very difficult to ensure merit and commitment at lower levels. The thrust of the Volcker Commission recommendations was that, with increasing numbers of political appointees, it becomes more difficult to ensure merit throughout the top of the executive leadership system.

B. The Public Service Ethic

The principles of merit as described above are negative in the sense that they are protections *from* bad management, that is personnel decisions based on factors other than merit are prohibited. But we really expect more than protections from abuse in the public service; citizens also expect a can-do spirit and a serious commitment to the public interest. Mission accomplishment needs to take precedence over minor inconvenience or monetary concerns. With the admission that the federal government (as in all large organizations) has its share of slackers and those retired in place, citizens expect the kind of dedication to duty that characterizes the best of the postal service, the armed services, the FBI, and the National Institutes of Health.

Many of the most talented and dedicated public employees join the public service in order to contribute to the public good. The most talented career executives have lucrative options in the private sector where they can make more money but many choose the public service because of the challenge, the nature of the work, and the chance to make a difference in the lives of others. How can Americans preserve the best of this public service ethic—a commitment to the public interest and a willingness to sacrifice in order to accomplish the mission—when much of the public's work is being carried out by nongovernmental organizations?

Incentive systems in the private sector are oriented to the bottom line. Business managers have commitments to stockholders and the future profitability of the company, and there may be times when these commitments override serving the public. But these times should concern business decisions about what business to pursue and which products to produce, not whether to fulfill the requirements of a contract or how well to do a job.

First of all, citizens have the right to expect the spirit of public service to prevail in private-sector organizations that carry out public purposes. That is, contractors who collect refuse ought to be as concerned about public health as are government employees. Private manufacturers of jet fighters ought to be just as careful about quality control as the military maintenance mechanics who service them. Drug manufacturers ought to be just as committed to public health and quality control as the Food and Drug Administration is about ensuring that they are safe and effective. One already sees much of this commitment in the private-sector companies that carry out public programs.

Realistically, most people have mixed motives, and the public service ethic is not universal in government employees, just as maximizing profit is not present in all employees of the private sector. But the commitment of workers ought to be determined by the mission to be accomplished, not who signs their paycheck. The challenge is how to engender the public service ethic and commitment to mission accomplishment in organizations that carry out public purposes, regardless of the legal arrangements of their organization (public, business, nonprofit). The answer is the instillation of public service values through effective leadership, informed management, and good recruitment—that is, merit.[37]

In seeking to instill these values in workers who carry out governmental policy, it is essential to take a broad, inclusive view of public administration. George Frederickson argues that "governance comprehends the full range of public activity—governmental, quasi-governmental, and nongovernmental." This fits with his definition of public administration: "Public administration includes the state; indeed, it is rooted in the state. But it is—and should be—more broadly defined to include the administration or implementation aspects of all forms and manifestations of collective public activity."[38]

Frederickson further argues that there is a danger in focusing too heavily on merely the efficient delivery of goods and services by private contractors to the neglect of the broader public service dimensions of doing the public's business. "The most destructive effect of equating public service with commerce has been the devaluation of public service to just another area in which individuals can achieve essentially private ambitions. . . . This tendency is particularly destructive in public administration, for it attacks the assumption that a special relationship should exist between public servants and citizens in a democracy. . . . The public expects something more from the bureaucracy, and rightly so."[39]

What is needed as the nature of governance changes in the United States is to ensure that the "spirit of public administration," or the "public service ethic" infuses all who do the people's work, regardless of who signs their paycheck.

C. Accountability

A major challenge that has not been fully thought out by the government or the public administration community is the question of accountability. Political accountability is ensuring that the government is doing what the people want it to do and is ensured (more or less) through regular elections. Managerial accountability is achieved through supervision of the work done to assure that policy directives are being faithfully carried out. Traditional accountability has been achieved through the processes of bureaucracy and hierarchy, but as has been pointed out above, the way that the government does business has been changing toward more contracting out. Thus accountability through hierarchy is being replaced by accountability through contract.[40]

In terms of efficiency, contracting out may save the taxpayers' money and may relieve the government of maintaining the personnel necessary to do many jobs itself. On the other hand, contracting for work attenuates the level of control that the government has over the provision of goods and services. If quality and quantity of what is contracted for are easy to specify in a contract, the management problem is relatively simple. But much of what the government acquires through contract is not simple to specify in a contract. If changes in the work are necessary, government leaders cannot give orders; they must renegotiate the contract. As Don Kettl argues, these new arrangements call for a new type of government manager.[41]

In addition to the problematic relationship between government managers and contractors in the era of contracting, there are real dangers of fraud and corruption. The history of U.S. governments at all levels demonstrates that fraud in contracting is a common problem. While most private-sector contractors are honest and competent, some will do their best to defraud the taxpayers.[42] Thus the government needs a new type of manager who can skillfully write contracts and oversee them for quality and to detect fraud. The dangers of fraud and the government programs at potential risk for abuse are specified by Don Kettl in his book on government contracting, *Sharing Power*.[43]

In his analysis of the implications of the new wave of contracting, George Frederickson argues that fraud will again become a major problem. "Hollowing out bureaucracy and eliminating regulations will make the seedbed for corruption and scandal . . . contracts have always made a tempting environment for kickbacks and fraud."[44] He goes on to predict another wave of reforms. "The reforms that are being adopted may, at the margins, make government more productive, but they will almost certainly result in less ethical government. This being the case, in the years ahead we will eventually see another reform movement emphasizing administrative expertise, a merit-based civil service insulated from political meddling, and the use of regulations to control corruption."[45]

CONCLUSION

As America enters the twenty-first century, those concerned with the quality and integrity of the public service have reason to be optimistic, but there are also reasons to be concerned. The trend of contracting out has created a strain in the federal public service because it has increased uncertainty and was based in part on the premise that government workers are inefficient.

But the more we learn about contracting the more we transcend this simplistic premise and the more we know about when contracting pays off and when it is inappropriate.

The great battles over the role of the national government in the last three decades of the twentieth century have been bruising to the public service. On the other hand, the pulling and hauling may have brought the political system to an equilibrium in which the general scope of governmental action will be accepted across the mainstream political spectrum despite disagreements at the margins. If this is the case, the public service can return to its mission of faithfully executing the laws.

Government still faces the continuing challenges of ensuring the status of merit within the public service and demanding nonpartisan efficiency in the contracting community. Accountability to the will of the people expressed in public law is essential. Finally, the public service ethic must be engendered in all those who do the people's work, regardless of who signs the paycheck.

NOTES

1. See Patricia Ingraham, *The Foundation of Merit* (Baltimore: Johns Hopkins University Press, 1995), 34.

2. Ingraham, *The Foundation of Merit*, 34. With the sudden increase in government programs and workers in the early years of the New Deal, not all new workers were covered by the merit system. Thus the percentage of workers covered dropped during Roosevelt's first term.

3. See Chester A. Newland, "Politics of Transition from the Administrative to the Facilitative State," in this volume.

4. For an analysis of presidential suspicion toward the career bureaucracy, see James P. Pfiffner, *The Strategic Presidency: Hitting the Ground Running,* 2d edition (Lawrence: University Press of Kansas, 1996), 74–6. The quote is from *Public Papers of the Presidents 1971,* 448.

5. Quoted in Pfiffner, *The Strategic Presidency,* 75, from *Congressional Quarterly Weekly Reports* (16 October 1976), 3009.

6. Ingraham, *The Foundation of Merit,* 71.

7. The self-interest claim, while partially true, was a narrow and cynical perspective, but the efficacy of bureaucratic efforts to protect their programs was belied by the significant domestic program and budget cuts of Reagan's first budget in 1981. See Pfiffner, *The Strategic Presidency,* chaps. 4, 5.

8. See James P. Pfiffner, "The National Performance Review in Perspective," *International Journal of Public Administration* 20, no. 1 (1997): 41–70.

9. See James P. Pfiffner, "President Clinton, Newt Gingrich, and the 104th Congress," in *On Parties: Essays Honoring Austin Ranney,* ed. Nelson W. Polsby and Raymond E. Wolfinger (Berkeley, Calif.: Institute of Governmental Studies Press, 2000).

10. Clinton's statement symbolized the Democratic acceptance of a more conservative political consensus in much the same way that President Nixon's statement that "We are all Keynesians now" symbolized the Republican acceptance of deficit spending and the welfare state.

11. Donald Kettl et al., *Civil Service Reform: Building a Government That Works.* (Washington, D.C.: Brookings Institution Press, 1996), 4.

12. A number of good reasons support contracting rather than directly providing government services. It can be done because expertise is needed that the government does not have. It can be done to gear up for a task for which the need for the workers will no longer exist once that task has been accomplished. Many goods can be produced more efficiently than the government could do it, and the competition of the marketplace may result in lower prices. Special expertise may be available that does not exist in the government. Private-sector companies can operate without many of the procedural rules and constraints that the government must follow.

13. See James P. Pfiffner, "The American Tradition of Administrative Reform," in *The White House and the Blue House: Government Reform in the United States and Korea,* ed. Yong Hyo Cho and H. George Frederickson (New York: University Press of America, 1997).

14. Donald Kettl, *Reinventing Government: A Fifth-Year Report Card* (Washington, D.C.: Brookings Institution Press, 1998), 18.

15. Paul C. Light, "The True Size of Government," *Government Executive* (January 1999).

16. U.S. General Accounting Office, "The Excepted Service: A Research Profile" (May 1997), GAO/GGD-97-72, 1.

17. Data can be found in U.S. Civil Service Commission, *Biography of an Ideal: The Diamond Anniversary History of the Federal Civil Service* (Washington, D.C.: Government Printing Office, 1958), and updates by OPM presented in Ingraham, *The Foundation of Merit,* 34.

18. GAO, "The Excepted Service," 11. This probably overstates the coverage, since employees of the CIA, DIA, and NSA are not included in the data used to calculate the percentages.

19. GAO, "The Excepted Service," 5.

20. *The President's Reorganization Project: Personnel Management Project—Final Staff Report,* vol. 1 (December 1977), 42, as quoted in GAO, 23.

21. Ingraham, *The Foundation of Merit,* 56.

22. See Carolyn Ban, "The National Performance Review as Implicit Evaluation of CSRA: Building on or Overturning the Legacy?" in this volume. The OPM workforce dropped from 6,861 in 1993 to 3,567 in 1998. (Patricia Ingraham and Donald

Moynihan, "Evolving Dimensions of Performance from the CSRA Onward," in this volume.) The number of personnelists in the government has decreased by 21 percent (8,900) from 1993 to 1998. Chester Newland, "Politics of Transition from the Administrative to the Facilitative State," in this volume.

23. Presentation of Diane M. Disney, deputy assistant secretary of defense for civilian personnel policy (May 15, 1998).

24. NAPA, *New Options, New Talent: The Government Guide to the Flexible Workforce*, HRM Series IV, Washington, NAPA (August 1998), xiv.

25. NAPA, *New Options, New Talent*, 14. While these three categories might simplify some aspects of federal hiring, chapter 2 of the NAPA report describes four types of relationships that might exist between an employee and the government that might be through intervening organizations such as a professional employer organization (PEO), consulting firm, temporary help company, or an independent contractor (17–21). This new workforce might be more flexible, but it would certainly not be more simple.

26. Ingraham, *The Foundation of Merit*, 56. A longer list of merit principles can be found in Title 5 (section 2302b) and is adapted in "The Merit System Principles," OPM pamphlet MES-97-2 (June 1997).

27. See the list of overlays on the merit system in Ingraham, *The Foundation of Merit*, 57.

28. We ought not to expect public servants, or political appointees for that matter, to be neutral with respect to program. We expect that since they have committed a portion of their careers to the carrying out of public purposes, they will be advocates for the accomplishment of those purposes. This expectation of legitimate advocacy does not, however, justify fanaticism, zealotry, or unethical practices in the protection of their "turf." We still expect that they will render their best judgment to political superiors in the executive branch and members of Congress and abide by authoritative policy decisions.

29. For an analysis of the reasons why federal managers often do not use the regulations available to remove poor performers, see U.S. Merit Systems Protection Board, Office of Policy and Evaluation, "Removing Poor Performers in the Federal Service (September 1995).

30. For an analysis of the changes in contracting achieved in the first term of the Clinton administration see Steve Kelman, "Implementing Federal Procurement Reform," in *The Managerial Presidency*, 2d ed., ed. James P. Pfiffner (College Station: Texas A & M University Press, 1999).

31. For the data on political appointments see James P. Pfiffner, *The Modern Presidency*, 2d edition (New York: St. Martin's Press), 117.

32. National Commission on the Public Service, *Leadership for America: Rebuilding the Public Service* (Washington, D.C., 1989. For a detailed argument for a reduction in the number of political appointees, see the *Task Force Reports to the Commission*, "Politics and Performance: Strengthening the Executive Leadership System"

(157–90). The Task Force on Relations between Political Appointees and Career Executives was chaired by Elliot L. Richardson; the staff director was James P. Pfiffner.

33. Paul Light, *Thickening Government* (Washington, D.C.: Brookings Institution Press, 1995), 7.

34. Light, *Thickening Government*, 7.

35. For a trenchant critique of our patronage system in the executive branch, see David M. Cohen, "Amateur Government," *Journal of Public Administration and Theory* 8, no. 4 (October 1998): 450–98.

36. For data on the pace of political appointments, see Pfiffner, *The Strategic Presidency*, Chapter 8 and Conclusion.

37. For an analysis of effective leadership in the public and private sectors, see Hal G. Rainey and J. Edward Kellough, "Civil Service Reform and Incentives in the Public Service," in this volume.

38. H. George Frederickson, *The Spirit of Public Administration* (San Francisco: Jossey-Bass, 1997), 225.

39. Frederickson, *The Spirit of Public Administration*, 195–96.

40. For a typology of different kinds of accountability and their implications, see Barbara S. Romzek, "Accountability Implications of Civil Service Reform," in this volume.

41. Donald Kettl, *Sharing Power* (Washington, D.C.: Brookings Institution Press, 1993).

42. For one egregious case, see Norma Riccucci, *Unsung Heroes: Federal Executrats Making a Difference* (Washington, D.C.: Georgetown University Press, 1995), Chapter 5, "Stephen Marica: Using the Wedtech Scandal to Establish Credibility."

43. Kettl, *Sharing Power*, 4–5.

44. Frederickson, *The Spirit of Public Administration*, 193.

45. Frederickson, *The Spirit of Public Administration*, 194.

CHAPTER TWO

WHAT WAS BEHIND THE 1978 CIVIL SERVICE REFORM?

DWIGHT INK

Twenty years after passage of the Civil Service Reform Act of 1978 and the reorganization plan that accompanied it, the original philosophy behind the reform has begun to fade and is often misconstrued. Since it still provides the legal framework for much of our federal civil service system, it may be useful to review the background for the reform and what it was intended to accomplish before deciding whether and how it should be changed. In this chapter I will provide my perspective as executive director of President Carter's Personnel Management Project, which had the task of designing the reform.

BACKGROUND FOR REFORM

Public Environment

Between the passage of the 1883 Pendleton Act and 1977 when President Carter took office, the civil service system never had a broadly based review. Many observers of good government, as well as those in government, had come to believe that an overhaul was long overdue. The level of respect for government service had declined sharply by 1977. One heard frequent comments about the "lazy bureaucrat" and "parasites feeding at the public trough." At the first meeting of a group of corporation vice presidents I convened, we were shocked when the first speaker thundered, "If you do nothing else in this reform, make sure you can fire the wasteful bureaucrats." In the public mind, we had a civil service system that fostered incompetent bureaucrats who could not be fired.

Red Tape

Over the years a myriad of laws, regulations, and procedures had accumulated. Most were well-intentioned measures to improve personnel management or to provide protection against discrimination or political abuse. But new procedures tended to be simply added to old ones rather than using new developments as an opportunity to eliminate or modernize outdated approaches. As a consequence, process dominated substance. Personnel officers were reduced to technicians with little time, and very little encouragement, to address the positive aspects of human resource management. Timely personnel actions grew so difficult in many agencies that program managers tended to regard the civil service system as a hindrance to securing and retaining good people rather than as a partner. As much as possible, they distanced themselves from the personnel offices and were often reluctant to even meet with personnel officers.

All this drove many agency personnel people to rely more on enforcement of procedures that limited program managers, rather than focusing on how to help them move their programs forward. Agency managers who were credited with being action-oriented were often those who had become skilled in shortcutting or ignoring those procedures, further weakening respect for the merit system.

Merit Concept Undermined

Much of this red tape had accumulated in the system as safeguards from political pressures that threatened the merit concept, a concept that had grown out of public revulsion against the corruption produced by the earlier spoils system. Yet during the Watergate period, we saw that neither the ever increasing protective processes nor the bipartisan Civil Service Commission prevented a major assault on the integrity of the civil service system. We concluded:

the entangling web of safeguards spun over the years often fails to protect against major political assaults and cronyism. . . . With each new protective measure, there seems to have emerged new techniques to manipulate the system as best illustrated by the so-called May-Malek Manual.[1]

These assaults were usually justified under the guise of developing more flexible management and making employees more responsive to public needs. Making government more like the private sector was often said to be the way in which to achieve those goals. The Civil Service Commission (CSC) had been unable to stem the tide that was undermining merit concepts until after Nixon and his White House political operatives resigned. Not surprisingly, the willingness of the CSC commissioners to compromise and to mute criticism of political forays into the career service were viewed by the White House as weakness, and they were treated with contempt.[2]

Further, the enormous burden of handling personnel complaints made it very difficult for the CSC to devote the time and effort needed to provide leadership for modernizing human resource management throughout the government. Our task forces believed the public was the biggest loser in this system that could neither promote effective management nor safeguard against political abuse. We argued:

> It is the public which suffers from a system which neither permits managers to manage nor provides employees adequate assurance against political abuse. Valuable resources are lost to the public by a system increasingly too cumbersome to compete effectively for talent. . . . It is families everywhere who suffer from mismanagement of social programs caused by incompetent and inexperienced executives appointed on the basis of personal friendships rather than managerial qualifications. It is hard-pressed neighborhoods and communities across the nation who are discriminated against on a massive basis by managerial decisions which divert grants elsewhere because of the influence of a mayor, governor, or member of Congress.[3]

ORGANIZING FOR CSRA

With the strong support of Bert Lance, Carter's first director of OMB, Carter's new chair of the CSC, Scotty Campbell, provided vigorous leadership in organizing the President's Personnel Management Project as a closely knit political/career team to design the reform. Scotty served as chair of the project and Wayne Granquist of OMB served as vice chair. I was granted six months leave from American University to serve as executive director.

For many reasons, particularly the desire to move forward at a rapid pace and to ensure the workability of the reform, the design was done largely by career men and women. Of the nine task forces that developed the recommendations, for example, distinguished career persons chaired all but one. Input from political appointees was welcomed and taken into consideration, but in no case was the staff directed or pressured by them to change its views. The Carter administration was not bound by what the task forces might recommend, but Scotty knew that having the reform developed largely by career men and women would reduce apprehension within the bureaucracy and increase credibility on the Hill. As it turned out, there was very little difference in the conclusions of the career and political participants in the process. The final staff report containing all 120 recommendations was forwarded to the president and Congress with no revisions by OMB or CSC.[4] It provided Congress with the rationale for reform.

Seldom, if ever, has development of a major reform been so open. At three different stages during the six-month design phase, the task force analyses and options for change were issued at press conferences. Under a broad outreach program designed by Dona Wolf, these were also distributed directly to as many as 1,400 groups and individuals for comment, and several public hearings were conducted in different parts of the country. Congressional staffs were invited to send representatives to our staff meetings and a GAO representative was free to visit with any of the task forces. As a result, the congressional committees were well informed as we developed our recommendations and there were no surprises in what President Carter submitted to Congress.

This open and consensus building approach, combined with the energetic leadership of Scotty Campbell and strong support from Jule Sugarman and OMB, resulted in the wide ranging reform legislation being enacted and implementation begun less than eighteen months after the task forces were organized.

PHILOSOPHY UNDERLYING CSRA

Few evaluations of CSRA have reflected the basic concept of those who designed the reform. Most of them have focused on only certain elements of what we had hoped to accomplish. Others have erroneously stated that we were trying to develop greater political control of the career service. The following statement in my final project staff report summarizes the staff philosophy that underlay our proposals:

The staff recommendations in this report are based on the premise that jobs and programs in the federal government belong neither to employees nor to managers. They belong to the people. The public has a right to have an effective government which is responsive to their needs as perceived by the president and Congress, but which at the same time is impartially administered.

Managers have no right to impose new spoils systems under the guise of flexibility. Neither do they have a right to mismanage public programs by hiring incompetent cronies. They must, however, be free to manage or there will be little accountability. . . . Employees have no right . . . to cling to jobs in which they cannot, or will not, perform adequately. They do, however, have a right to work in a public service that is free of discrimination and partisan political influence, and they have a right to expect advancement to be determined on the basis of merit.[5]

In other words, we attempted to proceed with twin objectives. On the one hand, we wanted to strip the system of its stultifying emphasis on detailed time-consuming processes so that managers were free to manage and the personnel community could focus on modernizing human resource management.

On the other hand, we wanted to put in place sufficient safeguards to minimize the new flexibilities being abused through discrimination or politicization of the career service. Congress agreed and underscored this philosophy in the purpose with which Congress began the 1978 statute. It should be kept in mind today by those administering the act.

It may be useful to review the breadth of the principal changes we sought. From my perspective the following elements represented the most significant changes embodied in the reform.

MODERNIZING HUMAN RESOURCE MANAGEMENT

Streamlining the System

- **Simplification.** In order to free managers to manage and to facilitate faster action, we urged drastic cuts in both government-wide procedures and those within agencies. This included simplifying reduction-in-force processes and the complex structure and procedures for appeals, grievances, and discrimination complaints. We knew from experience that streamlined systems outside the civil service could function without becoming politicized, given proper leadership and insulation from political pressures in administering programs.

- **Decentralization.** Personnel management authorities were to be decentralized to levels as near as possible to program operations in the agencies, including presidential authority that would permit assigning examining responsibility to agencies. Experience had shown that decentralization, when done properly, had contributed greatly to reducing red tape and accelerating action. We believed that it would also permit agencies to adapt personnel approaches to their specific needs, although we also believed that central standards, guidelines, and monitoring had to be provided.

  In retrospect, we should have said more about how to manage decentralization and greater agency flexibility. Effective decentralization, in contrast to devolution, has nearly always required a central leadership role that included (a) a few central guidelines explaining what the decentralized activities are designed to accomplish, (b) the ability to ascertain the capacity and readiness of an organization to exercise the new authorities, (c) the authority to monitor the decentralized activities in a constructive way, and (d) the capacity to assist organizations that encounter difficulty in handling their new responsibilities. This leadership role requires the retention of highly qualified professional men and women with the experience to command the respect of those they are monitoring and assisting. Unfortunately, we assumed these points were widely recognized and did not require repetition by us. Events have proven otherwise.

- **Central Controls.** Centrally mandated controls that inhibit good management, such as personnel ceilings, were to be eliminated for agencies with adequate accounting and other management systems. The recommendation to eliminate ceilings did not sell.

Better Management

- **Replace CSC.** In order to move forward vigorously with the range of changes we believed necessary to modernize the civil service system, the CSC was to be replaced by means of a reorganization plan with a single headed Office of Personnel Management (OPM). The new agency could devote its full energies to improving personnel management without the time-consuming function of handling employee appeals, a function many thought represented a conflict of missions. We believed the OPM director should have broad human resource experience in the private and/or public sector(s) with sufficient stature to provide government-wide leadership, a point we should have stressed more heavily.

- **Productivity**. We urged the strengthening of programs to measure and enhance productivity. Our recommendations did not specify whether this should be achieved through TQM, MBO, or some other mechanism, but the Senior Executive Service (SES) recommendations included a greater emphasis on progress toward the organization mission and objectives in measuring effectiveness, and less on personal traits or process and workload. (The Government Performance and Results Act [GPRA] has addressed this need more effectively than we did twenty years ago.)

- **Job Quality.** We were investing substantial taxpayer funds in federal salaries, but we had fallen far behind the private sector in providing for the quality of working life that could increase our return on that investment. The task forces recommended improvements, such as job redesign, bonus pay plans, flextime, and improved working environments.

- **Workforce Planning**. One of our task forces found that workforce planning was inadequate and sporadic. It was used primarily to implement budget decisions rather than as a basis for arriving at budget decisions. Agencies said that careful workforce planning was ignored by the budget cutters, so why bother? Budget personnel, on the other hand, complained that workforce plans were developed in a dream world unrelated to the realities of available resources. Nevertheless, we recommended systematic workforce planning in the hope that a government-wide effort would more likely result in the budget process working more in tandem with workforce planning rather than against it.

- **New Approaches**. Both CSC and those agencies in the civil service system had been quite limited in the extent new approaches to personnel management could be developed. We urged the expansion of basic and applied personnel research and new authority to pilot test new management techniques. Congress was wary of steps that might provide an opening wedge for new ways in which to undermine the merit system, however, and enacted only a very limited version.

45

- **Broaden the Talent Base.** Concerned that the government was failing to draw upon the talent represented by those other than white males, several recommendations were advanced to improve opportunities for women and minorities, including the setting of nonquota goals. Most of these recommendations did not require additional legislation.
- **Employee Development.** We urged the establishment of a government-wide effort to strengthen the systems within agencies for developing employees, including special emphasis on executive development programs. This was needed both to improve their job performance in their current assignments and to prepare them to fill positions of greater responsibility in the future. We found it particularly ironic that a number of those most vocal about reshaping government more like business nevertheless failed to be concerned that outside defense, government agencies rarely devoted more than a fraction of the effort to employee development that one found in successful corporations. Employee development was often viewed as an important company investment by the very same private sector leaders who regarded similar expenditures in government as too costly and fodder for budget cutters.
- **Training Contracts.** We recommended improvement in the procurement of training services, particularly greater assurance of competence of the contractor employees.
- **Broad Based Training.** We suggested the development of standards and ethics training for all government employees to provide a clear understanding of their responsibilities to the public. I doubt that our task forces would have endorsed the recent shift of emphasis from serving the citizen to that of serving the customer, but the issue never arose.
- **Mobility.** Several task forces agreed that most supervisory and management personnel lacked the experience and breadth of judgment gained through serving in organizations that were needed for advancement to higher levels of management responsibility. We recommended elimination of financial and other barriers that discouraged mobility, but I do not believe we gave enough attention to positive incentives to encourage mobility. And we should have warned about the damage of using mobility to achieve political objectives.
- **Performance Ratings.** Our task force recommended replacing the existing complex, centrally mandated performance-rating proce-

dures with broad guidelines allowing for streamlined evaluation processes. We recommended that awards for performance be related more closely to performance, which often seemed not to be the case. This area of recommendations turned out to be much more difficult to implement than we anticipated.

- **Probationary Period.** We recommended establishing a probationary period for initial assignment to a managerial position.
- **Compensation.** We concluded that pay comparability studies as then designed were vulnerable to criticism that weakened the case for comparability. We advocated a total compensation approach, which included both pay and benefits in pay comparability analyses. We also recommended the inclusion of state and local pay in these analyses.

In addition to the merit pay recommendations for the SES, we recommended that a merit pay system be pilot tested to determine the feasibility of rewarding performance of managers below the SES. In my view, during the implementation stage this concept was applied too broadly at the GS-13, 14, and 15 levels, before being tested adequately. The new performance evaluation systems were much too paper oriented, and were eventually abandoned. As our task force work progressed, it also became increasingly clear that the pay for performance concept was not nearly as well developed in the private sector as the literature implied, leading me to place more emphasis on pilot efforts and phased implementation than otherwise would have been the case. Because of the political realities of the need for producing results during a presidential term, neither Scotty nor OMB could afford the amount of merit pay testing I had envisaged.

- **Veterans' Preference.** We also urged that veterans' preference be limited to a one-time initial period to help returning veterans adjust to civilian life, except for disabled veterans who should retain lifetime benefits. Among other things, we believed that this preference worked against equal opportunities for women, few of whom were veterans. Despite an aggressive effort by Scotty to sell this change, Congress rejected most of our proposal.
- **SES.** A major result of President Carter's Personnel Management Project was the enactment of the Senior Executive Service legislation, which provided a new personnel management structure for selecting, developing, and managing top level federal executives. Beginning with the second Hoover Commission, efforts under sev-

eral presidents had been made to establish some type of senior service, but without success. Considerable CSC thought already had been given to the concept before our task force chaired by Sally Greenberg translated these earlier ideas into a workable proposal. Recommended SES characteristics included:

— A rank-in-person personnel system, with limitations on the number permitted to rise to the top of the ranks. In addition to the flexibility this would give agencies in assigning SES members, we believed this provision would permit highly qualified career men and women to be given greater responsibilities.

— A system of accountability for organizational performance linked with both compensation and tenure. We recommended elimination of longevity pay increases, and substitution of one-time bonuses based on performance.

We regarded the existing performance measurement systems as virtually worthless for linking with bonuses or other pay incentives, however. Because the evaluations had been based largely on personal characteristics and behavior of individuals, few managers had either the qualifications or the inclination to produce evaluations that were perceived as valid. I hoped our recommendations would lead to the more useful approach of basing evaluations of SES members much more on the extent to which organizations they supervised met their program goals and objectives. Today we call this moving from inputs to outcomes. In fact, I thought this recommendation was one of our most important from the standpoint of more effective government.

— A systematic executive development program, including a requirement that individuals demonstrate managerial capability before entering the service.

— Agency head authority to reassign senior executives to best accomplish the agency's mission.[6]

Management-Labor Relations

FLRA

In addition to the foregoing features, the CSRA provided a legal foundation, including the establishment of the Federal Labor Relations Authority to replace the more transitory executive order framework for federal management-labor relations activities. This was very advantageous to the unions, but not surprisingly they objected to our recommendation that certain management functions be excluded from the scope of bargaining. Several such functions were under negotiation at the time, and in at least one instance, already incorporated in an agreement.

I met jointly with all the federal union leaders even before our task force was organized, but most unions did not take our project seriously at first, believing we had no chance of passing such broad reform legislation. It was unfortunate that most of them did not take advantage of their opportunities for early participation. The chapter in this volume by Chester Newland who played a key role in this part of the reform addresses this topic in some depth.

NEW SAFEGUARDS AGAINST ABUSE

We all believed that, in the absence of new safeguards, streamlining the civil service system along the lines we were recommending would increase vulnerability to abuse and politicization of the career service. Still vivid in our minds was the Watergate period in which flexibilities in the system had been pressed to, and beyond, their legal limit. Also the linkage between patronage and corruption we had seen unfold in GSA and elsewhere simply had to be avoided by preventing the former. Integrity of the career service was to be protected at the same time it was to be revitalized. To counter the vulnerabilities to abuse which future leaders might exploit, we made new safeguards a key component of CSRA:

- **MSPB.** A critical part of the reform was the establishment of an independent bipartisan Merit Systems Protection Board and Special Counsel to adjudicate appeals, investigate possible merit violations, and perform special studies concerning the overall performance under the CSRA. Special emphasis was to be given to emerging systemic problems that threatened to violate the merit principles and undermine the integrity of the career services. Investigative powers not available to the CSC were included in the new law. I characterized the board and counsel as the "cornerstone" of our proposals and assured Congress that we had built into the law those safeguards that could prevent future politicization of the career service.

   Congress would never have enacted the CSRA without the promise of a strong and vigorous MSPB that Congress believed could discover and correct abuse on a timely basis.

- **Merit Principles.** The new legislation specified basic merit principles to be followed. Giving these the stature of law was deemed of critical importance.
- **Prohibited Practices.** The act also specified certain personnel practices that were to be prohibited. One who was especially anxious to see a more dynamic and creative civil service, Jule Sugarman, was also a leader in recognizing the need for merit principles and prohibited practices being given the force of law.
- **GAO Role.** Because the work of the GAO had been heavily focused on financial related issues, we recommended that GAO now assume heavier oversight responsibilities in the field of human resource management from a perspective broader than just money or compliance with regulations.
- **SES Safeguards.** Because of greater discretion afforded top management with respect to SES personnel actions, the following legal safeguards were specified for the SES, provisions not many people realize are all in the law:[7]
    - *Arbitrary Actions.* The act requires protection of career executives from arbitrary or capricious actions. Although the law granted considerable freedom to managers in administering the SES system, it is clear that Congress did not intend that flexibility to be misused through vindictive or other unreasonable actions toward SES personnel.
    - *Political Interference.* The law requires an executive system that is guided by the public interest and free from improper political interference. As we stated in our report, the SES positions belong to the public, not to the political party or special interest group to which a presidential appointee would feel obligated to put "their people" in key career positions.
    - *120 Day Get-Acquainted Period.* Except for misconduct, a new noncareer executive is prohibited from moving subordinate career executives out of their positions until at least 120 days after the noncareer executive is appointed. The purpose of this provision was to give the SES incumbent an opportunity to demonstrate what he or she could contribute to the programs and policies for which the new appointee had responsibility. It was intended to provide a "get acquainted" period during which the appointee could determine whether the relationship would be a positive one. And if the decision were then made to reassign the

person, the appointee would be in a better position to determine where that person could contribute most effectively.[8]

The current OPM interpretation that the decision to move an SES incumbent out of a position can be made immediately so long as the paperwork does not occur for 120 days is totally at odds with what Congress intended.

— *Prohibited Practices.* Not fully recognized by many, the law requires an SES merit personnel system free of CSRA prohibited personnel practices.

— *Limited Political Appointees.* The proportion of noncareer managers in the SES was limited by statute to 10 percent of the total in order to halt the steady increase in their numbers that was taking place in most nondefense agencies prior to CSRA. Sensitive positions requiring nonpartisan actions were to be reserved for career managers. My recommendation that field managers awarding grants and contracts be reserved for career people to help guard against politicizing the award process was not approved.

Based on our experience in the Atomic Energy Commission, I initially envisaged a separate subsystem within the SES for high level technical personnel who were hard to retain under the existing system. The type of incentives, the qualifications, and the mobility being considered for our proposed SES were tailored for managers, not technical men and women, although some technical people undoubtedly had the managerial talent to be trained for SES managerial positions. It soon became apparent, however, that these people were fearful that they would be exposed to political pressures in any component of an SES and would oppose any such arrangement, thereby placing the whole SES concept in jeopardy. I dropped the idea.

WHERE IS THE CSRA TODAY?

In looking at CSRA today, we need to remind ourselves that, important as the 1978 act and Reorganization Plan were, success of the reform required far more than laws. It relied upon an interrelated mix of legislative and executive branch actions. The recommendations on red tape cutting and decentralizing personnel management authorities, for example, depended heavily on how the new system would be managed. The same was true of reforms envisaged in such areas as workforce planning, productivity enhancement, executive development, increased mobility, and modernized agency personnel management. Success required highly qualified leadership. I have several observations concerning where I believe we are today:

Progress

Streamlining and decentralization are reform objectives that have been given new life in recent years. OPM and most agencies are taking many positive steps to take advantage of the flexibilities made possible by CSRA. A new spirit of experimentation and innovation is moving forward with strong support from the Vice President. The reinvention laboratories may lead to steps that have great payoff in the future. Personnel officers are encouraged to concentrate on better human resource management, and less on detailed procedures. Particularly since the passage of GPRA, considerable effort is being devoted to refocusing managers from outputs to outcomes.

All of this progress is in the spirit of the CSRA, while taking advantage of knowledge and experience gained since 1978.

These welcome steps deserve commendation and support.

Concerns

The positive dimension of current actions has been given extensive coverage, as they should. Because far less attention has been given to the problem areas, they will be given more coverage here.

OPM Role

As the decentralization authorized by CSRA has taken place, and OPM has downsized through NPR more than any other agency, many are concerned that OPM has not retained the leadership role contemplated by the reform. Greater attention seems to be given to how many employees can be eliminated (without much attention to the number and cost of contract employees and private consultants required to replace them) than to the effectiveness of the agency. Successful decentralizations in the past have shown the value of a strong central leadership capacity considerably stronger than we critics now see in OPM to monitor the decentralization and provide professional assistance where needed.

MSPB Role

The MSPB got off to a rocky start and has never recovered. No administration has regarded the board as sufficiently important to deserve decent funding. Neither has Congress. Appropriations committees have not shared the original concept of the oversight committees regarding the need for a counter weight to a politically motivated OPM. The board has certainly never developed as the "cornerstone" I had contemplated, and has often had difficulty in determining exactly what its role is. When the board does demonstrate courage, it generally comes under heavy political attack and few come to its defense. Today there seems to be very little constituency for MSPB and the preservation of a nonpartisan career service the MSPB is supposed to protect.

The MSPB Office of Policy and Evaluation has had excellent people but does not have anything approaching the resources needed to uncover systemic problems related to the merit principles and prohibited practices. Congress has tended to look upon the special studies as duplicative of OPM work. This is due in part to the fact that over its lifetime, so many of the MSPB studies, while useful, have been of the type that OPM should be doing rather than its primary mission under the law to conduct studies and report to the president and Congress on whether the "public interest in a civil service free of prohibited personnel practices is being adequately protected."

Office of Special Counsel

With the exception of whistleblowing cases, the Office of Special Counsel is seen as timid, in my view. Its processes involve too much secrecy (not to be confused with investigations that do require secrecy), and I believe the staff has developed very questionable views toward due process. At times its actions give the unintended appearance of protecting prohibited practices by political appointees rather than exposing them.

Presidential Appointees

Finally, experience since 1978 has once again shown how dependent effective implementation is on the quality of the appointees a president selects to provide the necessary political leadership. A number of those involved in the birth of CSRA believe the political leadership in OPM, MSPB, and the Special Counsel has been of very uneven quality. Both Scotty and I believed that some future changes in the law would be desirable from time to time. We also believed, however, that no changes in the law were likely to improve our civil service system to the potential envisaged by CSRA until presidents and cabinet members would come to regard government human resource management as important as major corporations regard vice presidents for human resource management.

GAO Role

The GAO has been hard-pressed to provide the added emphasis to assessing threats to the integrity of the public service that the reform intended. Because of the recent, ill-advised downsizing of GAO, it may be even less able to do so in the future.

These institutional shortcomings have contributed to other CSRA problems:

SES Abuse

Of particular concern to some of us is the seeming failure of OPM, MSPB, and the Special Counsel to take the law very seriously with respect to the legal safeguards that were enacted to protect SES against political and arbitrary abuse of the much greater management flexibility embodied in the reform. It seems clear that one of the reasons mobility has not increased as hoped, for example, is the bad name it has regained through the use of job reassignments for punitive purposes in recent years rather than executive development or better agency utilization and executive development as the reform intended. The 120-day "get acquainted" provision has been distorted beyond recognition. The important SES safeguard in the law against "arbitrary" actions is seen as ignored.

What have been the consequences? We know of cases of abuse in OPM and various agencies reminiscent of the Watergate days. However, there is no oversight capacity today to tell us whether there are only a few such cases or if the problem is more endemic. But the fact that these abuses occur without remedial action indicates that my assurances to Congress that the CSRA safeguards would be effective were overly optimistic.

Mobility

In addition to punitive actions poisoning the image of mobility, the movement toward balkanization of civil service systems may become a significant barrier to future efforts to facilitate mobility among agencies. The weakened condition of OPM and the budget focus of OMB management activities have reduced the likelihood of them regaining their role in facilitating the top level career mobility that began to emerge in the 1960s and early 1970s.

Training and Development

The emphasis on employee and executive development has not been given the impetus recommended in the reform, and after a temporary resurgence under OPM Director Constance Newman, many believe we have now lost ground. The current devaluing of a public service career reduces the incentive that agencies might otherwise have in investing resources needed to enhance the future contribution of career people. This decline is particularly unfortunate in view of the current need for greater efforts to support the large amount of change required by NPR and GPRA.

Privatizing the bulk of training that OPM used to provide is supported by some but perceived by others as a message that employee development is no longer a priority. Regardless of whether this is true, there should be an independent evaluation of the costs, quality, and adequacy of the privatized development program in comparison with the programs formerly conducted by OPM.

LOOKING AHEAD

With twenty years of experience behind us, it may be timely to review both the concepts and the implementation of CSRA, but it should be done with care and based on facts rather than assumptions. During the analysis phase of CSRA, for example, we found that many of the problems people blamed on the law turned out on more careful scrutiny to grow more out of poor agency management and weak leadership. We now need to review current problems in sufficient depth to determine which problems require new legislation and which can be solved through management and procedural changes under existing authority.

The next major review of the federal public service should include the political appointees as well as career men and women. It should consider the carefully developed recommendations of the Volcker Commission for fewer political appointees, the political thickening of government highlighted by Paul Light, and work done by organizations such as panels of the National Academy of Public Administration and the Council for Excellence in Government. It is unrealistic to believe that our public service can achieve peak performance without examining the enormous impact, both positive and negative, of our political leadership and how it can be improved.

As we move forward with adjustments and occasional reforms over the years, I would urge retention of the basic concept of CSRA even though it has been difficult to implement. Career men and women can carry out policies of new political leadership more effectively in a streamlined personnel system that relies more on developing and retaining highly qualified personnel than numerous checks and balances, *provided* these men and women have the opportunity to develop to their full potential and they are protected from political pressures in their nonpartisan execution of these policies and the laws.

NOTES

1. *Final Staff Report*, President's Personnel Management Project, December 1977, v.

2. Some of the senior career members of CSC were dismayed by the failure of their commissioners to take stronger stands.

3. *Final Staff Report*, vi.

4. Vol. 1, written by the executive director, was based heavily on the recommendations of the nine task forces that reported to him. The complete text of each of the task force reports made up Volume 2. Volume 3 consisted of detailed flow charts of actual personnel actions that illustrated the horrendous red tape involved in many basic personnel actions such as hiring and firing. They also revealed the surprising degree to which, in addition to detailed procedures, the processes were often extended month after month by inept management. This was especially true in cases of firings in which poor management contributed far more than procedures to the difficulty in removing incompetent employees.

5. *Final Staff Report*, vii.

6. Senator Stevens (R-Alaska) and Representative Mathias (R-Maryland) strongly dissented from this provision, arguing that it made the SES career members vulnerable to the type of abuses experienced in the Watergate period.

7. 5 USC Section 3131.

8. I thought a 90-day period was adequate for the purpose we had in mind, but recommended 120 days in the expectation that the White House or Congress would pare it back to 90 or 60 days. That did not happen.

CHAPTER THREE

THE NATIONAL PERFORMANCE REVIEW AS IMPLICIT EVALUATION OF CSRA: BUILDING ON OR OVERTURNING THE LEGACY?

CAROLYN BAN

INTRODUCTION

Twenty years ago, the Civil Service Reform Act was passed, with a combination of hype and hope. Five years ago, the National Performance Review proposed even more sweeping reforms in how the government conducts its business. This chapter examines the relationship between the two efforts as a way of exploring a key question in our understanding of the policy process: How do we know what worked? I argue that formal evaluation of programs with lofty goals and complex structures, such as CSRA, is difficult if not impossible, although some evaluation findings have informed the policy debate. But the drafters of the NPR proposals relied less on research by academics and more on the experience and wisdom of respected practitioners, leavened somewhat by outside consultants. If we consider the proposals that emerged from this process as a kind of implicit evaluation of CSRA, we see that the NPR gave CSRA mixed reviews, in some ways building on the foundation of CSRA while in others striving to reverse the course taken in 1978.

EVALUATING CSRA: THE PERILS OF LONG-TERM OUTCOME EVALUATION

I must begin with a personal note here. I write this section as a participant-observer, having spent just under three years at the Office of Personnel

Management as a member of the impressively titled Civil Service Reform Act Evaluation Management Division. Our lofty mission was to conduct and coordinate evaluation of CSRA government-wide. OPM committed serious resources to the effort, including a staff of twelve to fifteen and a budget of about $1,000,000 annually, which included funds for three independent evaluations conducted by academic teams and for periodic large-scale surveys of the federal workforce, to our knowledge the first such surveys ever conducted. The evaluation plan this team developed was fairly sophisticated and included both process and impact assessment approaches. The effort began shortly after the act was passed, so that there was time to collect baseline data before it was fully implemented. Yet, on balance, I would have to say that this evaluation effort failed. It did so for several reasons, some common to such long-term evaluation efforts and some unique to this historical moment.

First, CSRA was a complex piece of legislation, with multiple programs addressing multiple, and sometimes conflicting, goals. In the introduction to our book on CSRA, Patricia Ingraham and I summarized those conflicts as follows:

- The conflict between the desire for greater political responsiveness and the desire for greater managerial capability and independence.
- The conflict between the concept of a management cadre with a sense of identity and esprit de corps and the concept of competition to increase productivity.
- The conflict between the goal of increasing managers' ability to fire problem employees and the goal of protecting whistleblowers.[1]

These goal conflicts are the natural result of the policy process; when there is a "window" for reform, those putting together the reform package have an understandable tendency to create a "Christmas tree," adding in all the pet projects that have been gathering dust for years (such as the SES for example), while including elements that bring in needed constituencies (such as Title VII for labor). Drafters also float trial balloons to test the tolerance for controversial changes (such as proposed changes in veterans' preference and in procedures for dealing with problem employees, both of which were severely watered down from the original proposals). The net result, in the case of CSRA, was a package that was politically palatable but far from logically consistent.

Further, even where there is agreement as to goals, actually measuring end goals is often impossible. Can we really say that modifying the personnel system, and the system of incentives and rewards, particularly for senior executives and mid-level managers, has improved the efficiency or effectiveness of government? Most evaluations don't even try to measure such ultimate outcomes, focusing instead on measurable objectives, often seen as intermediate steps necessary to reach the ultimate goal. OPM's evaluation plan, which was very ambitious, had a creative and ambitious way of attempting to reach the outcomes question.[2] OPM selected, via competitive bidding, three university-based evaluation teams. Each carried out its study independently, but they all had the same charge: to examine the performance of specific federal installations over time and to find out whether the whole constellation of CSRA reforms that affected operations at the regional or local level had any effects on what the organizations actually did. This assumes, of course, that even at an installation level one can measure outputs and even outcomes. But it had, inherent in the design, assumptions that proved to be even more unrealistic.

The real downfall of the evaluation was political change. It is not uncommon for large-scale evaluations to falter because the political environment has shifted. This was certainly the fate of the very expensive and long-running experiments with a negative income tax, for example.[3] OPM and agency political leaders, as they implemented CSRA in 1978 through 1980, certainly didn't anticipate that Carter would shortly be voted out of office, and neither did the evaluators. Our assumption was that CSRA would change the personnel and management systems, but that the organizations being studied would not be facing other significant pressures to change. Nothing could have been further from the truth.

The Reagan revolution hit all parts of government quickly and dramatically and vitiated the logic of the evaluation. For example, one university-based study was tracking performance at a regional office of the Mine Safety and Health Administration, where one output being measured was number of lawsuits filed against mine operators by MSHA as a result of inspections that uncovered violations. The Reagan administration approach to this task was a 180-degree reversal. No longer would the agency immediately bring suit; rather they would work first with the mine owners to persuade them to make needed changes. While the goal of saving lives remained, the path for getting there had been dramatically altered, and changes in internal management systems were irrelevant to that process.

Other political issues made measuring the impact of CSRA unrealistic. Nationwide surveys of the federal workforce were designed to track such issues as employee morale, relationship of employees to their supervisors, and perceptions of changes in productivity. But periodic pay freezes probably had more impact on morale, particularly of those at the top, than any part of CSRA.

Finally, long-term evaluation requires a commitment to research and a willingness to devote the resources that are required. That commitment was uneven at best. While Alan Campbell and Jule Sugarman, the original director and deputy director of OPM, were committed to the evaluation effort and used the process evaluation aspects of it in guiding the implementation process, congressional support was weak. Indeed, one senior staff to the House Post Office and Civil Service Committee proposed that, in order to save money, the evaluation be stopped for a year, after which it could always be started up again, showing not only his lack of commitment but his lack of understanding of how the evaluation process worked.

President Reagan's first director of OPM, Donald Devine, clearly had a different set of priorities, and evaluating CSRA was not high on his list. I remember sending the proposal for the next scheduled survey of the federal workforce to him for review and getting a note back in the margin beside the discussion of merit pay that read something like, "We already know the news is bad, so why ask?" The formal evaluation effort ended when Devine shut down the major research units at OPM and laid off most of the staff, myself included.

It is interesting to note that the team leading the effort of drafting and implementing the National Performance Review (now dubbed the National Partnership for Reinventing Government) did not even attempt to accept responsibility for evaluating NPR's effects. When I met with spokespeople of the NPR effort, both at SUNY Albany and at the Brookings Institution, they took the position that it was up to academics to conduct any evaluations. Their own reports have been straight "good-news" boosterism.[4]

The difficulty we faced in evaluating CSRA were not unique. Indeed, I do not know of other large-scale administrative reforms that have been put to the test of a serious evaluation effort. The problem is that, absent hard data on what works, it is hard to sort out real success stories from hype. In an environment of inadequate information, the psychology of reform, where people follow what they perceive as best practices, feeds a kind of faddishness or band-wagon effect.[5] The public sector has sometimes been criticized as lagging the private sector just enough so that it is often picking up new management approaches (TQM, for example) just as the private sector is giving up on that and moving on to the next hot technique. Similarly, the CSRA served as a model for reforms at the state and local level and internationally, even though there was no hard data by which to judge its success.

THE NATIONAL PERFORMANCE REVIEW AS IMPLICIT EVALUATION OF CSRA

To what extent did the drafters of the National Performance Review proposals see the CSRA as having succeeded? While the NPR can certainly be critiqued as being heavy on hype[6] and as reflecting the current management fads, it nonetheless also is based on the assessment of experienced managers of what is currently working. Implicit in that assessment is a collective sense of the effectiveness of the CSRA reforms. The current reform efforts in the federal government, especially the National Performance Review, have significant parallels with the CSRA, but also major differences. The NPR is even more broad in its goals (and marked by similar goal conflicts), and both CSRA and NPR reflect a combination of genuine good-government values and political imperatives. But the management context to which the NPR is responding is one that reflects the changes created by CSRA almost two decades previously. As such, the NPR can be seen as an implicit set of evaluative statements. In some cases, the NPR is clearly building on and going farther than the CSRA. In others, it appears to be rejecting the CSRA models and going in a sharply different direction. And in some areas that were central to CSRA, the NPR is largely silent.

Given the breadth of both NPR and CSRA, I will focus this discussion on four areas that I consider central to CSRA:

- Decentralization of personnel management, particularly hiring
- Reliance on an "MBO-type" appraisal system linked both to merit pay or bonuses and to employee discipline
- The creation of the SES
- Reform of labor-management relations

I will address each of these areas below.

DECENTRALIZATION: YET ANOTHER SWING OF THE PENDULUM?

The CSRA Mandate for Decentralization and Its Interpretation

The classic visual aid produced by the president's Personnel Management Project (PMP) task force on staffing was a flow chart of the hiring process.

They selected a worst-case scenario, in which it took 374 days to complete the hiring process. The chart of the process looked like something created by Rube Goldberg (PMP, 1977, Appendix XII, chart 2). The CSRA argument was a simple and powerful one: the personnel processes in the federal government, particularly in the area of hiring, were too slow, too rigid, and too cumbersome. Further, those reviewing qualifications and ranking candidates were too far removed from the agencies and managers doing the hiring and did not always have the necessary technical knowledge of the job. Therefore, responsibility for a range of personnel actions, but most importantly for hiring, should be delegated to the agencies wherever possible.[7]

I have detailed elsewhere the pendulum swings that have taken place throughout the history of the U.S. civil service between centralized and decentralized approaches to hiring and the arguments in favor of each approach.[8] Each has its advocates because each emphasizes different values. Centralization provides economies of scale, standardized (and thus presumably fair) treatment of applicants, a single point of entry for applicants, and (at least before the courts intervened) a single test for most entry-level positions, which was seen by managers as providing high-quality employees. In addition, many personnel specialists have traditionally seen a centralized system as a necessary bulwark against pressure to subvert the system.

In contrast, decentralizing the process is seen as providing faster service that more directly reflects the needs of the agency or managers, but it complicates the process from the perspective of the applicant, and, in the eyes of some, opens the door to abuse (either pressure to hire for political reasons or simply cronyism).

While the PMP rhetoric was strong, the actual legislation was relatively mild, permitting delegation to agencies of authority to manage hiring only for positions that were unique to the agency. Hiring for common positions (such as secretary or computer programmer) was still to be handled centrally. While Alan Campbell and Jule Sugarman, the first director and deputy director of OPM, aggressively encouraged agencies to accept delegated authority, Don Devine, Reagan's first director of OPM, reversed course, defining narrowly the legislative mandate on delegation and withdrawing some delegated authorities.[9]

The NPR Approach to Decentralization: Radical Change

The CSRA attempts at decentralizing the system can be characterized as incremental change, complicated by the pendulum swings of implementation. The NPR proposals (many of which have been implemented) go much farther, virtually dismantling the traditional centrally managed system of hiring and linking decentralization explicitly with deregulation.

The initial NPR report called for complete decentralization of hiring. Specifically their recommendation was as follows:

> **Action:** Give all departments and agencies authority to conduct their own recruiting and examining for all positions, and abolish all central registers and standard application forms.[10]

The NPR proposal dramatically changes OPM's role. No longer would agencies be mandated to go through OPM to hire. They could, if they wish, develop their own testing mechanisms and maintain their own lists. This proposal has, in fact, been implemented. Hiring has been virtually completely decentralized, and the central registers maintained by OPM are gone. The result is to reduce OPM to serving as a consultant, developing tests or screening candidates only if agencies request (and presumably pay for) their assistance.

The NPR's solution to the challenges a completely decentralized system creates for job-seekers is to propose that OPM create a government-wide employment information system. The rapid growth of job listings on the web, as well as 800 numbers and phone systems that permit actual application by phone for some occupations, has reduced the burden on prospective job applicants somewhat.

The drafters of the CSRA portrayed a system mired in red tape, but the legislation did not call for any significant deregulation. The NPR, in contrast, linked total decentralization to drastic deregulation. One step that was taken early, with considerable media fanfare, was to abolish the Federal Personnel Manual, relied on by personnelists for guidance (in a series of notebooks that included roughly 10,000 pages), and to permit applicants to submit a resume (standard in the private sector) rather than the rather intimidating and confusing SF 171. The NPR report on human resources[11] fleshed out these proposals in more detail, calling for reducing the number of competitive service appointment types from over 300 to three, but also for extending probationary periods for initial appointment or for supervisory or managerial positions from one year to three years.

Both the supporters of CSRA and the drafters of the NPR reports had to address the fear that decentralizing and deregulating would increase abuse. The argument of CSRA proponents was that there is a trade-off between preventing abuse and efficient management, and that the system was weighted too heavily toward preventing abuse, whatever the cost in terms of timeliness and quality of hires. As Campbell put it, "Rules which originated as a defense against spoils and the ineffective government which widespread patronage provided have resulted in as much inefficiency as they were designed to prevent."[12] His argument was that abuse could be controlled adequately post-hoc by those who were the victims of abuse appealing to MSPB or blowing the whistle on prohibited personnel practices to the Office of Special Counsel, rather than before the fact by rigid regulations and over-centralization. In effect, he would agree with the economists studying corruption who have argued that it is not cost-efficient to strive for zero corruption or abuse.[13]

The NPR HR report addresses directly the charge that decentralization will open the door to merit system abuse. It argues that this will not be a problem because:

> [D]ecentralization of responsibility for recruitment and examining is expected to increase managers' participation in and control over the staffing process, thereby reducing their ability to blame the system for unsatisfactory outcomes. Managers will become even more accountable for adherence to merit principles and for prohibiting personnel practices as increased flexibility leads to correspondingly increased performance expectations.[14]

The report adds that "extensive training must be provided to ensure that managers understand how the merit principles are applied in the context of making personnel decisions."

As a former federal manager, I can personally attest to the fact that hiring was probably the most difficult and frustrating part of my job, and that it routinely took three to six months of constant pushing. But both the CSRA and, even more, the NPR were also playing to a populist, anti-government strain in American politics. The calls for decentralization and especially for deregulation were meant to counter the stereotypes of government as hopelessly mired in red tape and unable to act. In the case of CSRA, the message was combined with another stereotype: of a government filled with "deadwood." NPR picked a different scapegoat: the problem was good people trapped in a bad system.

I do not mean to say that the calls for decentralization, particularly of hiring, were just PR. Certainly the managers who have used previous decentralized systems found them to be faster and to yield higher-caliber employees without reducing diversity.[15] But, both reforms tended to gloss over

64

the down-side of decentralization. I would argue that reports of the demise of political abuse have been greatly exaggerated. In fact, there are two related problems: First, and foremost, political appointees do not receive the kind of extensive training described above. They typically come from outside government and are used to total flexibility in hiring. In most companies, hiring people you know is considered good business, based on an ethical system built on reciprocal favors. In government, that is illegal. And, as many personnel managers know, those who try to explain the difference to political appointees are not always appreciated.

Second, some agency cultures have been so politicized that abuse of the system is rampant. MSPB survey data from 1988 showed dramatic differences in the extent to which personnel specialists reported that they had observed hiring into the competitive service as a result of political party affiliation during the past twelve months. While government-wide, only 7 percent reported seeing such abuse, in the top four agencies (each of which has some reputation for having been politicized) the figures ranged from 30 percent at SBA and 31 percent at the State Department to 39 percent at HUD and a remarkable 47 percent at Education. In contrast, in the military agencies only 1 to 4 percent of personnelists reported seeing such abuse.[16]

I am not arguing that decentralization will lead to the widespread rape of the merit system. But the proponents of CSRA were perhaps more forthright than the NPR drafters in acknowledging that the cost of reform is likely to be some increase in politicization. And some senior personnel specialists say informally that they fear a drastic increase in direct pressure on them unless there is active oversight by OPM.

The NPR also took a far broader approach than did CSRA to both decentralization and deregulation. CSRA focused on hiring but ignored classification. NPR called for giving agencies the option of adopting a simplified and more flexible classification system. Here one might see NPR as the indirect heir of CSRA, since broad-banded classification plans build on models developed as a result of CSRA's provision for demonstration projects to test new approaches to personnel management. Several demonstration projects, most notably the navy demonstration project, have tested and honed this approach. The research and demonstration provision of CSRA was predicated on a logical model of the policy process: organizations would try out new approaches, and those that worked could be implemented system-wide. But broad-banding appears to be always the bridesmaid, never the bride. Although it has dominated the discussion of classification reform for well over a decade,[17] the long history of failed attempts to institutionalize it, even on a voluntary basis, attests to the lack of fit between this model of policy-making and the reality of the political environment.[18]

In many ways, the general approach of the NPR echoes this ethos of experimentation. Agencies could develop "reinvention labs" that could cut through red tape and find better (and cheaper) ways to conduct the business of government.[19] The difference is that these could be small-scale bottom-up efforts that did not require congressional approval, unlike demonstration projects under CSRA, which had to go through an exhaustive review and approval process. And most did not require changing laws to implement system-wide. But what I have not yet seen is whether those successful reinvention labs have, in fact, led to system-wide change.[20]

In sum, in its calls for decentralization and deregulation, the NPR can be seen as the heir of CSRA, building on its logic but taking the argument much further. In recent years, there has been a lively debate over the pros and cons of decentralizing the system. While some have argued in favor of letting agencies design individualized systems in line with their cultures,[21] others have seen decentralization as leading to "Balkanized chaos."[22] The NPR team has clearly come down on the side of the decentralizers and has already led OPM to decentralize the system far more dramatically than in even the early years of CSRA.

Performance Management: A Rejection of the CSRA Model

If NPR was the heir to CSRA in moving to decentralize personnel processes, in the area of individual motivation and effective management it appears on balance to be abandoning the approach taken by CSRA. The CSRA model of management relied heavily on individual performance appraisal, which was seen as the "keystone" of CSRA's management philosophy. Prior to CSRA, agencies were free to develop their own performance appraisal systems. Many relied simply on a "pass-fail" system, i.e., a form to be completed annually by supervisors on which they rated performance of individual staff members as satisfactory or unsatisfactory. CSRA, taking a page from private-sector management, called for each agency to develop a new system based on setting objectives for the year and then measuring achievement of those objectives.

The keystone analogy for performance appraisal was apt because CSRA envisioned linking performance appraisal results to pay, with merit pay systems for managers and bonuses for members of the Senior Executive Service (SES). Performance appraisals were to form the basis for decisions on training and promotion, but also on demotions, dismissals for unsatisfactory performance, and reductions in force (RIFs).

As we saw above, CSRA played to the negative stereotypes of government. That was nowhere more obvious than in the stress on improving the government's ability to get rid of "deadwood." The drafters of CSRA accepted the argument that the pendulum had swung too far in the direction of protecting employees' rights, that existing "adverse action" procedures were too cumbersome, and that actions were too likely to be overruled on appeal or grievance. Thus, they created a new category, "performance-based actions" in which disciplinary action, including dismissal, was linked to the results of the performance appraisal. Objectives within the performance appraisal plan were termed "job elements," and some were designated "critical job elements." Unsatisfactory performance on a single critical job element was grounds for dismissal. Further, the evidentiary standard was reduced from a "preponderance of the evidence" to a lower "substantial evidence," and procedural errors were to be considered grounds for reversal on appeal only if they were "harmful," thus, at least in theory, making it easier to make a case and harder to overturn it on appeal.[23]

This whole approach to management, based on individual performance appraisal and positive and negative incentives, appeared at the time to be "state of the art," based on private-sector research and on a theory base (expectancy theory) that was widely accepted and had strong face validity. But early in the implementation process some academic critics pointed out the problems in relying on such a "Theory X" approach. In particular, Fred Thayer pointed out that the reliance on private-sector models was questionable, and that "evidence indicates that industry and municipal government are not very successful at tying wage increases to productivity gains" and that the private sector was not, in fact, consistent in its approach to performance appraisal. He charges that the CSRA approach is based on "dubious mythology" and points out how difficult it is for managers to know what their subordinates are actually up to, particularly given the fact that much work takes place within what he terms "multiorganizational networks."[24]

As agencies began to implement the new systems, a whole range of problems was encountered. Agencies found that negotiating job elements with each employee individually was not only time-consuming but led to the perception of inequity, as individuals in the same job title were held to different standards. Thus agencies started to move to standard job elements for common jobs. At the same time, after a period of letting "1000 flowers bloom," OPM decided to impose standards, such as that all systems would have five levels. This undercut the individual plans that some agencies had already invested considerable resources and energy in developing. The original pay-out of merit pay was marred by a conflict with the General Accounting Office that resulted in a significant reduction in the amount of money available to agencies for pay-outs.[25] Thus, the system as implemented bore limited resemblance to that originally envisioned.

Later research failed to find any positive linkage between merit pay (or SES bonuses) and either morale or productivity. If anything, merit pay was found to be destructive of both morale and organizational commitment for the majority of employees who were not super-stars but who were the core of employees on which organizations depended.[26] Further, creation of the category of "performance-based actions" to make it easier to fire poor performers had no discernible effect on the willingness of managers actually to take such action.[27]

The NPR: Of (at Least) Two Minds

The performance management sections of the CSRA were rooted in a clear, consistent management philosophy, based on a belief in the efficacy of individual performance appraisal as a management tool that could be linked effectively to positive and negative incentives. Because of the tight logical connections between the component parts of this approach, one could argue that it should stand or fall as a piece.

The NPR addresses the legacy of CSRA, both in the main report and very directly in the report on human resources. But both its analysis of the failures of the CSRA approach and its proposals are ambivalent, presenting no single clear management philosophy, but rather at least two, with the conflicts between them unacknowledged and unresolved.

On the one hand, the NPR team was often harshly critical of the general thrust of the CSRA reforms as well as of its specific approach to performance management. The NPR purports to address a "performance deficit" in the federal government,[28] certainly an indirect admission that the CSRA reforms did not significantly improve the performance of the federal government.

The conflict embedded in the NPR diagnosis of problems and in its proposed solutions is between those who still buy in to the basic structure of the CSRA, which has now, after twenty years, become the "traditional" approach, rooted in individual performance appraisal, merit pay, and increased ease of firing, and those who support participative management philosophies, such as Total Quality Management, who recognize the corrosive effect of the Theory X approach, and who would like to scrap the whole traditional system, perhaps replacing it with group or team performance measures and rewards. In places, one can see the NPR drafters jumping back and forth between the two approaches, sometimes within the same section of the report.

The key section of the HR report embodies the conflict within its title: "Enable Managers to Empower, Develop, Train, Reward, and Discipline Employees." One might argue that the CSRA approach, especially toward rewarding and disciplining employees, was the antithesis of empowering. The three subsections address performance appraisal, incentive award and bonus systems, and dealing with poor performers. In each case, the need for change is made forcefully, based on a clear understanding of what has not worked. Briefly, the HR report states that "virtually all observers" agree that performance management systems "have not resulted in the desired improvements in individual and organizational performance."[29] It presents a whole laundry list of problems, portraying the systems as overly standardized and inflexible, and as top-down control mechanisms "rather than tools for empowering employees and supervisors to improve performance." It faults inaccuracies in ratings, overemphasis on dealing with poor performers, and lack of ownership by managers. And it points out that "systems emphasize individual performance and do not support emerging efforts to manage group and organizational performance."[30]

The critique of CSRA's pay for performance systems is equally hard-hitting. The NPR HR report states that they have had "mixed results in both the public and private sectors," and that observers "agree that (1) there is insufficient empirical evidence that pay for performance programs are effective, and (2) variable pay or bonuses are superior to base pay adjustments for improving employee performance."[31]

One might note the conflict displayed within this single paragraph, which could be paraphrased as "it doesn't work at all, but one method works better than others." Again here, the NPR HR team points out that programs are not responsive to individual, agency needs or cultures, and that the system emphasizes reward and incentives to the individual not organizational or team performance. They conclude that "[t]he current approach promotes competition, with winners and losers, rather than cooperation and cohesion, which are important elements in most successful government programs."[32]

The same themes are reflected in the critique of systems for dealing with poor performers. They, too, are described as inconsistent with agency cultures and not "owned by agency managers."[33] While the NPR report echoes the old CSRA argument that it takes too long to deal with poor performers, it also acknowledges that this is not just a question of law or policy; rather, the culture and the lack of managerial support for those who take action are central to the problem.

These are strong criticisms, and one might expect them to be followed by a call for dramatic changes. But the reform proposals are minimal, incremental at best, and demonstrate an unwillingness to let go of the individual-based appraisal systems and structure of rewards and punishments that CSRA put in place. In the section on performance management, the only major recommendation was to "authorize agencies to design their own performance management programs," essentially taking us back to the early days of CSRA before a standardized system was imposed. Related recommendations were that agencies be authorized to develop their own incentive programs and that agencies "develop a culture of performance that supports supervisors' efforts to deal with poor performers."[34]

The participative management so in evidence in much of the NPR appears here only in a recommendation that agencies be encouraged to establish productivity gainsharing programs "to support the reinvention and change effort."[35] In contrast, the lead recommendation on dealing with poor performers calls for reducing "by half the time required to terminate federal managers and employees for cause" and recommends doing so by cutting the required time for notice of termination from 30 days to 15.[36] This is almost ludicrously silly. The problem, from the perspective of most managers, is not with the 30 days but rather with the many months required to document a case and give the employee a chance to improve, a process that can drag on interminably in the case of marginal performers.[37] Cutting the notice period may reduce the time by a trivial amount, but at a cost to due process that the courts may not uphold.

In short, while the NPR criticisms of the status quo are frequently biting, the recommendations are, by and large, trivial, proposing few dramatic changes in the existing system. One exception is buried in a list of possible changes that agencies could make in their performance management systems: "At least two levels of performance must be identified: meets and does not meet expectations."[38] This seems to take us back to the status quo ante, or perhaps forward past many of the problems with individual performance appraisal detailed by Charles Fox, who recommended abolishing performance appraisal altogether or moving to a simple form with two categories: "unsatisfactory" and "fully satisfactory" if some formal system is necessary "in order to establish a defensible legal base for the occasionally needed adverse personnel action—firing or demoting, for example. . . ."[39] In fact,

OPM has already issued regulations permitting agencies to move to "pass-fail" systems, and several have done so, with mixed reports thus far. One can see, in this move, the demise of the traditional CSRA system; rating someone unsatisfactory may be sufficient basis for discipline, but such a system is almost impossible to use as a basis for merit pay (now defunct for managers anyway) or for other positive incentives. How such a system fits with the regulations for reduction in force, which give those with high ratings credits equivalent to extra years of service, is unclear.

Overall, there is a dramatic contrast between the tone of the human resource recommendations, which are both minimal and generally supportive of the traditional management paradigm, and the sections of the overall NPR report on empowering employees to get results. Here the authors of the NPR advocate, often eloquently, decentralizing decision-making power down as low as possible in the organization and empowering rank-and-file employees through such mechanisms as self-managed teams.

The SES: How Should We Define Silence?

Interpreting the NPR as an implicit evaluation of the previous reform efforts, especially the CSRA, poses a particular challenge when we look at the Senior Executive Service. It was one of the centerpieces of the CSRA, central to its probably conflicting goals of improving government performance while increasing political control. It has been one of the most studied parts of the CSRA, with extensive academic attention right from the beginning.[40] And it has remained controversial, with many observers maintaining that it has not lived up to its promise to create an elite cadre of generalist managers,[41] or to its commitments to individual SES members, including higher pay and greater prestige, opportunities for training and sabbaticals, and a chance to have a real effect on public policy.[42] In fact, scholars and practitioners have continued to come up with proposals for revamping the SES, some of them quite dramatic.[43]

Yet, the main NPR report is strangely silent on the subject of the Senior Executive Service. Nowhere is it even mentioned in the main NPR report. If one tried to understand the structure of federal leadership from that document, one might conclude that there were senior political appointees and line managers, with nothing in between. Certainly, the SES is not portrayed as having a central role in the reinvention effort.

That image is corrected, but only somewhat, by the NPR report on human resources, which does have one relatively brief section covering the

SES. It summarizes the past assessments of the SES, focusing on the fact that the majority of SES members do not fit the original mold of generalist managers but rather "serve in the SES because of their technical expertise."[44] The report also describes the "poor relationships that often exist between career SES members and political appointees," and agency weaknesses in managing the SES. Finally, it argues that the SES members will be the real drivers of the culture change needed to make reinvention a reality.[45]

Here too, however, the lofty rhetoric is followed by weak and vague recommendations for reform. This section of the NPR HR report recommends three actions. The first calls for creating and reinforcing a "corporate perspective within the SES that supports governmentwide culture change." It assigns to OPM the task of fostering this "corporate vision," via its curriculum for management development programs, via an executive information system, and generally by "recommending governmentwide SES policies and management development strategies in support of government culture change efforts."[46] This assumes, of course, that OPM knows what that corporate vision should be and is both strong and respected enough to promulgate it effectively. Both assumptions are questionable.

The other two recommendations concerning the SES are more specific but far from revolutionary: they call for promoting succession planning, again with the responsibility falling to OPM, and for enhancing voluntary mobility of SES members within and between agencies, with OPM acting as a catalyst.[47] This recommendation for mobility is one that has recurred from the early days of the SES. It is central to the model of the SES as a cadre of generalist managers, a model that has never been embraced by agency leadership. I would argue that it is based on fallacious assumptions about the nature of leadership positions in most agencies. Political appointees may, in fact, serve the function of generalist managers (although many come in to their positions with significant relevant knowledge and experience), but those hiring career SES members have frequently passed over candidates who completed SES training programs in favor of those with relevant technical knowledge and experience because SESers without that technical knowledge are seen as inappropriate leaders and spokespeople for highly technical organizations.

Why is so little attention paid to the SES in the NPR proposals, and why are the reforms proposed so modest, given that much more radical reforms have been proposed by others over the last several years? It is hard to interpret the relative silence of the NPR team on this topic. On the one hand, it could be a sign that they felt the SES was basically working well and just needed a little tweaking. On the other hand, it may mean that the model of management, and of leadership, central to the NPR was focused elsewhere. If the main thrust of the NPR's management philosophy is to delegate authority down as far as possible in the organization, then the focus becomes line managers interacting with rank-and-file employees, not SES members. In fact, although the NPR gives some lip-service to political leadership, that, too, is rather vague, as in the recommendation that "the President should issue a directive detailing his vision, plan, and commitment to creating quality government." Overall, the model of management in the NPR is oddly apolitical. It does not provide a sophisticated blueprint for how the several layers of leadership— high-level political appointees, SES members (some of whom are also political appointees), and line managers—can work together effectively.[48]

Reform of Labor Relations: The Political Imperative

While the creation of the SES and the performance appraisal sections of CSRA had roots in public administration and management theory, the section on labor relations (Title VII) reflected hard-nosed political calculations. Scotty Campbell and company understood that they needed the unions on their side. They tried to involve the unions actively in the process of drafting CSRA, which the unions resisted, but won at least passive support (or avoided union opposition) by responding to some key union concerns: placing the provision for collective bargaining in statute, rather than executive order, and expanding the scope of bargaining. The language on scope of bargaining that resulted was so vague that it spawned a raft of appeals to the newly created Federal Labor Relations Board.[49]

The NPR team went even further than did the CSRA group in trying to bring the unions into the process. Union leaders were invited to serve on the National Partnership Council (NPC), and agencies across the government set up their own councils, attempting to move beyond cooperation to full partnership with unions. Just how this partnership structure fit with on-going TQM efforts or other approaches to participative management was never made clear.[50] Via Executive Order 12871, issued in 1993, Clinton expanded the scope of bargaining. And the NPC explored such politically sensitive ground as requiring all employees in a bargaining unit to pay a union fee. But the Democratic loss of Congress in the 1994 election ended any chance for pro-union legislation.

More importantly, some have argued that the need for union support shaped the NPR in significant ways. In particular, the NPR's recommendations for downsizing focused more on managers (not included in bargaining units) than on rank-and-file employees, although some union members were clearly among the "oversight" workers in areas such as budget, personnel, and procurement who were slated for cuts. Cuts were to be made via improved efficiency, not by targeting any specific agency.[51] Overall, then, the unions were neutralized if not coopted.

In a political sense, then, the NPR can also be seen as the heir of CSRA. Both were reform proposals by Democratic presidents, and in both cases the unions were seen as key to the political coalition necessary for acceptance of reform efforts by Congress. The key difference, of course, is that union support became perhaps a liability for the Clinton administration's efforts to pass NPR-related legislation in the area of human resources management once the Republicans took control of Congress.

CONCLUSIONS

The NPR provides us with a somewhat cloudy but nonetheless useful lens through which to look at the impact of the CSRA. NPR was a much more ambitious effort at government reform than was CSRA. Reforming the formal systems of government—civil service, budgeting, and procurement—was only one part of an extraordinarily broad-ranging, if somewhat incoherent, effort. And this paper has made no attempt at assessing the NPR's impact.[52] I have argued elsewhere that in the area of personnel management the effects have been mixed, with no success in passing legislation, but some significant administrative changes, and real reforms forced by sharp downsizing of personnel staff.[53]

Looking at CSRA from the vantage point of NPR emphasizes the fact that reform is an on-going, iterative process in which successive reform efforts are responding to that which was tried before. Perhaps, given the uncertainties of program design and the challenges of implementation, it is inevitable that administrative reform is a trial-and-error process. While we look for models of "best practice" elsewhere—in other levels of government, in the private sector, and, increasingly, in other countries—it is hard to tell what is really working well in those settings (versus what is being hyped). It is even more difficult to know how it will work when transferred to a different setting.

The reforms proposed by the NPR show this iterative process, as well as the search for external models. Both the NPR and CSRA were based in part on external models, both from the private sector and from other countries. And the NPR built on and expanded the focus on decentralization and delegation that was articulated in CSRA. Thus, in evaluative terms, the NPR drafters were saying of the CSRA efforts, "Nice try, but you didn't go far enough." In many ways this thrust of the NPR was also shaped by the dialogue in the intervening years about the implications of decentralization. The NPR falls squarely on the side of decentralization, recognizing the importance of organizational culture and the failure of one-size-fits-all systems.

On the other hand, the NPR drafters don't appear to have been able to reach internal agreement on the success of CSRA's management reforms. In some places they are saying, "Good idea, but it wasn't properly implemented. Let's try it again," while in other places they are arguing that it was a failure of theory, not just of implementation. I should note that there has been a similar debate in the academic literature.[54] For example, while the NPR report recognizes that Congress has reiterated its support for merit pay, it offers only weak support for continuing individual merit pay and argues much more strongly for trying group reward systems, such as gainsharing. But the NPR drafters never really reconciled their continuing support for some kind of individual accountability system with their strong advocacy of participative management approaches, or with the NPR calls for labor-management partnership.

In spite of these inconsistencies, I see the NPR approach to management as a more positive one, at least in rhetoric, with more focus on ways to develop employee commitment and to tap the energy and creativity of employees. While the heavy emphasis on downsizing has seemed to dominate the implementation of NPR, recent reports show that, since much of the downsizing was done via buy-outs, the effect on morale has not been devastating, and that employees in the agencies where NPR was a high priority had both higher personal job satisfaction and were more likely to see improvements in both customer service and productivity in their organizations.[55]

In one key area, political control of the bureaucracy, it is impossible to use the NPR to glean an implicit assessment of the success of CSRA. The NPR is virtually silent on the broad issue of political control and has little to say about the role of top-level leadership in an entrepreneurial, participative environment where line managers and rank-and-file workers are empowered. It has only minimal and weak recommendations concerning the Senior Executive Service, focusing mainly on the perennial effort to make it a mobile corps of generalist managers, while ignoring the reasons that this model did not take hold, especially the technical nature of much of what the government actually does.

It is important to recognize the differing political environments of the two reform efforts. Carter, working with the Democratic leadership of Congress, was able to forge a political coalition in support of reform. While Campbell later noted that that support was a mile wide and an inch deep, nonetheless, the legislation was passed with only a few compromises. In contrast, while Clinton and Gore used the media effectively to garner broad support for their change agenda, the loss of Congress made major legislative efforts impossible and politicized what should have been a non-partisan "good government" effort.

Finally, if my argument holds, we should be looking at the life-cycle of administrative reform efforts and thinking about (and perhaps influencing) the next wave. One central question is whether the movement toward a decentralized model has gone so far that it is irreversible, or whether there will be pressure to recentralize, either because of perceived abuses or perceived efficiencies of centralization. Another is whether the SES will be subject to further changes. While the NPR ignored the subject, OPM has recently issued a draft proposal for fairly significant changes. What is driving that effort is not clear. What is clear is that the CSRA can be seen, from the vantage point of 20 years, as one in a chain of reform efforts, going back to the creation of the civil service system in 1883 and forward to the NPR and beyond.

NOTES

1. Carolyn Ban and Patricia W. Ingraham, "Introduction: Civil Service Reform: Legislating Bureaucratic Change," in Patricia W. Ingraham and Carolyn Ban, eds. *Legislating Bureaucratic Change: The Civil Service Reform Act of 1978* (Albany: SUNY Press, 1984), 3.

2. U.S. Office of Personnel Management, *A Strategy for Evaluation: The Civil Service Reform Act of 1978*, OPM Document 134-06-6 (Washington, D.C.: OPM, 1981).

3. David N. Kershaw, "A Negative Income-Tax Experiment," in David Nachmias, ed., *The Practice of Policy Evaluation* (New York: St. Martin's Press, 1980).

4. See, for example, National Performance Review, *The Best-Kept Secrets in Government* (Washington D.C.: USGPO, 1996).

5. Steven W. Hays and Richard C. Kearney, "Riding the Crest of a Wave: The National Performance Review and Public Management Reform," *International Journal of Public Administration* 20, 1 (1997): 11–40.

6. James P. Pfiffner, "The National Performance Review in Perspective," *International Journal of Public Administration* 20, 1 (1997): 41–70.

7. Carolyn Ban and Toni Marzotto, "Delegations of Examining: Objectives and Implementation," in Ingraham and Ban, eds. *Legislating Bureaucratic Change: The Civil Service Reform Act of 1978, op. cit.*

8. Ibid.

9. Ibid.

10. National Performance Review, *Creating a Government That Works Better and Costs Less* (Washington, D.C.: USGPO, 1993), 23.

11. National Performance Review, *Reinventing Human Resources Management* (Washington, D.C.: U.S. Government Printing Office, 1993).

12. Alan K Campbell, "Civil Service Reform as a Remedy of Bureaucratic Ills," in Carol H. Weiss and Allen H. Barton, eds. *Making Bureaucracies Work* (Beverly Hills: Sage, 1980), 153.

13. Robert Klitgaard, *Controlling Corruption* (Berkeley: University of California Press, 1988).

14. NPR HR Report, *op. cit.*, 13–14.

15. Carolyn Ban and Patricia W. Ingraham, "Retaining Quality Employees: Life after PACE," *Public Administration Review* 48, 3 (May/June 1988): 708–718.

16. Carolyn Ban and Harry C. Reed III, "The State of the Merit System: Perceptions of Abuse in the Federal Civil Service," *Review of Public Personnel Administration* 10, 3 (1990): 59. For a broader discussion of differences in agency cultures, see Carolyn Ban. *How Do Public Managers Manage? Bureaucratic Constraints, Organizational Culture, and the Potential for Reform* (San Francisco: Jossey-Bass, 1995).

17. See, for example, National Academy of Public Administration, *Modernizing Federal Classification: An Opportunity for Excellence* (Washington, D.C.: NAPA, 1991). Howard Risher and Charles Fay, eds. *New Strategies for Public Pay: Rethinking Government Compensation Programs* (San Francisco: Jossey-Bass, 1997).

18. Carolyn Ban, "Q.E.D.: The Research and Demonstration Provisions of CSRA," *Policy Studies Journal* (Winter, 1988–89), 420–434; Carolyn Ban, "Research and Demonstration under CSRA: Is Innovation Possible?" in David Rosenbloom and Patricia W. Ingraham, eds. *The Civil Service Reform of 1978: A Retrospective Evaluation* (Pittsburgh: University of Pittsburgh Press, 1992).

19. Beryl Radin, "Varieties of Invention: Six NPR 'Success Stories'," in Donald F. Kettl and John J. Di Iulio, Jr., eds. *Inside the Reinvention Machine: Appraising Governmental Reform* (Washington, D.C.: Brookings Institution Press, 1995).

20. On this point, James R. Thompson and Ronald Sanders present interesting case studies in "Reinventing Public Agencies: Bottom-Up Versus Top-Down Strategies," in Patricia W. Ingraham, ed., *Transforming Government: Lessons from the Reinvention Laboratories* (San Francisco: Jossey-Bass, 1998). They describe bottom-up reform from an invention laboratory in the Veterans Benefits Administration and conclude that "it appears that they are going to be adopted across the entire VBA" (p. 113).

21. Ray Kline, "Let the Cultures Grow," *Government Executive* (October 1998): 52–53.

22. Lucretia Dewey Tanner, "Fragmentation: A Quick Fix for a Failed Policy," ibid. 53–54.

23. Carolyn Ban, Edie N. Goldenberg, and Toni Marzotto, "Firing the Unproductive Employee: Will Civil Service Reform Make a Difference?" *Review of Public Personnel Administration* 2, 2 (Spring, 1982): 87–100; G. Jerry Shaw and William L. Bransford, *The Federal Manager's Handbook: A Guide to Rehabilitating or Removing the Problem Employee,* second edition (Huntsville, Ala.: FPMI Communications, 1994). Re burden of proof, see U.S. Office of Personnel Management, *Representing the Agency before the United States Merit Systems Protection Board: A Handbook on MSPB Practice and Procedure* (Washington, D.C.: USOPM, 1984).

24. Frederick Thayer, "The President's Management 'Reform': Theory X Triumphant," *Public Administration Review* (July/August, 1978), 311.

25. For a discussion of the early stages of implementation, see Robert W. Brown, "Performance Appraisal: A Policy Implementation Analysis," *Review of Public Personnel Administration* 2, 2 (Spring, 1982): 69–86. For a recent discussion of federal performance appraisal issues, see Doris Hausser and Charles Fay, "Managing and Assessing Employee Performance," in Risher and Fay, *op.cit.*

26. J. Edward Kellough and Haoran Lu, "The Paradox of Merit Pay in the Public Sector: Persistence of a Problematic Procedure," *Review of Public Personnel Administration* 13, 2 (Spring, 1993): 45–64; National Research Council, *Pay for Performance: Evaluating Performance Appraisal and Merit Pay* (Washington, D.C.: National Academy Press, 1991).

27. Thomas G. Robisch, "The Reluctance of Federal Managers to Utilize Formal Procedures for Poorly Performing Employees: A Case Study," *Review of Public Personnel Administration* 16, 2 (Spring, 1996): 73–85.

28. NPR, 1993 *op.cit.*, 9.

29. NPR HR 1993 *op.cit.*, 32.

30. Ibid.

31. Ibid., 36.

32. Ibid.

33. Ibid., 40.

34. Ibid., 41.

35. Ibid., 37.

36. Ibid., 41.

37. U.S. General Accounting Office, *Performance Management: How Well is the Government Dealing with Poor Performers?* GGD-91-7 (Washington, D.C.: USGAO, 1990); Carolyn Ban, *How Do Public Managers Manage? op.cit.*

38. Ibid., 33.

39. Charles J. Fox and Kurt A. Shirkey, "Employee Performance Appraisal: The Keystone Made of Clay," in Carolyn Ban and Norma M. Riccucci, eds., *Public Personnel Management: Current Concerns, Future Challenges* (New York: Longman Press, 1991).

40. See, for example, Carolyn Ban, Edie Goldenberg, and Toni Marzotto, "Controlling the U.S. Federal Bureaucracy: Will SES Make a Difference?" in Gerald E. Caiden and Heinrich Siedentopf, eds., *Strategies for Administrative Reform* (Lexington, Mass.: Lexington Books, 1982); Peter Colby and Patricia W. Ingraham, "Civil Service Reform: The Views of the Senior Executive Service," *Review of Public Personnel Administration,* 1, 3 (1981): 75–89; Bruce Buchanan, "The Senior Executive Service: How We can Tell If It Works," *Public Administration Review* 41, 3 (1981): 349–358; Naomi Lynn and Richard Vaden, "Federal Executives: Initial Reactions to Change," *Administration and Society* 12, 1 (1980): 101–120.

41. Mark W. Huddleston, "Background Paper," in *The Government's Managers* (New York: Twentieth Century Fund/Priority Press, 1987); Mark W. Huddleston and William W. Boyer, *The Higher Civil Service in the United States: Quest for Reform* (Pittsburgh: University of Pittsburgh Press, 1996); Toni Marzotto, "Whither the Generalist Managers: Reinventing the Senior Executive Service," paper presented at the Annual Meeting of the American Political Science Association (Washington, D.C., September, 1993).

42. Carolyn Ban, "The Crisis of Morale and Federal Senior Executives," *Public Productivity Review* 43 (Fall, 1987): 31–49; Mark Abramson, Richard Schmidt, and Sandra Baxter, "Evaluating the Civil Service Reform Act of 1978: The Experience of the U.S. Department of Health and Human Services," in Patricia W. Ingraham and Carolyn Ban, eds. *Legislating Bureaucratic Change: The Civil Service Reform Act of 1978, op. cit.*

43. Ronald P. Sanders, "Reinventing the Senior Executive Service," in Patricia W. Ingraham and Barbara S. Romzek, eds., *New Paradigms for Government: Issues for the Changing Public Service* (San Francisco: Jossey Bass, 1994).

44. NPR HR, *op.cit.,* 74.

45. Ibid.

46. Ibid., 75.

47. Ibid., 76.

48. For thoughtful discussions of the issue of political leadership in the SES, and its constitutional implications, see Ronald C. Moe, "The 'Reinventing Government' Exercist: Misinterpreting the Problem, Misjudging the Consequences," *Public Administration Review* 54 (March/April 1994): 125–136; James P. Pfiffner, *op.cit.*

49. Toni Marzotto, Charles W. Gossett, and Carolyn Ban, "The Dynamics of Civil Service Reform: The Case of Labor-Management Relations," paper presented at the Annual Meeting of the Association for Public Policy and Management (Washington, D.C.: October, 1981).

50. Carolyn Ban, "Unions, Management, and the NPR," in Donald F. Kettl and John J. Di Iulio, Jr., eds., *Inside the Reinvention Machine: Appraising Governmental Reform, op.cit.*

51. Carolyn Ban, "Reinventing the Federal Civil Service: Drivers of Change," *Public Administration Quarterly* (Spring 1998).

52. Donald F. Kettl, *Reinventing Government: A Fifth-Year Report Card* (Washington, D.C.: The Brookings Institution, 1998), CPM 98-1.

53. Carolyn Ban, "Reinventing the Federal Civil Service: Drivers of Change," *op.cit.*

54. Patricia W. Ingraham, "Of Pigs in Pokes and Policy Diffusion: Another Look at Pay-for-Performance," *Public Administration Review* 53, 4 (July/August 1993): 348–356.

55. Katherine C. Naff and John Crum, "Reinventing Government: The Reaction of the Federal Community," paper presented at the Annual Meeting of the American Political Science Association (Boston, September, 1998).

CHAPTER FOUR

SENIOR EXECUTIVES IN A CHANGING POLITICAL ENVIRONMENT

JOEL D. ABERBACH

BERT A. ROCKMAN

The Senior Executive Service (SES) was created as part of the Civil Service Reform Act (CSRA) of 1978. Like most political reforms, the provisions of the Civil Service Reform Act are sometimes inconsistent. And implementation has not always been smooth or in line with expectations. One student of the Senior Executive Service sees it as containing a "kaleidoscope of images." These include images of the SES as different from one another as a European-style elite corps of administrative generalists, a political machine-like mechanism to promote political responsiveness, and a corps of executives serving in essence as corporate managers utilizing private sector practices.[1] Another observer of the SES argues that its creators never resolved the tension between the desire to have SES career civil servants serve as expert advisors who participate in policy making and to have them be fully and completely responsive to political direction (the political control model).[2] It would not be surprising, then, to find that SES executives themselves have varied notions about the success or failure of SES. Nor would it be surprising that the SES has been used in different ways by different administrations.

After a brief description of SES and of our data source, our paper looks at two sets of issues. The first focuses on how top executives in the federal government evaluate SES. How do they believe it has worked in practice? What do they like and dislike about SES? How have evaluations changed over time? And why have they changed?

The second set of issues focuses more directly on the politics of SES. What is the relationship between the partisan predispositions of senior executives and their evaluations of SES? How have administrations used the Civil Service Reform Act to impact the placement of SES civil servants within agencies? Have administrations been able to manipulate the career service and to move civil servants across agencies more effectively than before?

We will conclude with a brief evaluation of the system, focusing on the political implications of the changes that have occurred.

SES

The major features of the SES are relatively easy to describe.[3] SES set up a rank-in-the-person system to replace the previous rank-in-position system. This promoted the image of an elite corps, but could also be used to manipulate personnel politically because members of the SES would ordinarily not lose status if moved from position to position. SES members are to be eligible for a variety of performance bonuses and cash awards. This feature has elements of private sector management practices (pay for performance), mixed with obvious possibilities for using the bonus system to ensure political responsiveness. Executives are to be evaluated systematically using performance criteria. Those who do not measure up and do not show improvement can be removed from SES. While removal has been exceedingly uncommon, the possibility provides evaluators with significant potential power. SES executives are to be given expanded training and development opportunities. This is in line with their status as senior executives in an elite corps of managers occupying sensitive (policy relevant) and important positions. It is also consonant with one of the goals of SES, which is to offer career executives increased opportunities for advancement.

A variety of safeguards were written into the law to prevent the politicization of SES. While SES allows for noncareer appointments, no more than 10 percent of SES appointments (total) and no more than 25 percent in an agency can be noncareer. The Act requires that certain positions, where impartiality or public confidence is essential, be listed and reserved for careerists. And it establishes two 120-day waiting periods—one after a new administration begins and the other after a new agency head or noncareer supervisor takes over. The former requires a wait before commencing performance appraisals and the latter a wait before a career executive can be involuntarily reassigned or transferred.

The SES became operational in 1979. Most eligible executives joined, some with enthusiasm and others under pressure to be part of the new corps. The provisions of SES were sufficiently complex and contradictory and the changes possible under it sufficiently significant, especially if an administration came to power determined to exert control over the career service, that there were bound to be disagreements in evaluating it.

THE DATA

The main data we report here come from surveys of top federal executives done in 1986–7 and in 1991–2. In each period, we interviewed samples of political appointees and SES career civil servants drawn from agencies of the federal government primarily concerned with domestic policy.

In 1970 we had interviewed similar samples of political appointees and top civil servants. The sampling universe consisted of upper level political appointees (below the rank of undersecretary) and supergrade career civil servants who were the *top* career executives in their particular administrative hierarchy and reported to political appointees. We modified our sampling design somewhat when we went into the field again in 1986–7 and in 1991–2. Because of the changes in the system brought about by the Civil Service Reform Act, we selected two samples of career federal executives. One consisted of a group occupying the top rung of their administrative units and reporting to political appointees. This group represents the closest parallel to the senior civil servants interviewed in 1970. We label them Career I (or sometimes Civil Servants I) in the text. The second group, labeled Career II (or Civil Servants II), is a sample of SES career civil servants who report to other civil servants rather than to political appointees.

Comparison of the attributes and views of the two career SES samples gives us a way to examine the impact of the CSRA and the ways administrations have used opportunities presented by it as such. For example, under the SES rank-in-the person system administrations now have the ability to shift senior career executives from position to position within an agency without fear of charges of "adverse action." This gives administrations a strategic tool, should they choose to use it, to determine which civil servant will hold the top career positions in programs of particular interest to them.

HOW EXECUTIVES EVALUATE THE SES

The introduction of any significant change in a well-established system is bound to unsettle many of those who work in it. On the other hand, change also provides opportunities for effective and ambitious people, and the individuals eligible to join SES had already navigated their way through difficult

Table 1 Evaluating SES by Status and Year
(Percent saying SES has worked well)

	Political Executives	Civil Servants I	Civil Servants II	
1986–87	59	22	21	*(G = .30)*
(N)	(46)	(59)	(56)	
1991–92	57	49	44	*(G = .06)*
(N)	(42)	(53)	(52)	

Question: One recent change in the personnel system has been the creation of SES. In general, how do you think SES has worked?

waters to reach high positions in the federal government. Therefore, by 1986, seven years after the initial implementation of SES, one would expect relatively little opposition to the new system based solely on its relative recency.

As Table 1 indicates, however, career executives in 1986–7 took a dim view of how well SES was working. A clear majority (about 60 percent of both the Career I and Career II SES executives), in fact, thought that it was not working out well at all, with the balance indicating that it was not an improvement over the previous system. Political appointees, on the other hand, generally gave SES high marks, although close to 40 percent of them also felt that SES had not worked well.[4]

The career executives sampled in 1991–2 were decidedly more positive about SES than their counterparts had been in 1986–7. Almost half of the Career I SES executives and close to 45 percent of Career II executives now said that SES was working well. Still, a majority felt that SES was not working well or had made little difference. Why? For what reasons? What accounts for the difference between the two time periods? And why were so many political appointees still unlikely to say that SES was working well?

To answer these questions, we coded executives' explanations about why SES has or has not worked well. Our interviews were conversational in nature, and respondents were encouraged to elaborate on their answers to our queries. This provided a rich source for understanding their evaluations of SES, both positive and negative.

Positive comments about SES were hardly lacking in 1986–7 (see Table 2), but the proportion of executives who had nothing positive to say about SES is the most notable aspect of the data. Fully a third of the Career I executives and more than 40 percent of the Career II executives had no positive comments. Contrast this to the data in Table 3 on negative responses about SES by the same respondents. Just about all of the Career I and Career II ex-

Table 2   Positive Aspects of SES, 1986–87, by Job Status
(Entries are percent giving response)[a]

	Political Executives	Civil Servants I	Civil Servants II
Greater status	13	16	17
Bonuses	21	28	20
Managerial flexibility and adaptability	17	10	15
Greater mobility	14	9	12
Leave time; sabbaticals	4	25	31
High quality of SES personnel	16	2	0
Enables more effective interface between bureaucrats and politicians	12	7	3
Pay/salaries	8	5	2
Greater collegiality among senior careerists	0	3	4
No positive aspects of SES	24	32	42
(N)	(55)	(60)	(65)

[a] Totals do not add to 100 because of multiple responses. Response categories mentioned by fewer than 10 percent of all types of executives in both surveys deleted.

ecutives made at least one negative comment about SES, and most had several negative things to say. (The entries in the table do not sum to 100 percent because multiple mentions—positive and negative—were coded.) Only political appointees differed. While about 25 percent mentioned no positive aspects of SES, over 40 percent had nothing negative to say about it.

What career executives in 1986–7 liked best about SES were the benefits the reform promised—particularly leave time/sabbaticals and bonuses for superior performance (both mentioned by more than 20 percent of the career executives). They also mentioned the greater status SES brought and the increased managerial flexibility and adaptability that accompanied it, but with lesser frequency. Political appointees also liked the bonuses and managerial flexibility, and they were more likely than career executives (although fewer than 20 percent mentioned these things) to talk about the high quality of SES personnel and the greater mobility between agencies that the creation of SES allowed.

The contrast to the negative mentions is striking. Top career executives were angry at the way bonuses were given out—almost half of them believed that the distribution was unfair and manipulated for political purposes. They expressed general indignation about the lack of incentives for

Table 3 Negative Aspects of SES, 1986–87, by Job Status
(Entries are percent giving response)[a]

	Political Executives	Civil Servants I	Civil Servants II
Concept of mobile category of executives unrealistic or inappropriate	6	16	32
Has not resulted in greater mobility of executives	19	41	29
Lack of incentives for performance	20	28	34
Bonuses are unfair or manipulated	11	48	49
SES not exclusive enough	11	10	7
Allows for political manipulation of personnel	2	15	15
System demeaning to senior civil servants	4	7	19
Overpromised benefits (general mention)	17	38	38
No negative aspects	42	10	7
(N)	(53)	(60)	(60)

[a] Totals do not add to 100 because of multiple responses. Response categories mentioned by fewer than 10 percent of all types of executives in both surveys deleted.

performance in a system that put a heavy emphasis on material rewards. And many believed that the concept of a mobile corps of executives was either unrealistic or inappropriate, or that the reform had not yielded results in this area. (The combined totals for these two sets of beliefs which some executives expressed alone and other in combination was 48 percent for Career I executives and 47 percent for Career II executives. Twenty one percent of the political appointees made similar mentions.) The rest of their complaints were scattered over the other topics in the table.

Political executives, as indicated, were much less likely to have negative things to say about SES, but their negative comments tended to focus on the lack of incentives for performance and what they saw as insufficiently frequent mobility of executive personnel.

All in all, career executives and political appointees in 1986–7 were split about how well SES had worked out. Career executives tended to be unhappy with it, and their discontent focussed on the lack of performance incentives and what many perceived as a failure of the reform, either conceptually or in practice, in the area of personnel mobility. Political appointees were much more likely to approve of the way SES had worked out, but they tended to focus their negative comments in the same areas as the career executives.

Anger about performance incentives, particularly the bonus system, was quite understandable in 1986–7. The original legislation contained a provision that 50 percent of the SES executives would be eligible for bonuses each year. After NASA awarded bonuses to the full percentage permissible, "Congress, which had paid little attention to the numbers in hearings on the bill, reacted angrily, indicating that 50 was an outside boundary, not a required level. Congress reduced the number of those eligible from 50 percent to 25 percent six months after the reform was put in place."[5] And then OPM used its rulemaking authority to further reduce the number eligible to 20 percent. Since many of the original group of career SES executives had joined because pay caps and compression had made SES "financially 'the only game in town,' " the "compensation issue framed, and probably distorted, expectations for the SES among its charter members."[6]

SES executives were, according to Patricia Ingraham, relatively unlikely to cite other reasons as incentives to join. And many were, she says (consonant with our data), skeptical about the mobility provisions of SES which they viewed either as a potential punitive tool or as inappropriate to the traditions of the American federal service where program or technical expertise has been highly valued.[7]

The situation was so bad that OPM, under its new leader Constance Horner, began to make changes in the bonus system in 1987. These included increasing the percent of SES members eligible to receive nominations for the Presidential Rank Award and removing the limit on the number of executives who could receive annual performance bonuses.[8] Legislation also raised base pay significantly starting in 1991.

The results are apparent in the way executives evaluated SES in 1991–2. As Tables 4 and 5 show, executives were now very positive about salaries and much less negative about the bonus system. Where only a tiny percentage (5 percent or less) of career executives mentioned pay as a positive aspect of SES in 1986–7, the percentage was 28 percent for Career I executives and 36 percent for Career II executives in 1991–2. And the figures on bonuses also changed greatly. Where close to 50 percent of the career executives complained about bonuses being unfairly given out or manipulated in 1986–7, the percentages dropped to six and two for the Career I and Career II executives respectively. General complaints about over-promised benefits also

Table 4 Positive Aspects of SES, 1991–92, by Job Status

(Entries are percent giving response)[a]

	Political Executives	Civil Servants I	Civil Servants II
Greater status	9	21	21
Bonuses	5	9	4
Managerial flexibility and adaptability	9	11	4
Greater mobility	9	13	2
Leave time; sabbaticals	2	11	6
High quality of SES personnel	39	13	8
Enables more effective interface between bureaucrats and politicians	2	2	6
Pay/salaries	23	28	36
Greater collegiality among senior careerists	11	4	6
Great idea, but has not worked in practice (coded in 1991–92 only)	16	15	10
No positive aspects of SES	21	25	23
(N)	(44)	(53)	(52)

[a] Totals do not add to 100 because of multiple responses. Response categories mentioned by fewer than 10 percent of all types of executives in both surveys deleted.

dropped considerably for career executives, down from 38 percent for both groups of career personnel to an average of 5 percent. And there were many fewer complaints about lack of incentives for performance.

Beyond pay and other compensation issues, career executives in 1991–2 were still negative about mobility issues which, as noted above, can be interpreted as having elements of a punitive political tool about them. However, they were less likely than the executives sampled in 1986–7 to make negative comments about SES allowing for the political manipulation of personnel. Political executives remained generally positive about SES, with a greater emphasis in 1991–2 than in 1986–7 on the high quality of SES personnel.

Four things about executives' views about SES are reasonably clear. First, political executives sampled in 1986–7 were more positive than career executives about the way the SES system was working out and they remained more positive in 1991–2. Second, the margin of difference between the views of political and career executives about SES dropped considerably between the two waves of our study. Third, much of the drop in dissatisfac-

Table 5 Negative Aspects of SES, 1991–92, by Job Status
(Entries are percent giving response) [a]

	Political Executives	Civil Servants I	Civil Servants II
Concept of mobile category of executives unrealistic or inappropriate	7	13	13
Has not resulted in greater mobility of executives	16	43	28
Lack of incentives for performance	14	9	8
Bonuses are unfair or manipulated	2	6	2
SES not exclusive enough	9	6	4
Allows for political manipulation of personnel	7	4	6
System demeaning to senior civil servants	0	4	0
Unable or difficult to remove SES incompetents (1991–92 only)	23	8	0
Overpromised benefits (general mention)	5	2	4
No negative aspects	46	28	37
(N)	(44)	(53)	(52)

[a] Totals do not add to 100 because of multiple responses. Response categories mentioned by fewer than 10 percent of all types of executives in both surveys deleted.

tion on the part of career SES people seems to have come from improvements in the pay and bonus systems. Fourth, while the career executives interviewed in 1991–2 were much more positive about SES than those interviewed in 1986–7, the system was still not particularly well regarded. Less than half of the Career I and Career II executives said that the system was working well. And, while the percentage that could think of nothing positive to say about SES had dropped noticeably, the figure still hovered around 25 percent for both groups (see Tables 2 and 3). In addition, a category we added in 1991–2 to record a general sentiment that SES was a good idea, but had not worked in practice garnered an additional 10 to 15 percent of the respondents.

The data clearly indicate that SES has been better received over time, but career executives can hardly be described as enthusiastic about it. In fact, to the extent they are satisfied, much of the cause seems related to improved material rewards. Political appointees, for reasons we discuss in the next section, had more cause to be positive about SES from the start, but even they have reservations.

POLITICS OF SES

CSRA (including SES) was passed by a Democratic Congress and signed by a Democratic president. However, it is not a partisan tool in the narrow sense that it advantages only one party. Rather, it presents the party in control of the presidency with opportunities to use its provisions to advance its agenda.

Republicans controlled the presidency in 1986–7 and 1991–2, the two times we interviewed high level executives after SES was established. Table 6 shows the relationship in each round of the study between executives' party affiliations and their views on whether SES was working well. As the table clearly shows, the relationship between party affiliation and evaluation of SES was quite marked in 1986–7 and was almost nonexistent in 1991–2.

The relationship in the table between party affiliation and evaluation of SES in 1986–7 is partly explained by the fact that political appointees were more positive about SES than career executives, and almost all political appointees in 1986–7 were Republicans. (There was one independent.) Consistent with that explanation, the disappearance of the relationship in 1991–2, when the political appointees in our sample were all Republicans, can be explained by the increased approval of SES among career executives (Table 1.)

However, there is more to it than that. In 1986–7, career members of SES who were Republicans were more likely to say that SES was working well than career executives who were Independents or Democrats. The relationships between party and evaluation of SES presented in Table 6 are more modest within each career sample, but controlling for job status does not eliminate them. (The average *gamma* coefficient between the two variables for the two groups of SES career executives is .26, with the stronger relationship for the Career II sample.) There is, however, no relationship between party and evaluation of SES in 1991–2 for any of the samples. (The average *gamma* coefficient between the two variables for the two groups of SES career executives is actually .00, with the two component coefficients mirror images at .02 and −.02.) In short, there was something different going on in 1986–7 than in 1991–2.

Table 6 Evaluations of SES by Party and Year
(Percent saying SES has worked well)

	Republican	Independent	Democrat	
1986–87	46	16	18	*(G=.41)*
(N)	(82)	(19)	(51)	
1991–92	52	54	41	*(G=.03)*
(N)	(85)	(24)	(37)	

The difference, of course, is that Ronald Reagan was president in 1986–7 and George Bush in 1991–2. The Reagan administration was dedicated to producing far-reaching changes in the scope and operation of government. It was self-consciously inspired by the "administrative presidency" doctrine of the Nixon administration, and aimed to use all the tools available to it to influence policy by administrative means. George Bush's administration, in contrast, was basically a maintaining administration, and tended to endorse the status quo. As we noted in an earlier article about the political views of senior federal executives: "Not surprisingly, the career civil servants we interviewed in 1991–2 seemed comfortable with the stability and relative moderation they were now experiencing."[9]

The effects of partisanship were muted in the Bush administration in contrast to the Reagan administration. Concomitantly, partisan differences in evaluations of the Senior Executive Service were also muted. Though many federal executives still were not enthusiastic about SES, their views were more positive and no longer related in any direct way to their partisan attachments.

Analysis of our data give us an insight into the ways in which the Reagan administration used the rank-in-the-person feature of SES to influence who occupied key positions in the bureaucracy. Figure 1 presents data on the percentage of career civil servants in 1986–7 and 1991–2 who were Republicans, broken down by agency type and job status. Career I and Career II civil servants are grouped separately, as are those in what we call the social service agencies (the departments of Education, Health and Human Services, and Housing and Urban Development) and those in all other agencies.

The agency data are divided into social service agencies and others because the Reagan administration was particularly interested in controlling policy in these agencies. The social service agencies have primary responsibility for the New Deal and Great Society programs the administration was dedicated to thwarting. And, as our past work demonstrates, during the

Figure 1   Party Affiliation of Career Civil Servants by Agency Type, Job Status, and Year

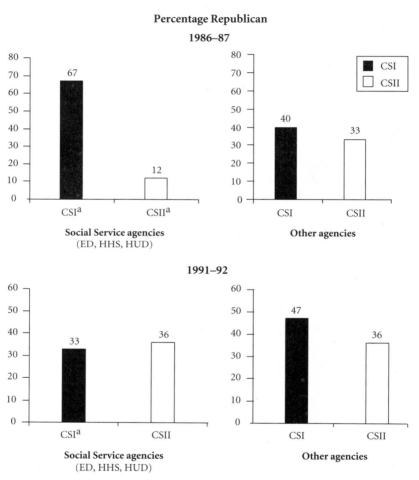

Percentage Republican

1986–87

Social Service agencies
(ED, HHS, HUD)

Other agencies

1991–92

Social Service agencies
(ED, HHS, HUD)

Other agencies

[a] CSI = career civil servants who occupy the top rungs in their administrative units and report to political appointees. CSII = career Senior Executive Service members who report to other civil servants, not political appointees.

Adapted from Joel D. Aberbach and Bert A. Rockman, *In the Web of Politics* (Washington, D.C.: Brookings Institution Press, 2000.)

Nixon administration these agencies were more likely to have Democrats than other agencies.[10] If one believes, as the Reagan administration did, that having the right personnel in key administrative positions (including, where possible, career positions) is vital to having administration priorities carried out, then focusing on who served in what position would be especially important in targeted agencies.

Here is where the rank-in-the person feature of the SES provided a potential lever. Recall that under the provisions of the CSRA, SES career executives could now easily be moved from one position to another within an agency without fear that such an action could successfully be challenged as an "adverse action." If one had an interest in putting career executives who shared one's views into the top positions within any hierarchy, that could now be accomplished—provided, of course, that the administration could determine the political views of top civil servants. And the data in Figure 1 suggest that this was not all that hard to do.

What the Reagan administration apparently did was to take advantage of the opportunity provided by the CSRA to place Republican-oriented career executives in Career I positions, that is, those positions whose incumbents reported to political appointees. The Career II positions in the social service agencies, those whose incumbents reported to other career civil servants, were the province of the considerable number of Democrats and Independents who held SES positions in these agencies. The distribution of personnel was quite different in the other, less sensitive agencies. Here the percentages of Republicans in Career I and Career II positions were much closer to even.

The pattern in the Bush administration was quite different. In line with its lesser emphasis on litmus tests and its more civil service–friendly position, there is no indication that the administration used the available opportunities to influence the partisan makeup of what we call the Career I and Career II levels in the agencies. In fact, while the differences are tiny, the Bush administration data actually show a smaller percentage of Republicans in Career I positions in the social service agencies than in the other agencies.

In brief, the SES reform gives an administration with a will to use it a powerful new tool for getting the types of career people it prefers into key positions in the bureaucracy. It may or may not choose to use the tool or have the skill to employ it effectively, but that is another matter.

MOBILITY

As we noted above, SES executives frequently made negative comments about mobility under SES. Some thought the mobility goal of the reform inappropriate and others were convinced that it had been ineffectively implemented. Judgments about the appropriateness or inappropriateness of the

Figure 2 Career Mobility of Federal Executives, by Year

Percentage who have served in a department/agency other than the present one

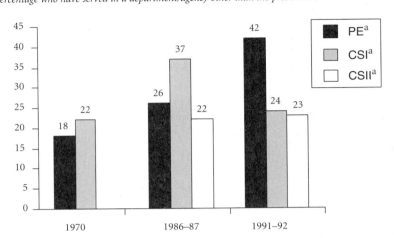

[a] PE = political executives. CSI = career civil servants who occupy the top rungs in their administrative units and report to political appointees. Members of this group were called supergrade career civil servants in 1970; in 1986–87 and 1991–92 they were drawn from career civil servants in the Senior Executive Service (established in 1979). CSII = career Senior Executive Service members who report to other civil servants, not political appointees. Data for 1986–87 include only line personnel for purposes of comparability.

From Joel D. Aberbach and Bert A. Rockman, *In the Web of Politics* (Washington, D.C.: Brookings Institution Press, 2000).

goal is to a significant degree a matter of one's views about how an elite civil service corps should operate, but how much mobility there has actually been and whether it has varied between administrations can be measured.

Figure 2 makes clear that mobility has varied quite a bit over the years between administrations and job statuses. It also makes clear that mobility in the U.S., even after the introduction of SES, has not come close to the level of Great Britain whose civil service system places emphasis on generalized intellectual skills rather than specialized expertise, and where 51 percent of top civil servants in one of our studies reported that they had served in a ministry other than their present one.[11]

The data in Figure 2 cover the Nixon administration as well as the Reagan and Bush administrations. The percentage of political appointees who have served in more than one department or agency in 1991–2 is particularly high because the Bush administration moved many of the people who had served in the previous administration into new agencies. Doing this was part of the Bush administration's effort to put its own stamp on the government. But the most interesting fact is that the mobility data for career civil servants was generally the same across all three administrations except for Career I executives in the Reagan administration. While the percentage of these individuals who report serving in more than one agency may not be overwhelming by British standards, it is sufficient to suggest what the SES reform enables a determined administration like that of Ronald Reagan to accomplish if it wants to move executives around.

In brief,

> The Reagan administration wanted to shake up the agencies, and one way to do so was to put into top positions people who agreed with its political agenda or people who, due to the variety of their experiences, would be less likely to identify strongly with an agency's mission. The Bush administration was much less zealous than the Reagan administration and therefore had less interest in moving civil servants from agency to agency or in selecting SES executives within an agency who were sympathetic to its views. The opportunity is now there, however, as it has always been in the more generalist-oriented British civil service, to more easily promote the interagency mobility of career executives.[12]

JOB SATISFACTION

Finally, after all is said and done, how much is an executive's satisfaction with SES related to his or her overall job satisfaction? The short answer is relatively little. Executives who say SES has worked well are slightly more likely than executives who have negative views on the success of SES to like their jobs, but the relationship is quite modest.

As Figure 3 shows, in fact, most federal executives like their jobs no matter what they think of the way SES has worked.[13] The SES system is clearly not the defining element in the way senior executives evaluate their jobs.

OVERVIEW AND CONCLUDING COMMENTS

The creation of SES initiated a complex set of changes at the top of the federal bureaucracy. The reform aimed to create an elite corps of career civil servants (and a limited number of noncareer SESers also) who would be expert and politically responsive advisors, mobile within and between agencies, and subject to the types of performance evaluations and incentives typical in the private sector.

Figure 3 Job Satisfaction by Evaluation of SES, by Year

Percent who like their jobs

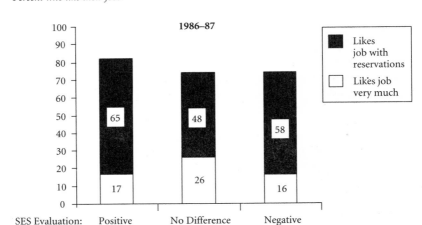

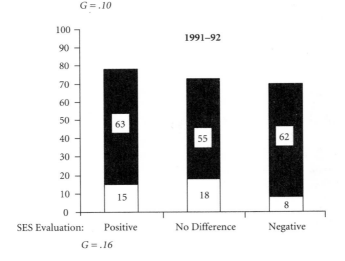

Our study is based on two samples of top executives, one drawn in 1986–7 and the other in 1991–2. The data indicate that executives in SES were, on average, not very pleased with it in 1986–7. Evaluations improved by 1991–2, but even in that sample only slightly less than half of the career respondents thought that SES was working well.

Initially, executives were disillusioned with the failure of the compensation system, especially with the way bonuses were given out, and many were unhappy about either the appropriateness or implementation of the agency mobility provisions of SES. Negative feelings about SES abated somewhat by 1991–2, due mainly, it appears, to improvements in the level of compensation and in administration of the bonus system.

SES has been better received over time, but career executives can hardly be described as enthusiastic about it. At the same time, their views of SES have not appreciably dampened their high levels of job satisfaction, so SES has apparently done little damage to morale.

Politically, the SES appears to be a success. *If it so desires,* the administration in power can use SES effectively to get career people more to its liking into key positions or those it does not like away from their current positions. SES definitely gives presidential administrations a tool to promote responsiveness. By that criterion, it has accomplished one of the major objectives of those who designed it.

The SES reform, like most reforms, has not achieved all its initiators hoped for. Given the tensions in the reform's images of what the SES should be, that was probably never possible or desirable. Many originators of SES are probably disappointed that the reform has not increased the *esprit* of the top civil service or produced a corps of elite generalists. On the other hand, SES has given politicians added (and effective) tools to promote responsiveness, at little apparent cost to morale or quality.[14]

The senior civil service in the U.S. is situated in a uniquely politicized government in which control of the bureaucracy is always uncertain and contested. As a consequence, it is likely that civil servants will always be wary about what any reform means for them. It is not surprising that they would be skeptical. Similarly, given the nature of our system, it is not likely that the aspects of any reform package designed to enhance the status of the civil service will dominate over the aspects designed to enhance political control. Viewed in the light of such expectations, the SES provided tools to presidential administrations to help achieve their policy aims without apparently causing significant damage to the senior civil service. That is not a great report card, but it is also by no means a bad one. One could imagine far worse evaluations of a reform at the age of twenty.

NOTES

The authors thank Constance Horner and James King for comments on the original draft of this chapter, Jim Pfiffner and Michael Lacey for inviting us to participate in the symposium, and the National Science Foundation and the Brookings Institution's Governmental Studies Program for their support of our research. Joel Aberbach also gratefully acknowledges support from the Center for American Politics and Public Policy and the Academic Senate at UCLA.

1. Mark Huddleston, "To the Threshold of Reform: The Senior Executive Service and America's Search for a Higher Civil Service," in Patricia W. Ingraham and David H. Rosenbloom, eds., *The Promise and Paradox of Civil Service Reform* (Pittsburgh: University of Pittsburgh Press, 1992), 180–91.

2. Patricia W. Ingraham, "The Design of Civil Service Reform: Good Politics or Good Management?" in Ingraham and Rosenbloom, eds., *The Promise and Paradox of Civil Service Reform*, 31.

3. See Report to the Congress by the Comptroller General of the United States, *Civil Service Reform—Where It Stands Today* (Washington, D.C.: Government Printing Office, 1980), Report FPCD-80-38, May 13, 1980, especially pages 35–47, for a brief description of the main features of SES. Also see Mark W. Huddleston and William W. Boyer, *The Higher Civil Service in the United States: Quest for Reform* (Pittsburgh: University of Pittsburgh Press, 1996). In addition, the features of SES are described in several of the articles in Ingraham and Rosenbloom, eds., *The Promise and Paradox of Civil Service Reform*.

4. Only 2 percent said that they noticed little difference from the previous system, a not unexpected finding since most had not served prior to the CSRA.

5. Patricia W. Ingraham, *The Foundation of Merit* (Baltimore: Johns Hopkins University Press, 1995), 85.

6. Ibid., 84.

7. Ibid., 85.

8. Kirke Harper, "The Senior Executive Service after One Decade," in Ingraham and Rosenbloom, eds., *The Promise and Paradox of Civil Service Reform*, 271–2.

9. The quote is from Joel D. Aberbach and Bert A. Rockman, "The Political Views of U.S. Senior Federal Executives, 1970–92," *Journal of Politics* 57 (August 1995): 850. On the administrative presidency, see Richard P. Nathan, *The Administrative Presidency* (New York: Wiley, 1983).

10. Joel D. Aberbach and Bert A. Rockman, "Clashing Beliefs within the Executive Branch: The Nixon Administration Bureaucracy," *American Political Science Review* 70 (June 1976): 459.

11. See Joel D. Aberbach, Bert A. Rockman, and Robert D. Putnam, *Bureaucrats and Politicians in Western Democracies* (Cambridge: Harvard University Press, 1981), 70–2. In general, it is the British case rather than the American one that is the anomaly regarding interagency mobility.

12. Joel D. Aberbach and Bert A. Rockman, *In the Web of Politics: Three Decades of the U.S. Federal Executive* (Washington, D.C.: Brookings Institution Press, 2000).

13. Controls for job status have no effect on the statistics reported in Figure 3 in 1991–2. In 1986–7 there is a tendency for political appointees who evaluate SES positively to like their jobs somewhat less than those who evaluate it negatively, but job evaluations are decidedly positive within all categories of the SES evaluation measure.

14. For data and analysis on the quality issue, see Aberbach and Rockman, *In the Web of Politics,* chapters 3 and 4.

PART TWO

PERFORMANCE, INCENTIVES, AND ACCOUNTABILITY

CHAPTER FIVE

EVOLVING DIMENSIONS OF PERFORMANCE FROM THE CSRA ONWARD

PATRICIA W. INGRAHAM AND DONALD P. MOYNIHAN

INTRODUCTION

Performance, or more accurately, efficient performance, has been a long-term concern in the American federal bureaucracy. Legislation in 1916 created a Bureau of Efficiency within the Civil Service Commission. The creation of the Bureau of the Budget in 1923 emphasized the efficient use of personnel, as well as of financial resources. Classification reforms in 1949 and performance appraisal provisions in 1953 were intended to facilitate not only the efficient use of federal personnel, but appraisal and assessment of individual performance in pursuit of public objectives. The Civil Service Reform Act (CSRA) of 1978, however, addressed the problem more directly and more comprehensively than any previous effort. In addition, the CSRA attempted to move from personnel administration to the specific linking of human resource management to broader management activities and performance. The CSRA recalibrated the focus of public management in the contemporary era, focusing intently on the concept of performance, and developing human resources systems that would contribute directly to performance.

That first bold step was an important advance; it was also, however, only the first step in a continuously emerging definition of performance in the federal government. Although the centrality of performance has remained largely unquestioned, the way by which to achieve that goal—and, by implication, the CSRA's definition of performance—has been shifting since 1978. One year after passage of the reform, Scotty Campbell observed that, "Standing alone, the changes embodied in the Civil Service Reform Act will not suddenly and dramatically improve the quality of performance in the federal workforce. They will have to be combined with effective performance appraisal systems, with a productivity measurement system, and with other techniques which will help answer the question 'How well are we doing?' "[1]

The Campbell statement reflected an awareness of the need to link the essentially individual based performance emphasis of the CSRA to broader organizational and policy goals. In the twenty years since the passage of the Act, those linkages have developed along three major dimensions: the focus of performance, the standardization and co-ordination of performance, and method of accountability for performance. From 1978 to 1998 there are apparently marked shifts in these three different dimensions: the focus of performance has shifted from the individual to the organization while having the potential to incorporate both; standardization has shifted from cross-government regulations to agency-based flexibility while co-ordination has become largely a function of the Office of Management and Budget; and an individual, confidential version of accountability has given way to a more public, organizational perspective. It may be suggested that the change in each dimension is based on a cyclical relationship rather than a clear movement forward, with different dimensions being in the ascendancy at any one point. In this way the extremes of the different dimensions have a relationship similar to the one between Kaufman's cycle of values (representativeness, political neutral competence and executive leadership): "None of these values was ever totally neglected in any of our past modifications of governmental design, but each enjoyed greater emphasis than the others in different periods."[2] What should also be clear is that the dimensions are closely interrelated to each other, and discussion of one concept will often overlap with, and provide insights to, other dimensions.

In this chapter, we analyze changing definitions of performance as they have evolved since 1978. Part one of the chapter, *The Role of the CSRA in Defining Performance,* looks at the dimensions of performance in how they are presented in the various provisions—and visions—of the CSRA. Reflective of the CSRA's definition of performance, and its position on each of the three dimensions, was the Senior Executive Service. A discussion of the history of the Senior Executive Service serves to highlight the limitations of the CSRA's emphasis on the role of the individual. We then examine *The Shifting of Dimensions,* considering how subsequent legislative efforts reflect a move towards a more organizational, rather than individual, definition of performance. The third part of the chapter, *The Current State of Performance,* examines how the different dimensions of performance are represented in contemporary public management initiatives such as reinvention and Government Performance and Results Act (GPRA). In addition, the evolution of the different central coordinating institutions, the Office of Management and Budget (OMB) and the Office of Personnel Management (OPM), is given attention. We close by discussing what the different strands of performance-related reform in the previous twenty years suggest for the future of public administration.

THE ROLE OF THE CSRA IN DEFINING PERFORMANCE

The Foundation of the Civil Service Reform Act

When Jimmy Carter proposed civil service reform in his presidential campaign, he emphasized the need for improved performance. The federal workforce, he argued, lacked the will and/or the ability to focus on two important objectives: productivity and quality. Burdened by over-regulation, "dead wood," and excessive emphasis on protecting employees, the civil service system was perceived to be desperately in need of repair. "There is no merit," said Carter, "in the merit system."

To address these problems, the Civil Service Reform Act contained a heavy dose of reforms specifically tailored to performance issues. Performance appraisal, merit pay, performance bonuses, emphases on whistle-blowing and removal of poor performers, the research and development provisions of Title VII, and the separation of the merit protection function from the managing of the civil service were all intended to sharpen the focus on what public employees did and how well they did it. In a manner that was unprecedented in the history of public sector reform in the Unites States the focus of change rested almost exclusively on improving performance.

The definition of performance that permeated the Civil Service Reform Act was influenced by several factors. First, was the generalized sense that government employees were simply too insulated from the real world idea of linking pay with effort. If promotion was essentially automatic and seniority the key factor in most promotion decisions, the personal incentives to "do better," Carter argued, were very limited.

Second, the civil service system was described as too rigid and too protective of employee rights. Indeed, as the system had grown, it had become encrusted with more rules and regulations to the point where the *Federal Per-*

sonnel grew to more than ten thousand pages before being scrapped by the Office of Personnel Management in 1994.[3] The Civil Service Commission was charged with both protecting merit and ensuring that the civil service system was well run and productive. There was little question, however, that the merit perspective on fairness and fair treatment of employees often translated as sameness—that treating everyone the same equated fairness.[4] Sameness, not surprisingly, did not emphasize performance. In fact, rewarding good performance could easily be viewed as favoritism in this context.

Third was a belief by Carter and many of his advisors that injecting better performance into the public service was essentially a technical problem. Evidence from the private sector was interpreted to mean that the thorny issues related to improving performance were measurement issues. To put it a bit too simplistically, calibration, not culture change, was viewed as the primary challenge for performance appraisal and measurement systems.

When it was drafted, the Civil Service Reform Act reflected the most current thinking about performance and reward. The heavy reliance on private sector perspectives and techniques did not foresee the difficulties of translating private practice into public reality.[5] Many of the Act's performance provisions had never been tested in a public setting; in many respects, government-wide implementation was a giant pilot experiment. Indeed, later research for the Office of Personnel Management demonstrated that many of the assumptions about how well performance appraisal worked in the private sector were not accurate.[6] While the CSRA pioneered an intense focus on performance as a theme for government reform, its approach proved to be too simplistic and narrow.

Individual Performance in a Standardized Context

Individual performance appraisal was the cornerstone of the design and the essence of CSRA's definition of performance. Ten years after the enactment of the CSRA, Campbell commented that: "The primary purpose of personnel policies and practices is to enhance quality performance among all public employees. Every policy and practice should be measured against this standard and performance should be measured against pre-established individual and organizational goals."[7]

This view was slightly revisionist, however. The CSRA largely failed to examine performance in larger program or organizational terms, and did not provide for direct links between individual efforts and organizational performance. Its heavy reliance on financial incentives targeted only individual

Table 1 The Evolving Dimensions of Performance from 1978 to 1998

Dimension	1978	1998
Focus of performance	Individual	Organizational—with potential for individual also
Standardization and coordination of performance	Cross–government standardization; central co-ordination on personnel matters with OPM	Greater agency flexibility and control; central co-ordination on management efforts with OMB
Method of accountability	Individual, confidential	Organizational, public

performance and reward. To the extent that the reform addressed the problem of "dead wood," that too was an individual perspective. The provisions, in short, were intended to ensure that individual performance was being monitored at the negative and positive ends of the performance spectrum but did not specifically address how this would matter to the overall capacity of the organization. As noted in Table 1, the focus of performance, quite clearly, was on the individual rather than the organization as a whole.

The entire performance system contained in the CSRA needed to operate within the confines of civil service law, as exemplified by standardized classification and compensation systems and by complex appeals procedures. As a result, the nature of performance assessment and the appraisal process and format was designed to be rigidly standardized. This standardization applied both within the organization and across government organizations. The standard five point rating system that was a part of the appraisal process and the formula that was adopted for determining amounts of money available in the merit pay pools are leading examples of this focus. In later years this dimension of performance would become more flexible, with far greater levels of discretion delegated to the agency level. A reflection of the central standardization and the emphasis on personnel matters was the proposed strong central coordination of the Office of Personnel Management. The section of the chapter titled *Standardization and Coordination: The Role of Institutions in Defining Performance* discusses the changing (and largely declining) role of the OPM.

Given that the focus of performance was on the individual, it was logical that accountability systems were similarly focused.[8] Under the CSRA, supervisors were to decide employee performance goals, ideally in conjunction with the employee involved. The implication was that goals were generated within the organization and the actual performance of the employee was a largely private matter between the employee and supervisor. This style of performance appraisal did not lend itself to useful aggregate measures and told the outside world little in terms of how well the organization as a whole was doing. This may reflect the perception that employee performance was a technical problem, best left to supervisors working within the organization to develop and appraise.

The Senior Executive Service: Exemplars of Performance?

The Senior Executive Service, and provisions in the legislation for evaluation and reward of its members, were also important parts of CSRA's performance definition. The pivotal role played by the SES in the initial CSRA design mandated two things: first, that performance be valued and performance appraisal be taken seriously by both members of the SES and their political superiors; and, second, that the experience with the new definitions of performance be a generally positive one for members of the SES. Understanding the role envisioned for the SES underscores where the CSRA was on the three dimensions of performance outlined in Table 1. It also highlights the limitations of focusing on performance at the individual level, both in the unsuccessful implementation of the SES concept and the very narrow view of the role of individual performance.

Members of the SES were technically removed from many of the protections of the civil service; their financial incentive package was larger, and many reported to, and were evaluated by, political appointees. This dimension of political responsiveness, therefore, became an integral part of the definition of performance for SESers. The SES had the ability to become a key institutional link between individual performance and broader organizational objectives (as defined by political executives). This potential is exemplified by the implementation strategy for the new performance systems. The SES played a central role. The legislation provided that the SES performance appraisal and financial incentive package be implemented immediately upon passage of the reform. The mid-level management plan, the merit pay scheme, was to be implemented three years later. Thus, members of the SES, as initial targets of performance reforms, were also envisioned as the champions of performance inside the organization and the implementers of the system within each federal agency.

For the individual performance triggers to fire throughout the organization as the CSRA framers intended, the performance system and incentives had to be embraced by members of the SES and then cascade down through the organization to other levels of management. For the individual/organization links to be forged, political executives and members of the SES had to concur on the program and policy directions and changes that created the performance objectives for the SES.

The strategy did not work as intended, either for the SES or for the mid-level Merit Pay Plan.[9] Indeed, current efforts to reform the SES indicate that the link the SES could have provided still has not been created in most agencies. This does not mean that the original concept of the SES has been invalidated, merely that there has been a lack of success in practical terms in fulfilling this concept. The implementation history of the SES never saw it evolve into a core cadre with broad management experience who enjoyed a high-risk, high-reward culture. This has been recognized by the OPM, whose recent suggestions to reform the SES have promised to "reinforce the original Civil Service Reform Act concept of a senior executive corps" rather than to redirect the SES away from its founding vision.[10] If the challenge for effective government performance is to link the individual efforts so that they are effectively contributing to the broader organizational goals, a reinvigorated SES might a key element of a successful union.

It has been proposed that the current SES be divided into two elements, the Senior Executive Corps (SEC) and the Senior Professional Corps (SPC). The SEC will be limited to those who perform executive managerial functions, while the SPC will be made up of more technical and professional experts. This is a reflection of the fact that many of those who are in the SES are there due to the technical expertise of the individual, rather than broader management ability. The Personnel Management Project, which provided the basis for the CSRA, warned against just such an outcome when it stated: "Some of the personnel management measures which are highly suitable for managerial staff do not apply equally well to individuals whose grade levels are based on a high level of professional or technical expertise. The greatest need for a special executive personnel system centers on the managerial group."[11]

Other proposals call for the SEC to sign three year performance agreements that are to be specific enough to assess level of performance, suggesting that agreements will be linked to agencies' missions and judged on program results. Performance agreements will be used to decide whether an executive should continue in a current position, be reassigned or removed at the end of the three years. There would be provisions for greater mobility of managers between departments and significant changes to the compensation system that would have the result of increasing the size of rewards but decreasing the likeliness of receiving one.

THE SHIFTING OF DIMENSIONS

As discussed in the previous section, the different aspects of the CSRA legislation saw certain dimensions of performance in the ascendancy. The focus of performance rested on the individual, there was high cross government standardization of personnel matters and accountability was largely confidential and based on individual performance. This part of the chapter discusses how these emphases on these dimensions have shifted to a much more organizational perspective. This section traces the shift in dimensions from the individual to the more organizational perspective. Title VII of the legislation offers a starting point, allowing agencies greater discretion and fostering a sense of performance scrutiny at a level above the individual. The proposed Civil Service Simplification Act (CSSA) of 1986 more fully represents the changing attitudes towards the performance, and reflects what would become the orthodoxy of the organizational perspective on performance.

Title VII and Experimental Flexibility

Although the CSRA followed a generally standardized path, Title VII of the Act provided potential flexibilities under Research and Demonstration provisions. Some of the projects approved under Title VII used the flexibilities to begin to define performance in organizational terms and to link individual and group performance and reward to organizational productivity. In cases such as the navy's China Lake demonstration project, the air force's Pacer Share project, and the demonstration project at the National Institute of Standards and Technology, individual performance became less central.[12]

In these experiments, the conditions for organizational performance began to be considered and the links between human resource performance and organizational outcomes explored. Recruiting and retaining the right people, group appraisal and reward, and the direct linking of rewards to organizational productivity emerged as new themes in the definition of performance, but only in the limited cases of the experimental projects themselves.

The Civil Service Simplification Act: Isolated Flexibility

Efforts to emphasize and reward individual performance were altered profoundly by Jimmy Carter's defeat at the polls in 1980. During the bureaucrat bashing of the Reagan presidency, it is fair to say that the performance of the public service was not carefully considered. Very early into the implementation of the Civil Service Reform Act, performance—particularly for the SES—became defined in very narrow and simple terms: political responsiveness. Those who argued that the performance of the public service deserved recognition and possibly additional rewards drew little popular or political support.

In the second term of Reagan's presidency, however, some additional consideration was given to personnel reform and its relationship to organizational performance. In 1986, in collaboration with some agencies from the Department of Defense, the Office of Personnel Management supported proposed legislation entitled "The Civil Service Simplification Act." Under its provisions, agencies with demonstrated performance capacity and special needs (or, in some cases, just special needs) were to be exempt from most civil service laws on an agency by agency basis.

The Civil Service Simplification Act did not pass, but its clear movement away from the idea of standardization of personnel and performance criteria is a notable step in the gradual redefinition of necessary conditions for improved performance in federal agencies. For the first time, legislation was discussed that would focus on implementing performance reforms not on the whole civil service, but on specific organizations. Further, those agencies that participated in the proposal made a very clear and specific link between the configuration of individual and group performance systems and the performance of the entire organization. The 1980s and the thinking behind the CSSA would provide a bridge that allowed the shifting of the focus of performance from the individual within a standardized civil service to broader organizational flexibilities.

The underlying idea was compelling and simple: if performance is to be improved, federal agencies must carefully consider what they need to do and how they intend to do it; individual, group, and executive performance and reward must all tie directly to the organizational strategy. The constraints of the civil service system, even as reformed, do not permit the flexibility necessary to achieve the desired results. As agencies demonstrate their ability to consider improved organizational performance, they "earn" the right to the flexibilities necessary to achieve it.

Although the CSSA did not pass, it defined the origins of the idea of "isolated flexibility." The central presence of this idea is demonstrated by the case of the Federal Aviation Administration (FAA). That agency argued to Congress that it could not meet the many demands on the agency without sweeping personnel and performance improvements. The FAA was excepted from most federal personnel laws by the provisions of the 1996 Department of Transportation (DOT) budget bill; it is now proceeding to define performance in agency specific terms and to create compensation and incentive structures quite different from those of the general civil service.

The move to provide greater flexibilities to a handful of organizations was a shift influenced by agencies in a strong position to argue that such measures made sense—that they were, in fact, both different and capable of higher performance. What kind of agencies could successfully make such arguments?[13] Generally, they fell into the following categories:

- Agencies with major resources; the ability to hire and develop employees in the 1980's; and strong political clout, e.g., selected agencies in the Department of Defense
- Agencies with broad and routinized functions, e.g., the Social Security Administration
- Agencies with a private sector style, commercial functions, and a bottom line against which to judge performance, e.g., the Patent and Trademark Office

One clear result of the "flexibility by exception" approach was the reality of different potential and therefore different performance expectations for federal agencies. Flexibilities recognized different concepts of performance, which were based on the particular functions and abilities of a specific organization. These include group awards, gain sharing and private sector style executive benefits. Many of these reward concepts were undertaken under the auspices of Title VII of the CSRA.

This idea of performance at the organizational level has continued, and is a central concern in some current reforms. The Government Performance and Results Act, for example, mandates that all organizations define their mission, objectives and the performance measures used to gauge success or failure. Those agencies that had been successful in gaining flexibilities and developing a concept of organizational performance were at an advantage when GPRA legislation required agencies to follow the model that they had previously pioneered. The agencies that did not enjoy special treatment or special recognition during the 1980s now suffer a double disadvantage in the current organizational context of performance: they lack both the experience and the "suitability" to easily adapt to strategic plans and performance measures.

THE CURRENT STATE OF PERFORMANCE

Combining New Flexibility in a Traditional Setting: Reinventing Government

Both of the two main reform efforts of the 1990s, Reinventing Government and the Government Performance and Results Act, are clearly about performance. Reinventing Government (formerly known as the National Performance Review, or NPR) is more difficult to categorize and describe, however, because it has embraced many different definitions of performance and has done so within the confines of an unreformed civil service system.

The scattergun of reforms that NPR favors call for a variety of changes of different scope, and at different levels, of organizations and programs. In some ways, Reinventing Government also supports the rewarding of "performance winners"—or those who are already ahead—the model that underpinned the CSSA. Perhaps the best demonstration of this was the concept of reinvention laboratories, proposed as commonsense, bottom up reforms. While all agencies were eligible to develop reinvention labs, the reality was that a disproportionate number of the labs came from the Department of Defense, a well-funded leader of innovations in the 1980s.[14] In cases where labs had reinvention ideas that might contradict existing agency-specific and governmentwide regulations they were promised regulatory waivers.[15] Other "exception" legislation was aimed at developing Performance Based Organizations. Organizations such as the Patent and Trademark Organization, which had particularly commercial functions, were to be given broad flexibilities including private-sector style levels of freedoms and performance contract relationships with their parent department and their employees.[16]

While Reinvention did advance some comprehensive reform legislation, most efforts at performance reform have been informal, small scale, and agency or program specific. Failed legislative efforts, however, would have allowed specific government organizations exceptional levels of freedoms. After the Personnel System Reinvention Act did not gain Congressional approval, the Clinton administration introduced the Omnibus Civil Service

Reform Act in 1996. This legislation proposed that fifteen demonstration projects be delegated significant exemptions from central rules.

These various elements of the reinvention effort underline the fact that the Clinton administration has emphasized performance at the organizational level for organizations that 1) were already performing relatively well, or 2) had a clear means of measuring performance. Standardization remains the norm for those agencies that have lagged behind.

However, NPR was also designed to impact individual performance: employees were to become empowered, less encumbered by arcane regulations, to pursue organizational objectives as the employees themselves defined them. The Blair House Papers[17] outlined the three principles that agencies were to employ to ensure individual empowerment:

1. Don't decide anything in headquarters that can be decided somewhere else
2. Move high-grade positions to the fields
3. Push dollar controls to the front line

Still other NPR reforms were focused on simplifying organizational processes to improve performance governmentwide. A good example of this—and one of NPR's few notable legislative successes—has been the Federal Acquisition and Streamlining Act. This legislation allowed government organizations a more businesslike approach to their purchasing, e.g. making "off-the shelf" purchases or using an Agency credit card for small purchases.

As noted NPR has encompassed: (I) giving government organizations increased freedoms to enhance performance; (II) placing an emphasis on individual empowerment, and by assumed connection, individual performance; (III) improving organizational processes. In addition NPR has attempted to (IV) provide a flexible definition of performance based on specific goals developed by different organizations. The vice president recently asked 32 of the most prominent government agencies to develop goals that people could understand and which could be measured. These High Impact Agencies have provided, in conjunction with GPRA efforts, a series of specific goals to be achieved by 2000. For example, a goal of the Health Care Financing Administration is:

- Increase from 34 percent (17 states) to 100 percent (all states) those states conducting maternal AIDS information projects to inform women of childbearing age of the importance of HIV testing and, if necessary, treatment as part of prenatal care, and that these services are covered for Medicaid-eligible women.

With the High Impact Agencies NPR has borrowed the fruits of GPRA related work and attempted to publicize its most digestible elements. This reflects the fact that the stated goal of the NPR is to ultimately restore public trust in government, and communicating what government performance means in concrete and understandable terms is, therefore, important. It also highlights the fact that the Reinvention effort has now embraced a specific type of performance definition that is exemplified by GPRA.

The above discussion illustrates a somewhat ambivalent attitude toward the various means of improving performance. To a certain extent the ambiguity of NPR can be observed in how it relates to the three different performance dimensions. With regard to the focus on performance the message has been both to empower the individual and the need for measurable organizational performance with the High Impact Agencies. The Reinvention movement is more consistent on the other dimensions. A strong advocacy for greater flexibility at all levels of government has seen a rejection of cross-government standardization. The NPR goal of restoring public trust in government underscores a rhetoric that encourages openness and public accountability by governmental organizations.

While NPR seems to have had a positive overall effect it has had a problem in providing a central definition of its performance strategy. It could be argued, with much merit, that many of these different strands could be pulled together to create a comprehensive and comprehensible model of government reform, contributing to an overall goal of improved organizational performance. However, the most comprehensive piece of reform legislation offered by the NPR, the Personnel System Reinvention Act, was a failure. Since then NPR has maintained the position that the myriad reform efforts proposed could be incrementally and separately implemented; a sort of reform menu from which agencies could pick and choose.

Flexibility and Appraisal Frameworks at the Organizational Level: GPRA

A purely congressional initiative, and one whose focus is substantially better defined than that of reinventing government, the Government Performance and Results Act legislated the concept of performance very much from an organizational perspective. GPRA has provided some marked contrasts with earlier reforms. The CSRA attempted to improve performance by creating incentives for individuals and measuring their efforts. It did this right across a standardized civil service. GPRA was designed to define and improve organizational performance, with little reference to the role of the individual public servant. There is, however, an element of standardization in GPRA in that it legislates the same requirements for all agencies regardless of their function or size. In its own way it has standardized performance measurement, but at the organizational level rather than at the individual level. All agencies are required to produce a five-year strategic plan that must be updated every three years. Each plan must contain the following:

1. A comprehensive mission statement
2. General goals and objectives, including outcome-related goals and objectives
3. A description of how the goals and objectives are to be achieved
4. A description of how performance goals in annual agency performance plans will be related to the general goals and objectives
5. Identification of key external factors that could affect achievement of the general goals and objectives
6. A description of program evaluations used in establishing or revising the general goals and objectives, as well as a schedule for future program evaluations

Additionally, all agencies have to provide annual performance plans and annual program performance reports. The performance plans map out agency goals for the year ahead and how they expect to achieve them. The program performance reports provide a review of how agencies fared in meeting their goals in the previous year. With all agencies facing such similar requirements it is fair to say that GPRA has "restandardized" performance definition and measurement at the organizational level. This standardization is, however, married with the particular functions of each individual agency, so that agencies are asked to produce outputs or outcomes specific to what they do. Agencies should, therefore, have enough flexibility to create appropriate quantitative performance measures within a common performance framework. In this manner we can see an effort to balance the requirements of standardization and advantages of flexibility. Each agency must answer to Congress and the people in a similar manner, but with substantial flexibility.

From Protection to Scrutiny: Individual to Agency Accountability

With the CSRA, we saw the enactment of an individually based, confidential method of accountability, where accountability measures and appraisal were largely a matter between the manager and employee. The accountability elements associated with GPRA are organizational and very public. Objectives that the agencies put forth need to be outputs or outcomes that can be easily understood and measured. This is not necessarily inconsistent with the value of confidentiality at the individual level, but suggests that employees direct their efforts in a manner consistent with the agency mission. Such stringent detailing of goals is hoped to allow Congress and the public to get a better understanding of outputs and outcomes that agencies produce with federal funding. It also reflects an attempt to improve the management of government by shifting the focus of decision making from input and process (including such issues as staffing) to tangible outputs and results.

This accountability model has also enhanced the influence of Congress and other stakeholders whom agencies are obliged to consult when formulating strategic plans.[18] The GAO has prepared critical questions on different aspects of agencies' strategic plans to aid Congress when consulting with agency officials.[19] The requirement for agencies to consult with Congress in the formulation of their strategic plans formally provides Congress with enhanced input into the planning process of executive agencies. The presentation of such detailed plans to Congress also provides the legislature with ample material to provide post-event analysis and input. The GAO has also prepared a guide to aid Congress in the assessment of the Annual Performance Plans produced by agencies,[20] as well as offering its own assessments of Annual Performance Plans and Strategic Plans. This illustrates the public nature of GPRA accountability, and the extent to which it requires agencies to interact with the environment outside the bureaucracy, especially Congress,[21] making them more open to external influence.

STANDARDIZATION AND COORDINATION: THE ROLE OF INSTITUTIONS IN DEFINING PERFORMANCE

As different definitions of performance have evolved since the CSRA, so too have the roles of the key central institutions charged with the management of the federal government—the Office of Personnel Management and the Office of Management and Budget. The CSRA was concerned with improving performance through an improved personnel system. Within this context the OPM was envisioned as having a central role in improving government and individual performance measures. Scotty Campbell predicted that the OPM would perform "for the President relative to personnel management what the Office of Management and Budget does for financial management."[22] Recent reform efforts have largely overlooked personnel reforms, the natural area of expertise for the OPM, in favor of results based measures, making the OMB the key central agency.

The reform efforts that we have seen in the 1990s have relied principally on the OMB as the coordinating central agency (see appendix 1). As the OMB has become an increasingly important focal point for issues of agency performance the other main central agency, the OPM, seems to have diminished in stature. Indeed the role of the OPM was never as extensive as originally envisaged, with the Reagan years limiting the extent of its activities by reducing the emphasis on the development of the public service, and subsequently its personnel. OPM has also felt the effects of downsizing in recent years, seeing a loss of 48 percent of employees in just over a five year period.[23]

The agenda-setting power of the OMB already provides it with enormous strength. By preparing the president's budget the OMB has a considerable influence in setting the policies that agencies will follow. The management record of the agency has been more uneven, lacking a central mechanism such as the budget to ensure that management concerns were regularly addressed. In recent years the legislative framework that has developed around performance-based management and accountability—most conspicuously GPRA—has given a statutory role to OMB's management efforts. Appendix 1 offers a more detailed account of the OMB's widening statutory role in federal management in the 1990s. GPRA tasked OMB with developing a performance plan for the entire federal government to be presented in conjunction with the president's budget submission to Congress. This allows a forum for the integration of management and budget issues. The OMB published the first Government-Wide Performance Plan in 1998. Included in this were a series of Priority Management Objectives. The Priority Management Objectives, to a far greater degree than GPRA or High Impact Agency measures, set themselves the goals of improving *capacity* and *management* rather than narrow, mission-related goals. This should, in turn, allow agencies to be better positioned to meet more specific and more outcome based goals demanded by the current emphasis on organizational results-based performance.

The GAO[24] identified four key factors in supporting and sustaining the OMB's efforts to improve federal performance:

- Support from the top of the OMB and the White House for management improvements
- Linking management initiatives with the budget process
- Effectively collaborating with agencies
- Congressional support for management improvements

Taken together, these factors have been essential in prioritizing quality management in the federal government and in singling out the OMB as the central agency that will oversee and coordinate reform efforts.

Ironically, from the perspective of the OPM, these are also the factors that appear to have been in short supply in recent years. The OPM has been neglected when the White House and Congress looked to improve the performance of its federal structure. During the era of politicization in the 1980s the original role of the OPM was severely constricted. During the reinvention period the main function of the OPM appeared to be the downsizing of its own operations, with Director King defining OPM success in terms of being a smaller organization.[25] As personnel functions have been decentralized and the OMB has become the key central agency for government reform; the role of the OPM has become increasingly unclear. OPM downsizing raises questions regarding the capacity of the OPM in developing human resources and providing leadership on these issues. It has been pointed out that the most influential new ideas on human resources have been coming from agencies themselves or interested parties outside the government such as Brookings and NAPA. This occurs despite the fact that the current situation creates a vacuum for a central body that can provide leadership in the promotion of the use of human resources management in linking individual performance with organizational goals and wider government policy.

CONCLUSION AND FUTURE DIRECTIONS FOR PERFORMANCE

Since 1978 we have seen both an increasing emphasis on, and differing approaches to, performance in the federal government. While efficiency has been a concern for public sector reformers in the twentieth century, the

CSRA represented the most serious attempt to address performance issues since the merit system was first devised. We have identified three different—yet interrelated—dimensions of performance: the focus of performance; the level of standardization and coordination; and the method of accountability. Differing aspects of each of these dimensions are present and identifiable since the enactment of the CSRA, with certain elements in the ascendant during different periods.

During enactment of the CSRA legislation there was some discussion with regard to the importance of organizational performance, yet the CSRA ultimately focused on the individual, and structured its reforms with the intent of improving individual performance. The assumption was that improved individual performance would take care of overall organizational performance. The definitions of reform that have emerged since the CSRA have focused more intently on the organizational unit, and recent reform efforts have concentrated on measuring and improving organizational performance. The implicit assumption of this approach is that demand for organizational performance will make the organization, and its employees, improve performance. The challenge for delivering effective performance is finding a balance between the two extremes, rather than choosing between a false dichotomy. This is indeed possible, and while the organizational focus of performance is in the ascendancy at the present time, the CSRA has laid an adequate groundwork to ensure the potential for linking focused individual performance within a broader organizational framework. A revamped SES, organized more closely to the original intent of the CSRA, but compatible with current performance reform, could be a leading element in developing individual-organizational linkages.

The level of standardization and the aspects of central coordination have certainly changed since the CSRA. This is perhaps best reflected by the nature of performance assessment that public managers face. Currently the key indicators of government performance are the GPRA goals and not standardized individual performance measurements. Organizational measures of performance are not monolithic, but are comparable frameworks that are flexible enough to permit agency-specific measures. The central role of the OMB (see appendix 1), and increased agency flexibility, underpins a shift from the cross-government standardization of the CSRA to a situation typified by the guiding role of a central institution and a high degree of agency autonomy and control.

With regard to the method of accountability there has been an apparent movement from individual and confidentially held evaluations to organizational evaluations intended for public scrutiny. The emphasis on public accountability and clear measures of performance is not necessarily incompatible with a continuing level of confidentiality for employees. What is important is that individual performance can no longer be insular, but must be contributing in an active and demonstrated way toward organizational mission and goals.

What implications do the dimensions of performance, as described by the CSRA and subsequent legislation, offer for the future of management in the federal government? The most obvious implication is that future legislative efforts toward improving public management will be couched in the context of improved performance. However, such efforts will be well advised to take note of the success (or lack thereof) of previous efforts that produced narrow definitions of performance. The jury is still out on the validity of concentrating goal definition, discretion and accountability at the organizational level. The quite limited success of the CSRA suggests that concentrating efforts solely at the individual level is certainly not the magic formula for overall success. One can conclude that the modesty of CSRA achievements may be explained in two ways. The first explanation may be that the CSRA focused on the wrong level; by emphasizing the individual level there was no guarantee that the higher level performance would follow. A logical conclusion of this perspective would be that current public sector initiatives are focusing on the correct level, and are destined for success. An alternative explanation is perhaps more plausible: the CSRA was unable to create fundamental remapping of the bureaucratic landscape because of the uni-dimensionality of its focus on performance, the fact that it concentrated on a single level. The conclusion of this perspective is that the current focus on performance is also largely uni-dimensional, and will ultimately encounter problems similar to the CSRA, regardless of the fact that its focus is on a different level.

The need to widen the focus of performance has clear messages for current and future reform efforts. It is a statement of the need to include all levels of the organization in the performance process. Each level needs to provide a contribution appropriate to its position and in light of the wider organizational needs, as illustrated in appendix 2, the Cascade-Down Model. Simply discussing individual performance is no guarantee of direction, and setting goals and measuring results tells us little about agency capacity and potential to perform in a civil service system that still has the same essential underlying structure as it had after the CSRA. The challenge is to ensure practical linkages and communication throughout the organization, to enable each level with the necessary incentives and direction. Although we describe this approach as a Cascade-Down Model it is likely that relationships will need to move both upwards and downwards, and possibly across different levels. While the nature of such relationships may vary by organization, an inescapable point is that all levels have to be present and linked if ongoing performance is to be achieved.

Despite those differing definitions of performance, there is no disputing the now central role of the performance concept in public management. CSRA's first bold steps were, in retrospect, bolder and more important than even the designers believed. To be sure, the initial designs and definition did not fully succeed—and perhaps did not succeed at all—but the shift in emphasis from protection to performance that the CSRA initiated was one of the most important in modern public management. The definitions of performance posed by the CSRA are still influential, and have potentially profound impacts if effectively married with more recent definitions. Performance, despite its many contemporary definitions, can no longer be left out of any debate on public management reform—that train has left the station.

APPENDIX I[26]

The Widening Statutory Role of the OMB in Federal Management

Legislation	OMB Requirement
The Government Performance and Results Act of 1993	• Agencies submit 5-year strategic plans to the OMB by September 30 1997; must be updated within three years. • Agencies submit performance plans to OMB annually beginning in FY1999. • Incorporating the agency's performance plans, the OMB must prepare a federal performance plan to be included with the president's budget when presented to Congress.
Chief Financial Officers Act of 1990 and Government Management Reform Act of 1994	• The OMB's Deputy Director for Management and the Office of Federal Financial Management are given oversight of federal financial management policies and practices. • OMB decides which components of federal agencies must prepare fully audited financial statements. • The OMB presents to Congress a federal 5-year financial management plan detailing future improvement efforts for federal financial management. • By January 31 of each year OMB presents to Congress updates of the 5-year financial plan and a financial status report.

Appendix I   *(continued)*

Legislation	OMB Requirement
Clinger-Cohen Act of 1996	• The OMB issues directives to executive agencies regarding capital planning and investment control, revisions to mission-related and administrative processes, and information security. • The OMB is tasked with promoting and improving the acquisition and use of IT through performance-based and results based management. • The OMB uses the budget process to analyze, track, and evaluate the risks and results of major agency capital investments in IT/information systems, and enforce accountability of agency heads. • The OMB also reports to Congress on the agencies' progress and accomplishments.
Paperwork Reduction Act of 1995	• In consultation with agency heads, the OMB sets annual goals for the reduction of information collection burdens. • In consultation with other agencies, the OMB develops and maintains a federal Information Resources Management plan. • The OMB also reports to Congress on the agencies' progress and accomplishments.
Federal Managers' Financial Integrity Act of 1982	• In consultation with the Comptroller General, the OMB establishes guidelines for agencies to follow in evaluating their systems of internal and administrative control (OMB Circular No. A-123, "Management Accountability and Control"). The OMB issues annual format instructions every summer.

APPENDIX 2   CASCADE-DOWN MODEL

Different Levels and What They Offer to the Performance Process

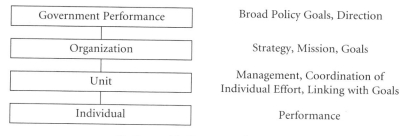

Government Performance	Broad Policy Goals, Direction
Organization	Strategy, Mission, Goals
Unit	Management, Coordination of Individual Effort, Linking with Goals
Individual	Performance

Challenge: To Guarantee the Linkages

NOTES

1. Alan K Campbell, "Civil Service Reform as a Remedy of Bureaucratic Ills," in *Making Bureaucracies Work*, ed. C. H. Weiss and A. H. Barton (Beverly Hills: Sage Publications, 1980), 165.

2. Herbert Kaufman, "Administrative Decentralization and Political Power," in *Classics of Public Administration*, ed. J. M. Shafritz and A. C. Hyde (New York: Harcourt Brace College Publishers, 1997), 289.

3. Al Gore, *Creating a Government That Works Better and Costs Less: September 1994 Status Report*. Report of the National Performance Review (Washington, D.C.: US Government Printing Office, 1994), 38. For an account of the buildup of internal rules and regulations, see Patricia W. Ingraham, *The Foundation of Merit: Public Service in American Democracy* (Baltimore: John Hopkins University Press, 1995), 55–72.

4. *U.S. President's Reorganization Report Project*, Personnel Management Project, vol. 1, Final Staff Report (Washington, D.C.: Government Printing Office, 1977).

5. See Patricia W. Ingraham, "Of Pigs in Pokes and Policy Diffusion: Another Look at Pay for Performance," *Public Administration Review* 53 (1993): 348–56; Patricia W. Ingraham and Carolyn Ban, eds., *Legislating Bureaucratic Change: The Civil Service Reform Act of 1978* (Albany: State University of New York Press, 1984).

6. G. Milkovich and A. Wigdor, eds., *Pay for Performance: Evaluating Performance Appraisal and Merit Pay* (Washington, D.C.: National Academy Press, 1991).

7. Alan K. Campbell, "Reflections on CSRA's First Decade," *The GAO Journal* (Spring 1989): 9–13.

8. In this, as in many other elements of reform the CSRA took its cue from private-sector practices. *The President's Reorganization Report Project* noted that: "The private sector has a wide variety of performance appraisal plans. Corporations have developed performance evaluation designed programs to fit their compensation, career development, and other personnel system requirements" (op. cit., 142).

9. Mark W. Huddleston, "To the Threshold of Reform: The Senior Executive Service and America's Search for a Higher Civil Service," in *The Promise and Paradox of Civil Service Reform*, ed. Patricia W. Ingraham and David Rosenbloom (Pittsburgh: University of Pittsburgh Press, 1992); P. W. Ingraham, J. R. Thompson, and E. F. Eisenberg, "Political Management Strategies and Political/Career Relationships: Where Are We Now in the Federal Government?" *Public Administration Review* 55 (1995): 263–72; James Perry, "Merit Pay in the Public Sector: The Case for a Failure of Theory," *Review of Public Personnel Administration* 7 (1986): 57–69.

10. U.S. Office of Personnel Management, *An Outline of OPM's Proposed Framework for Improving the Senior Executive Service* (Draft) (Washington, D.C.: U.S. Office of Personnel Management, 1998), 1.

11. *U.S. President's Reorganization Report Project*, op. cit., 108.

12. U.S. Office of Personnel Management, *Results of Title VI Demonstration Projects: Implications for Performance Management and Pay-for-Performance* (Washington, D.C.: U.S. Office of Personnel Management, 1991).

13. As will be discussed later in the chapter these are also the type of agencies that are in a position to perform strongly according to GPRA requirements. Beryl Radin, "The Government Performance and Results Act (GPRA): Hydra-Headed Monster or Flexible Management Tool?" *Public Administration Review* 58 (1998): 307–15, examines characteristics of such agencies that closely parallel the typology that we present: "In many ways; the process (GPRA) is designed for agencies that actually deliver services, or production agencies in James Q. Wilson's categorization; have relatively stable histories that are amenable to the planning approach; have cultures of data production (with agreement on typologies and belief on the accuracy of information); and have manageable levels of conflict between the external actors (or stakeholders) interested in the program."

14. U.S. General Accounting Office, *Management Reform Status of Agency Reinvention Lab Efforts.* GAO/GGD-96-69 (Washington, D.C.: Government Printing Office, 1996).

15. The GAO (1996, op. cit.) found that 60 percent of lab officials had found that they had not needed regulatory waivers that NPR officials believed would be necessary to develop their labs. The report also found that lab officials had frequently found it difficult to obtain regulatory waivers, especially from the central governmental agencies (the OPM, the OMB and the GSA). Perhaps in response to this on April 21, 1998, President Clinton issued a memorandum to the head of all agencies and executive departments instructing that:

- Waiver requests are acted upon within 30 days or less. After 30 days, the originating entity within the agency can assume approval and implement the requested waiver.
- Those officials having authority to grant or change internal agency rules can approve waiver requests, but only the head of an agency can deny a waiver request.
- Officials who have the authority to grant waivers are encouraged to identify potential waiver opportunities and extend waivers to their own agencies.

16. Patricia W. Ingraham, "A Laggard's Tale: Civil Service and Administrative Reform in the United States," in *Developments in Civil Service Systems,* ed. H.A.G.M. Bekke, J. L. Perry and T. A. J. Toonen (Bloomington: Indiana University Press, forthcoming).

17. William Jefferson Clinton and Albert Gore, *Blair House Papers: The National Performance Review* (Washington, D.C.: Government Printing Office, 1997).

18. David H. Rosenbloom. "The Context of Management Reforms," *The Public Manager* 24 (1995): 3–6; U.S. General Accounting Office, *Managing for Results: Enhancing the Usefulness of GPRA Consultations between the Executive and Congress.* GAO/T-GGD-97-56 (Washington, D.C.: Government Printing Office, 1997).

19. U.S. General Accounting Office, *Agencies' Strategic Plans under GPRA: Key Questions to Facilitate Congressional Review.* GAO/GGD-10.1.16 (Washington, D.C.: Government Printing Office, 1997).

20. U.S. General Accounting Office, *The Results Act: An Evaluator's Guide to Assessing Agency Annual Performance Plans.* GAO/GGD-10.0.20 (Washington, D.C.: Government Printing Office, 1998).

21. Congressional leadership has also been extremely active in highlighting the quality (or lack of it) in agency Strategic and Performance Plans, developing scorecards that graded the quality of GPRA related documents.

22. Campbell (1980), op. cit., 161.

23. Office of Personnel Management, Office of Workforce Information, *Monthly Report of Federal Civilian Employment (SF113-A)* (Washington, D.C.: U.S. Office of Personnel Management). The OPM dropped from 6,861 employees in January 1993 to 3,567 in April 1998.

24. U.S. General Accounting Office, *The Results Act,* op. cit.

25. G. S. Marshall, "Whither (or Wither) OPM?" *Public Administration Review* 58 (1998): 280–82.

26. Information comes from U.S. General Accounting Office, *Managing for Results: The Statutory Framework for Performance-Based Management and Accountability.* GAO/GGD/AIMD-98-52 (Washington, D.C.: Government Printing Office, 1998).

CHAPTER SIX

CIVIL SERVICE REFORM AND INCENTIVES IN THE PUBLIC SERVICE

HAL G. RAINEY AND J. EDWARD KELLOUGH

The Civil Service Reform Act of 1978 (CSRA) targeted the improvement of incentives for individual performance in the federal service as one of its most important objectives, and this objective has been central to civil service reforms at all levels of government in the United States and in nations around the world. The CSRA and related developments—such as later efforts to implement the Performance Management and Recognition System—sought to strengthen the relationship between individual performance and pay, to provide performance bonuses for executives, to streamline procedures for firing and disciplinary action against poor performers, and in other ways to combat alleged problems due to weak incentives for performance in the federal service.

In this chapter, we consider the problem that many of these efforts to enhance incentives did not work out well. We suggest a broader, more comprehensive approach to conceiving and reforming incentive systems in the federal government and other governments. We first discuss some general challenges in mounting reforms of governmental incentive systems, and then discuss, as examples of those challenges, limitations of past and current reforms aimed at improving incentives. We contend that some of the reforms, such as pay-for-performance, concentrated too narrowly on one or a few dimensions of the incentive systems of government agencies. Searching for alternative and broader perspectives on incentives we then review recent studies of excellent public organizations, that identify the characteristics of such organizations. These organizations emphasize such factors as leadership, organizational mission, task design, and employee development. While they emphasize recognizing and rewarding performance, they do not concentrate narrowly on pay-for-performance. Ultimately, we contend that enhancement of incentives in the civil service must be conceived more broadly, in relation to such matters as the public image of the civil service, political leadership, and additional or alternative incentives related to leadership development, task design, career development, public service motives and other factors. We propose changes in relation to these matters that are required for truly effective and enlightened incentive systems in the public sector. The steps we propose are actually consistent with the original goals of some of the designers of the 1978 civil service reforms, and would help to bring those goals to fruition.[1]

SOME KEY CHALLENGES IN REFORM

Our position on human resource reforms and reforms of other types reflects certain observations we have about the politics of reform and the current status of government and the civil service in the United States. These observations have important implications for our assessment of previous reforms and our proposals for reforms or developments currently needed.

The Problem of the Pretty Good: Reform and the Current State of the Civil Service

It is widely known that Garrison Keillor includes fictitious, droll advertisements as part of his National Public Radio show, *A Prairie Home Companion.* Many of the advertisements are for small businesses in the imaginary town of Lake Wobegon. One of these establishments is "Ralph's Pretty Good Grocery Store," whose slogan is, "if you can't get it here, you probably don't need it anyway."[2] Why is this amusing? In this age of hyperbole, who can imagine selling a product, service, or organizational reform proclaimed to be "pretty good"? Imagine a governmental reform presented to the Congress, the media, and the public as a pretty good idea. As we have all observed repeatedly, proponents of reforms and new programs must aggressively sell the initiative in a market crowded with issues and problems contending for a place on the public agenda. The challenge of creating a sense of urgency for reform is common to the public and private sectors.[3] Pretty good reforms sound wan, as do reforms that target anything less than a dire crisis.

This challenge of urgency complicates civil service reforms and other governmental reforms because, in spite of many assertions to the contrary, the government and the civil service system function well. The challenge involves devising and selling reforms that are not that badly needed in the broad scope of the public agenda. In this regard, we assert the following:

The administrative institutions of government in the United States are not in crisis and have not been in recent decades. Problems and shortcomings abound, and they can always be labeled crises, but no general, severe crisis exists. Nor is the personnel system of the federal government in crisis; it has served the country well and continues to do so. Nor is the motivation and performance of government employees and managers causing generally weak performance of government agencies, especially due to protections for poorly performing employees. Nowhere in government, for example, can one find a human resource–related system as wasteful and poorly designed as the compensation system for high-level executives in private sector industrial, financial, and commercial firms in the United States, or in certain professions. All systems need reform and improvement on a continuing basis, but one of the primary challenges in mounting reforms of the human resource management systems in governments at all levels in the U.S. arises from the absence of genuine crisis or verifiably serious performance deficit. This creates difficulties in stimulating well-conceived and well-designed reforms, because of a lack of urgency that would elicit a broad consensus and attentiveness to truly comprehensive and careful reform. This paper addresses the challenge for true reform of the incentive systems of government, the challenge of mounting well-integrated, carefully developed, successfully implemented reform in this context.

No one has produced convincing evidence that U.S. government agencies perform poorly because of large accumulations of poorly performing employees who remain in their jobs because civil service regulations protect them from discipline or dismissal. The university and college system of the United States is broadly accepted without dispute as the leading system of higher education in the world. Yet, myths abound about the damaging role that the institution of faculty tenure plays in that system. The Social Security Administration has an abundance of problems, but overall performs very effectively and efficiently in administration of the social security programs. The United States Department of Defense has weaknesses whose identification and virtual celebration provides employment and entertainment for many Americans. Yet that agency provides the most effective military force in the world, and many of its units perform virtual miracles in pursuit of their missions. These two agencies account for about half of federal budget outlays. In neither agency can one find an "employment at will" doctrine in force. In neither agency can one find managers who can easily and readily fire problem employees, or easily and readily bestow significant pay increases on exemplary employees.[4]

The Temptation to Tinker

The foregoing discussion implies that the challenge for true reform of the incentive systems of government involves mounting well-integrated, carefully developed, successfully implemented reforms, under conditions where there is no genuine crisis to generate attention to such reforms and support for them. Under these conditions, and because of the complications of mounting reforms of any kind in our complex, pluralistic political system, we have had a tendency to tinker with personnel systems, by targeting reforms at several dimensions of the system, such as pay systems, firing and discipline, or general decentralization of personnel rules. The implicit assumptions are that we can identify a superior practice that purportedly exists in the private sector, apply it to government agencies, and significantly improve the personnel system by fixing several dimensions of it, thereby improving agency performance—all dubious assumptions. As elaborated below, such reforms have not worked out well. We need to consider why and what we should do differently.

REFORM AS CHIMERA AND FAD: LESSONS FROM PAY-FOR-PERFORMANCE

The history of pay-for-performance reforms in the federal government and other governments provides examples of our tendency to embrace reforms without thinking carefully about the full range of less-than-desirable effects they may have. At first glance, the logic of such a reform is compelling and politically appealing because it symbolizes political officials' efforts to make the bureaucracy operate more efficiently. Whatever the underlying motivation, however, pay-for-performance initiatives have provided many examples of reform occurring precipitously, without full consideration of all ramifications. The federal government's experience with this type of pay reform is particularly illustrative.

As is widely understood, the federal experiment with merit pay was initiated as part of the Civil Service Reform Act of 1978. The basic idea was and is attractive: employees who perform at higher levels should receive larger pay increases than those who are poorer performers. In other words, pay increases should be made contingent on performance. As it turns out, however, this logic is deceptively simple. The first federal program, known as the Merit Pay System, was fraught with difficulty. The program targeted mid-level federal managers (i.e., managers in G.S. and equivalent grades 13–15), but those covered failed to perceive any credible link between pay and performance established by the program.[5] Because the system was required to be budgetarily neutral, and because supervisors often found it difficult to make sharp distinctions between employees with respect to performance, pay increases under the system were frequently quite small and the motivating potential of those increases was obviously questionable.[6] Employees also perceived that nonperformance factors were influencing performance ratings and subsequent pay decisions.[7] That perception no doubt rested, at least in part, on the employees' knowledge of the inherently subjective nature of the performance appraisal process. Additionally, a desire to avoid conflict and the extra work that may have been necessary to justify lower ratings for poorer performers may have led some supervisors to inflate ratings.[8] The attraction of this path of least resistance can be overwhelming to supervisors who already feel they have more than enough to do in their jobs. Later studies have demonstrated that in some federal agencies nearly every employee was rated "fully successful" or higher.[9]

Empirical studies of the federal effort to implement merit pay failed to find evidence that the reform significantly increased employee motivation or productivity.[10] Indeed, some studies found that the reform was dysfunctional in that it eroded trust between employees and supervisors and led to decreased organizational commitment and heightened levels of alienation on the part of numerous employees.[11] As we know, the Merit Pay System was abolished in 1984 and replaced by the Performance Management and Recognition System (PMRS). That new system was revised in 1989 and again in 1991, but ultimately the concept of merit pay was abandoned in late 1993. Reforms of this type have come to similarly disappointing ends at other levels of government and in other nations as well.[12]

We do not mean to criticize unnecessarily the concept of pay-for-performance or those who attempted it, but we wish to emphasize the need to consider the difficult challenges of mounting such programs, that include the problem of carefully considering the potential weaknesses of the reforms. The potential problems with merit pay were obvious from the outset.[13] Experts on the implementation of such pay systems in private firms have for decades pointed out that the success of such systems depends on the existence of certain preconditions. These include a reasonably high level of trust among members of the organization and especially between management and employees. Consultants working on such systems currently call for an appropriate "culture" as a prerequisite. The conditions also include adequate funding—a problem with many of the efforts in the public sector—and a reasonably well-accepted set of performance measures and evaluation processes. All these conditions were clearly not in place in many of the agencies told to implement pay-for-performance systems. While there may well have been some valiant efforts to do so, leaders in most agencies could not create such conditions in time to support the reforms that they were mandated to undertake. Indeed, in many instances the reform itself led to an erosion of trust and satisfaction necessary for improved performance.

This challenge of considering the "downside" of reform, and the potential implementation problems, continues. It is exemplified in other reforms and reform proposals currently in vogue, some of which have the same potential for damaging employee trust and morale that can result from the faulty implementation of a pay-for-performance scheme. The current movement toward greater decentralization of authority over personnel policy provides a case in point. The idea that managerial authority should be decentralized as far as possible is one of the more pervasive themes of recent discussions regarding civil service reform. It is a central component of the set of prescriptions for change associated with the concept of reinventing government. The notion is that managers should have as much authority as possible to carry out their responsibilities. In the view of David Osborne and Theodore Gaebler, managers should be empowered and encouraged to find innovative solutions to problems of program implementation.[14] The reinventors suggest that we should set goals and objectives for managers and give them the authority to do whatever it takes (within broad limits) to to see that those goals and objectives are achieved. "Let the managers manage," is the credo that best describes this philosophy.

Under this entrepreneurial approach to public management, civil service rules regarding such practices as selection, promotion, transfers, classification, and compensation are typically viewed as impediments. The constraints imposed by civil service rules and procedures are thought to restrict unduly the capacity of management to respond flexibly to various organizational contingencies. But rules and procedural constraints on public managers are designed to enhance accountability and fairness in the exercise of government authority. As B. Guy Peters and Donald J. Savoie remind us, "one person's red tape is often another's due process."[15] H. George Frederickson has echoed this point, arguing that "rules prevent some abuse and result in greater fairness."[16] Frederickson continues, suggesting that when we prefer efficiency and flexibility to the prevention of abuse and the promotion of fairness, "the results will be predictable—more efficient, innovative, and flexible government, *and* government that is less fair and open to [more] abuse or corruption" (emphasis in original).[17]

The nature of the constraints placed on public managers and the possibilities of reform are reviewed thoroughly in a recent book by Carolyn Ban.[18] Ban considers how procedural rules imposed on managers can reduce efficiency by consuming managers' time and directing resources away from tasks associated more directly with the accomplishment of agency missions, but she notes that formal constraints are not the only restrictions on management and are often not the most important restrictions. Public managers are also constrained by what Ban calls organizational culture, i.e., the shared pattern of values and beliefs about proper roles and behaviors for managers in an organization, the lack of managerial ability or expertise, and the lack of time or other resources. While formal restrictions are sometimes skirted, these informal constraints are more pervasive and unavoidable. Consequently, Ban makes the point that efforts to ease formal constraints on management authority may not always produce the results intended. Managers may still face other (informal) constraints, so there may be no net gain in organizational efficiency.

Nevertheless, proponents for reinvention argue that greater decentralization of personnel policy and the placement of increased authority into the hands of line managers is needed. Among the personnel processes targeted for reform, position classification systems have been particularly maligned. Traditionally, these are systems in which positions are evaluated, based on an analysis of job content and requirements, and placed into classes or grades that in turn determine compensation levels. The standard criticism is that such systems are too rigid—that they rob management of desirable flexibility in dealing with questions of work assignment and compensation. The proposed solution is a concept known as broad-banding. Under this approach, several pay grades are collapsed into fewer broader pay bands. Thus a set of very wide pay classes is established with a correspondingly wide range of jobs and salaries. As a consequence, managers may exercise considerable discretion in determining compensation levels for particular positions within each band, provided, of course, that they stay within their overall budget ceiling. The concept of rank-in-position is essentially supplanted by the idea of rank-in-person within the various pay bands. At the federal level, the National Performance Review (NPR) headed by Vice President Al Gore strongly advocated adoption of a broad-banding approach to classification.

The potential difficulty with this reform, and other ideas that are designed to decentralize authority and increase managerial flexibility, is that they may cause employees to feel that under such systems rewards are based on factors other than actual meaningful differences in work. Within each "broad" pay band, for example, one can find a larger array of different jobs than would have existed previously in more narrowly defined pay grades. Presumably "managerial flexibility" will lead to differences in pay levels for jobs that had previously had very similar pay levels. Conversely, jobs that had been treated differently in the past may be treated similarly. This kind of outcome would appear to be an objective of increased managerial discretion. As a result, unless management proceeds very carefully, perceptions of inequity and actual instances of inequity may increase. So far, federal experiments with broad-banding have found mixed evidence about levels of perceived inequality in compensation under that approach, as compared to traditional classification systems. When employees involved in broad-banding experiments were asked whether they perceived that individual differentials in pay reflected real differences in levels of responsibility and job difficulty, approximately one-fifth to one-third (depending upon the experimental site) agreed that they did as compared to one-fifth to one-fourth of the control site employees classified in traditional pay systems.[19] Of course, the most striking observation is that large majorities of employees under both approaches found pay differentials generally inequitable, and the potential for perceived inequity remains if reforms mandating wide and rapid implementation of broad-banding systems are implemented. Such perceptions will erode employee trust, satisfaction, and motivation.

Excessive decentralization of personnel policy authority may also give rise to important legal questions. The constitutional guarantee of equal protection of the law, for example, may require some degree of centralization and the application of consistent standards across government organizations. When agencies or bureaus are given authority to determine for themselves the compensation levels for jobs within their boundaries, significant pay discrepancies between similar jobs across different organizations could easily emerge. Employees might press questions of equal protection, through legal channels. In addition, the elimination of civil service rules will necessarily be limited by the constitutional imperative that procedural due process be afforded employees who have property interests in their jobs because of statutory merit system provisions or implied contracts based on promises made in personnel procedure manuals, and similarly, when employee liberty interests are damaged because of the nature of adverse actions taken by public employers, due process must also be provided.

Again, we intend no aggressive condemnation of broad-banding or efforts to decentralize personnel authority. Indeed, the demonstration projects and experiments with broad-banding represent commendable efforts to proceed carefully with assessment of such reforms rather than immediate across-the-board implementation. We suggest, however, that decentralization and increased managerial flexibility will not necessarily translate into better operating agencies. It is interesting to note that federal managers have been calling for more flexibility and authority over personnel decisions for a long time.[20] Significantly, the pursuit of more decentralization of personnel authority was an objective of the CSRA itself, and it emerged as an important theme of the NPR a decade and a half later. Although attractive in some ways, problems can arise if such reforms are pursued in isolation from other major considerations and in the absence of a more comprehensive view of reform that considers necessary preconditions and implementation challenges.

SEARCHING FOR ALTERNATIVES: STUDIES OF WELL-PERFORMING GOVERNMENT AGENCIES

If we want to consider incentive systems from a more comprehensive perspective, we face the challenge of suggesting what the alternative approach should involve. One place to look for alternatives is the recently-developing literature that seeks to characterize excellent, well-performing government agencies. These profiles represent efforts to develop models of excellent organizations, that specify their attributes. Table 1 summarizes some of these profiles.[21] An elaborate review and critique of these efforts is beyond the scope of the present paper, but the row headings on the left of the table indicate common topics in the profiles, that include the following: aspects of

Table 1   Characteristics of High Performance Government Agencies

	Gold (1982)	STEP (1985)	Wilson (1989)
Mission/ public orientation	Emphasize clear mission and objectives	Closer contact with customers to better understand their needs	Mission is clear and reflects a widely shared and warmly endorsed organizational culture
Leadership/ managing employees	Employees take pride in the organization and its product Focus on treating employees fairly and respectfully through honest and open communication Emphasize delegation of responsibility and authority as widely as possible Management aims at challenging and encouraging people Management emphasizes innovative ways of managing	Increased discretionary authority for managers and employees for greater control over accountability Increased employee participation taps their knowledge, skills and commitment	External political support Executives command loyalty, define and instill a clear sense of mission, attract talented workers, and make exacting demands of subordinates Leaders make peer expectations serve the organization Maximize discretionary authority for operators Executive takes responsibility for organizational maintenance Bottom-Up Implementation Perspective
Task design/ work environment	Places great value on the people in the organization Job task and goals are clear	Partnerships to allow the sharing of knowledge, expertise and other resources State-of-the-art productivity improvement techniques Improved work measurements to provide a base for planning and implementing service improvements and worker evaluation	Clearly defined goals Widespread agreement on how critical tasks are performed Agency autonomy to develop operational goals from which tasks are designed Ability to control or keep contextual goals in proper perspective

Note: Portions of this table are adapted from Hal G. Rainey *Understanding and Managing Public Organizations,* 2d ed. (San Francisco: Jossey-Bass, 1997), 359, and from Sandra J. Hale, "Achieving High Performance in Public Organizations," in *Handbook of Public Administration,*

Denhardt (1993)	Alliance (1994)	Hale (1996)	Holzer and Callahan (1998)
Dedication to public service and understanding public intent Serving the public which represents democratic values	Mission clarity and understanding Maintain open and productive communication among stakeholders	Focused mission that is clarified and communicated to organization members	Customer focused Build partnerships with public and private organizations and citizens
Leader demonstrates commitment to mission Manager builds sense of community in organization Manager clearly articulates values Managers insist on high ethical standards Empowered and shared leadership Employees accept responsibility and performance accountability	Empowered employees Organizations allocate resources for continuous learning Employees accept accountability to achieve results with rewards and consequences Motivate and inspire people to succeed	Enabling leadership that emphasizes learning, communication, flexibility, sharing and vision development	Manage for quality using long-term strategic planning with support from top leadership Develop human resources and empower employees through team building, systematic training, recognition, and balancing employee and organizational needs
Pragmatic incrementalism (change is natural, appropriate) Approach to change is creative and humane Commitment to values	Defined outcomes and focus on results (performance measures) Institute new work processes as necessary Flexible and adjust nimbly to new conditions Competitive in terms of performance Restructure work processes to meet customer needs	Emphasize learning and carefully support learning, risk taking, training, communication and work measurement Nurturing-community culture that is supportive and emphasizes teamwork, participation, flexible authority, and effective reward and recognition	Adapt technologies which includes open access to data, automation for productivity, cost-effective applications and cross-cutting techniques that deliver on public demands Measure for performance by establishing goals and measuring results, justifying and allocating as necessary resource requirements, and developing organizational improvement strategies

2d ed., ed. James L. Perry (San Francisco: Jossey-Bass, 1996), 139, with portions using Hale's terminology and summary.

the agency mission, especially its clarity and public orientation (including an emphasis on public service); characteristics of the leadership, and of the primary emphases in leading and managing employees, with particular emphasis on empowerment, employee involvement and participation, and employee development; and task design and work environment, with emphasis on clarification of work and task goals, effective measurement of results, and effective utilization of technology and productivity techniques.

One notes a number of interesting aspects of these profiles. The initial impression is that some of these aspects have the appearance of being consistent with certain of the reform efforts noted above. The emphasis on empowerment would seem to be broadly consistent with the emphasis in reforms on relaxing rules and constraints on managers, and decentralizing authority over personnel decisions. The emphasis on measuring and rewarding performance may be consistent in some ways with pay-for-performance initiatives. But on the other hand, the contrast in emphasis with some of the reforms described above is most striking. Rather than focusing on employee evaluation and pay systems, and on managerial discretion within the personnel rules, and on firing and discipline, the profiles heavily emphasize the roles of effective leadership, mission orientation, and of valuing, developing, and involving employees, and on giving them well-designed tasks and providing them with effective technology and productivity techniques. In this sense, the profiles tend to echo the point in Thomas J. Peters and Richard H. Waterman's *In Search of Excellence* that the excellent corporations they observed placed a general, high value on their people.[22] They did not so much emphasize clearing out the dead wood as inducing "extraordinary results from ordinary people," by generally encouraging, stimulating, caring for, and involving their employees. Similarly, the profiles underscore the importance of factors other than pay, discipline, and managerial discretion over personnel decisions, such as the incentive value of the organization's mission, and the work that people do.

The most noteworthy aspect of these profiles, moreover, is their occurrence in existing government organizations. That is, most of these profiles draw on examples and cases of organizations that operate under governmental civil service personnel systems. These organizations apparently proceeded with their drives for high performance even within the systems that reformers have attacked as debilitating and constraining to the pursuit of the very profiles described in Table 1. This again raises the question of whether emphases in reforms described earlier are too narrow.

While the contents of the implicit models in the profiles are of interest, also significant are some omissions. (In the parlance of organizational effectiveness researchers, they mostly represent "internal process models".) Additional factors receive emphasis in other research on agency effectiveness. Patrick J. Wolf analyzed forty-four case studies of federal agencies to construct measures of the agencies' characteristics and their relationships to the organization's effectiveness.[23] As do most of the profiles in Table 1, his findings indicated the importance of leadership and "sense of mission." In addition, however, he found important a variable representing political autonomy (that included "universal political support" and/or freedom from direction by political authorities). This variable indicates the importance of relations with oversight authorities and other external stakeholders, a topic that receives little or no emphasis in most of the profiles in Table 1 (with the Wilson entry as a prominent exception). It also suggests the need for a supportive and delegative role by those authorities that allows the agency reasonable autonomy to develop and pursue its mission.[24] This again indicates the incentive value of an agency's mission, and its operationalization into the work that people do in the agency, and suggests the *dis*incentives that can come from intrusions by external stakeholders. It more generally calls for a perspective on incentives in public agencies that includes the roles of external authorities and stakeholders.

Still another omission from the profiles, especially as summarized and oversimplified in Table 1, involves a fundamental question about incentives in government. What provides the incentive for people to do this noble work of creating high performance government agencies? Our political economy draws on the theory—implicit in the design of our institutions, and explicit in much of economic theory—that economic markets provide incentives and controls on business firms because people in them can make more money by performing well. Such incentives and controls are absent for most government agencies, and they must be controlled through political oversight. Lacking the opportunity to get high financial rewards, what motivates government executives and managers to lead the development of these high performance government organizations? Holzer and Callahan conducted a survey of people in government agencies that won prizes for innovativeness, about why and how they did it.[25] Asked why they felt motivated to innovate, the respondents gave the highest ranking to the response choice, "to do the right thing." Asked about factors important to innovation, they gave highest rankings to support of top agency executives, committed personnel, and support of political officials. Here again, we are prompted to consider the roles of political leadership, agency leadership, and incentives other than pay and discipline, incentives such as public service motivation and the intrinsic value of the work itself, in our discourse about effective incentive systems in government agencies.

PROPOSALS FOR MORE EFFECTIVE INCENTIVE SYSTEMS IN GOVERNMENT

What, then, can we propose for improving incentive systems in government, taking this broader view that we have touted? Dispensing for brevity with the articulation of their links to the preceding discussion, and dispensing with a thousand concerns over whether these developments are likely or feasible, we suggest the need for the following developments:

A Better Public Discourse on the Public Service and Improvements in Its Image

We need an enhanced public image of the civil service that would confer greater prestige and respect on its members, that in turn would strengthen the sorts of intrinsic, intangible, and service-oriented incentives mentioned above.[26] This proposal is hardly original. It would involve increased investments in the sorts of efforts represented by the Volcker Commission, the Partnership for Trust in Government, and some of the current activities by the National Association of Schools of Public Affairs and Administration (NASPAA). It would also involve, moreover, efforts to encourage a more sophisticated general discourse about the public service, in which participants in it, such as journalists, political candidates, and others, would countenance the need for an effective public service.

Political Leaders as Leaders of the Public Service

We need a corresponding change in the role of elected political leaders and politically-appointed executives, to conceive their roles as leaders and stewards of the civil service rather than as mere critics and cutback managers. Political leaders should embrace more seriously their role in supporting agencies in achieving their missions, and their responsibilities to act as real leaders who avoid intrusive interventions in agencies and micro management.

Increase Support for Leadership and Management
in the Federal Government

A more sensible public discourse about the federal service, together with a greater sense of leadership responsibility on the part of political officials, should lead to greater support for leadership and management. For a long time and up until very recently, expert observers, associations, and commissions have lamented the inadequate investment in developing and supporting leadership and management in the federal government. Some critics have pointed to weak development of the concept and role of leaders and managers in government. For example, this problem shows up in managerial assignments that still involve nonmanagerial duties, such that they assume the status of "worker-manager" or "pseudo-supervisor."[27] Other observers note the weak incentives and weak tendencies for higher-level executives to devote attention to the development and nurturance of the agencies they lead, especially in such matters as leadership development. Still others have pointed out that there has been too little central and institutional support for leadership development and for dealing with managerial challenges and issues—that, for example, there is not much M in OMB.[28] (They thus imply that it would be symbolically accurate to print the m in the acronym in the lower case, or even eliminate it.) For years, still others have pointed out that federal agencies spend much less on leadership development than the most successful and profitable private firms.[29] Addressing such challenges as these can produce better results for leadership, management, and performance of federal agencies than can reforms concentrating narrowly on pay-for-performance and streamlining disciplinary procedures.

Increased Salaries and Other Incentives for
Governmental Agency Executives

While intrinsic incentives are important, extrinsic incentives such as pay levels cannot be ignored. Currently, executive compensation levels are vastly higher in the private sector than in government. The pay of all high level executives and officials in the federal government, including the president, justices, the Congress, and top agency executives, should be increased to at least one third of the average annual salaries of the top executives in the top one hundred firms in the Fortune 500. With stock options and performance bonuses, the industry executives' compensation would still vastly exceed those of public sector counterparts. This step would also be symbolic of the acceptance of the essential nature of an effective public service.

Increased Investment in Leadership Development

Given the importance attributed to leadership in excellent agencies, and the common observations about the weaknesses of leadership development in government, we should sharply increase investments in leadership development to a level approximating that of major private firms.

Creative Developments of Incentives Besides Pay and Disciplinary Action

This would include investments in such areas as the following: career development; work design and enhanced working conditions; dissemination of high performance models involving enhanced culture and empowerment; and improved systems for rewards that satisfy public service motives through such steps as increased investments in recognition systems for excellence in service delivery and for dissemination of information about service accomplishments.[30] Current efforts to enhance organization performance measurement in government, through GPRA and other initiatives, also need to be considered in relation to providing incentives for performance and performance recognition.

CONCLUSION

We need more careful and comprehensive consideration of reform in government. Many of the reforms that have been fashionable recently will not accomplish the objectives their proponents seek. Reforms associated with pay-for-performance systems and the greater decentralization of authority over personnel policy in general are not likely to lead to higher levels of performance in government organizations. Indeed, such measures have the potential to damage productivity and morale by creating perceptions of inequity in the way individual employees are treated. The nation needs a broader concept of reform in the public service, based on a more sophisticated assessment of the critical role public servants fill in our society. Reforms also need a more sophisticated grounding in contemporary management thought, that recognizes the value of such priorities as leadership and employee development, managerial training, adequate and fair compensation. Political leaders and opinion leaders in public discourse need to embrace their responsibilities for providing constructive oversight and support for such developments.

NOTES

1. See Dwight Ink, Chapter 2 in this volume. According to Ink, the reformers envisioned a more comprehensive and sensitive approach to the reform of incentive systems than the reforms we critique in this paper, and than the one that emerged in the complex process of implementing the reforms. Those involved in the original design of the reforms sought to enhance executive and employee development and mobility in the federal system, and to enhance training, quality of working life, pilot testing and evaluation of new human resource procedures, and other enlightened measures. They could not, however, protect the original conception of the reforms amid the complex and shifting processes of implementation.

2. See Garrison Keillor, *Lake Wobegon Days* (New York: Viking Penguin, Inc., 1985). The reader can find discussion of Ralph and his store in several places in this book.

3. Larry E. Greiner, "Patterns of Organizational Change," *Harvard Business Review* 45 (1967): 119–28; John P. Knotter, "Leading Change: Why Transformation Efforts Fail," *Harvard Business Review* 53 (March/April, 1995): 59–65.

4. These arguments are elaborated, and further examples provided, in Hal G. Rainey and Paula Steinbauer, "Galloping Elephants: Developing Elements of a Theory of Effective Organizations," *Journal of Public Administration Research and Theory* 9 (1999): 1–32.

5. U.S. General Accounting Office, *A 2-Year Appraisal of Merit Pay in Three Agencies* (Washington, D.C.: U.S. Government Printing Office, 1984).

6. J. Edward Kellough and Haoran Lu, "The Paradox of Merit Pay in the Public Sector: Persistence of a Problematic Procedure," *Review of Public Personnel Administration* 13 (Spring 1993): 45–64; George T. Milkovich and Alexandra K. Wigdor, *Pay for Performance: Evaluating Performance Appraisal and Merit Pay* (Washington, D.C.: National Academy Press, 1991), 27–8; Jone L. Pearce, "Rewarding Successful Performance," in *Handbook of Public Administration,* ed. James L. Perry (San Francisco, CA: Jossey-Bass, 1989), 401–41; James L. Perry, "Making Policy by Trial and Error: Merit Pay in the Federal Service," *Policy Studies Journal* 17 (1988–9): 389–405; James L. Perry, B. A. Petrakis, and T. K. Miller, "Federal Merit Pay, Round II: An Analysis of the Performance Management and Recognition System," *Public Administration Review* 49 (1989): 29–37; Gilbert B. Siegel, "The Jury Is Still Out on Merit Pay in Government, *Review of Public Personnel Administration* 7 (1987): 3–15.

7. Milkovich and Wigdor, *Pay for Performance,* 28.

8. Kellough and Lu, "The Paradox of Merit Pay in the Public Sector."

9. Perry, Petrakis, and Miller, "Federal Merit Pay, Round II."

10. Kellough and Lu, "The Paradox of Merit Pay in the Public Sector."

11. Karen N. Gaertner and Gregory H. Gaertner, "Performance Evaluation and Merit Pay: Results in the Environmental Protection Agency and the Mine Safety and Health Administration," in *Legislating Bureaucratic Change: The Civil Service Reform Act of 1978*, ed. Patricia W. Ingraham and Carolyn Ban (Albany: State University of New York Press, 1984), 87–111; Jone L. Pearce and James L. Perry, "Federal Merit Pay: A Longitudinal Analysis," *Public Administration Review* 43 (1983): 315–25; Perry, Petrakis, and Miller, "Federal Merit Pay, Round II"; U.S. General Accounting Office, *A 2-Year Appraisal of Merit Pay in Three Agencies*.

12. Patricia W. Ingraham, "Of Pigs in Pokes and Policy Diffusion: Another Look at Pay-for-Performance," *Public Administration Review* 53 (1993): 348–56; Hal G. Rainey, "Assessing Past and Current Personnel Reforms: The Pursuit of Flexibility, Pay-for-Performance, and the Management of Reform Initiatives," in *Governance in A Changing Environment*, ed. B. Guy Peters and Donald Savoie (Montreal: McGill-Queen's University Press, 1998), 187–220; J. Edward Kellough and Sally Coleman Selden, "Pay-for-Performance Systems in State Government: Perceptions of State Agency Personnel Managers," *Review of Public Personnel Administration* 17:1 (Winter 1997): 5–21.

13. Hal G. Rainey, "Perceptions of Incentives in Business and Government: Implications for Civil Service Reform," *Public Administration Review* 39 (September/October, 1979): 440–48. See p. 446: "Attempts to accord more managerial discretion in the administration of pay will create as many problems as they solve."

14. David Osborne and Theodore Gaebler, *Reinventing Government: How the Entrepreneurial Spirit Is Transforming the Public Sector* (Reading, Mass.: Addison-Wesley, 1992).

15. B. Guy Peters and Donald J. Savoie, "Managing Incoherence: The Coordination and Empowerment Conundrum," *Public Administration Review*, 56 (May/June 1996): 281–89.

16. H. George Frederickson, "Comparing the Reinventing Government Movement with the New Public Administration," *Public Administration Review* 56 (May/June 1996): 266.

17. Ibid.

18. Carolyn Ban, *How Do Public Managers Manage? Bureaucratic Constraints, Organizational Culture, and the Potential for Reform* (San Francisco: Jossey-Bass Publishers, 1995).

19. Brigitte W. Schay, K. Craig Simons, Evelyn Guerra, and Jacqueline Caldwell, *Broad-Banding in the Federal Government: Technical Report* (Washington, D.C.: Government Printing Office, 1992), 31–3.

20. John Macy said that when he was head of the Civil Service Commission the most frequent complaints he received from federal managers concerned the constraints they faced in trying to reward and discipline their subordinates. See John W.

Macy, *Public Service: The Human Side of Government* (New York: Harper and Row, 1971), 20 and 266.

21. The references for the headings on the table are as follows: K. A. Gold, "Managing for Success: A Comparison of the Public and Private Sectors," *Public Administration Review* 42 (1982): 568–75; Robert B. Denhardt, *The Pursuit of Significance* (Belmont, Calif.: Wadsworth, 1993); Sandra J. Hale, "Achieving High Performance in Public Organizations," in *Handbook of Public Administration,* 2d ed., ed. James L. Perry (San Francisco: Jossey-Bass, 1996); Marc Holzer and Kathe Callahan, *Government at Work* (Beverly Hills, Calif.: Sage, 1998); James Q. Wilson, *Bureaucracy* (New York: Basic Books, 1989).

22. Thomas J. Peters and Richard H. Waterman, *In Search of Excellence: Lessons from America's Best-Run Companies* (New York: HarperCollins, 1982).

23. Patrick J. Wolf, "Why Must We Reinvent the Federal Government? Putting Historical Developmental Claims to the Test," *Journal of Public Administration Research and Theory* 7 (1997): 353–88; Patrick J. Wolf, "A Case Study of Bureaucratic Effectiveness in U.S. Cabinet Agencies: Preliminary Results," *Journal of Public Administration Research and Theory* (April 1993): 161–81.

24. Wilson, *Bureaucracy*; Kenneth J. Meier, *Politics and the Bureaucracy* (Pacific Grove, Calif.: Brooks/Cole, 1993).

25. Holzer and Callahan, *Government at Work.*

26. See, in this regard, U.S. General Accounting Office, "The Public Service" GAO/OCG-89-2TR (Washington, D.C.: U.S. General Accounting Office, November, 1988).

27. Ban, *How Do Public Managers Manage?* 63–9. See also Robert T. Golembiewski, *Humanizing Public Organizations* (Mt. Airy, Md.: Lomond, 1985), 28–9.

28. Dwight Ink, Testimony before the House Subcommittee on Management, Information, and Technology, May 12, 1998. Peter M. Benda and Charles H. Levine, "The 'M' in OMB: Issues of Structure and Strategy." Presented at the annual meeting of the American Political Science Association, Washington, D.C., 1986.

29. Frederic V. Malek, "The Development of Public Executives—Neglect and Reform," *Public Administration Review* 34 (May/June, 1974): 230–33.

30. For example, see James L. Perry, "Revitalizing Employee Ties with Public Organizations," in Patricia W. Ingraham and Barbara S. Romzek, eds., *New Paradigms for Government: Issues for the Changing Public Service* (San Francisco: Jossey-Bass, 1994), 191–214.

CHAPTER SEVEN

ACCOUNTABILITY IMPLICATIONS OF CIVIL SERVICE REFORM[1]

BARBARA S. ROMZEK

Reform of the merit system after passage of the Civil Service Reform Act (CSRA) was not a one-time event but rather the beginning of a process that has been ongoing ever since. While many of the changes in the past twenty years derive from mandates of the original legislation, there have been numerous experiments, elaborations, and modifications in federal human resources management practices since (Thompson 1993). The result is a record of two decades of change, during which the federal civil service system has been reformed and federal agencies have been reinvented—all in the hope of increasing the efficiency, effectiveness and accountability of government employees.

While the merit system was initially designed to insulate civil servants from undue pressure from elected officials, the sentiment behind civil service reform was that the pendulum in the United States had swung too far in the direction of insulation and rigidity, resulting in a cumbersome, unwieldy and unresponsive merit system. The "promise" of CSRA was to increase the responsiveness of civil servants to elected officials and rationalize human resource administration through various mandated management practices, including performance appraisal and pay-for-performance policies (Ingraham and Ban 1984, Ingraham and Rosenbloom 1992, Ingraham 1995). Early assessments of CSRA noted the failure of CSRA to live up to this promise, due in part to the nature of the public policy process

(Ingraham 1984). Later analysis noted that the CSRA had "come to represent a new generation of rules and regulations, a new wave of presidential appointees, pay freezes, grade creep, overlayering, and unfulfilled promises— more harm than good" (Light 1992, 305). Despite these patterns the spirit of reform survived in various demonstration projects (Federal Quality Institute 1994; Schay 1993, Siegel 1994; Thompson 1993).

Reforms in the 1990s have goals similar to those of the CSRA, including greater administrative flexibility, heightened responsiveness, and increased accountability (Kravchuk and Schack 1996). But they encompass much broader ambitions, namely, to change the way agencies pursue their missions generally (Gore 1993, 1994, 1995), not just how they manage their human resources. These later reform proposals, which seek to remove layers of regulations and constraints on how public agencies and employees operate, also have important implications for civil service practices and accountability (Moe 1994). Reforms which call for eliminating red tape, streamlining procedures, reducing middle management, adopting a customer service orientation, and engaging in entrepreneurial management encompass civil service practices as well.[2] A recent report by the U.S. General Accounting Office (July 1998, p. 5) characterized recent civil service reforms as focused on "emphasiz[ing] mission, vision, and organizational culture . . . Hold[ing] managers accountable for outcomes . . . rather than for adhering to a set of minutely defined procedures . . . choos[ing] an organizational structure appropriate to the organization rather than trying to make 'one size fit all.' " The presumption is that removing layers of constraints and empowering public employees will change how they do their jobs—and increase the chances that government employees will do what is expected of them.

At its most fundamental level, the impact of these various reforms on accountability has been to heighten interest and visibility of agency and individual accountability. Yet most reforms have concentrated on easing administrative constraints and presumed that accountability concerns would somehow take care of themselves once the reforms were successfully implemented.

Accountability practices represent a form of reality check for management's commitment to administrative reforms. Successful reforms require that management change the behaviors that are expected, evaluated, rewarded and/or punished, so that they match up with intended reforms. Without changing the nature of performance expectations and accountability practices, the chances are weak for successfully embedding the new cultural assumptions which undergird reforms (Schein 1992). If administrative rewards and punishments are not aligned with appropriate accountability practices, then the reforms may never move beyond rhetoric toward reality.

The reality of administrative reform is that there is often a gap between the rhetoric of reform and the reality of administrative practice. The rhetoric of reform emphasizes a "can do" mindset. The reality of administrative practice continues to operate within an accountability culture that encourages risk-averse behaviors and retains a punitive approach to accountability. The heart of the current management challenge is to close this gap, a task which is much easier to articulate than to accomplish. It involves emphasizing accountability practices that are appropriate for the types of behaviors envisioned under the reforms, including evaluating performance in terms of outputs and results rather than rules and process.

The analysis which follows provides insight into the difficulties of this challenge. First, the discussion places federal personnel management within the context of public sector accountability generally. Next, it examines several dimensions of accountability that have been affected by civil service reforms. Finally, it considers the questions of accountability alignments in light of these reforms. Is the rhetoric of reform matched in reality by changes in accountability practices?

ACCOUNTABILITY OF PUBLIC EMPLOYEES

Accountability is always a challenge for management and it is even more so in a time of reform when the potential for sending employees mixed signals about expectations is especially great. The rhetoric of reform usually poses questions of accountability in terms of whether government employees are *more* accountable after the reform than they were before the reform. While it is not impossible to discuss accountability in terms of *more* or *less*, doing so implies a unidimensional, linear concept that does not reflect the complexity of American public management. A more useful approach, which is employed in this analysis, recognizes the various dimensions of accountability and the complex context of public accountability.

There are numerous governance problems related to accountability issues (Romzek and Dubnick 1998).[3] Exploring the accountability implications of civil service reform requires special attention to those governance issues related to: determining the masters, delegating tasks and establishing expectations, verifying performance, and managing under conditions of multiple accountability relationships. The first of these, determining the masters, is a constant challenge for American public management. The challenge on this dimension comes from the fact that public employees typically are answerable to multiple sources of "authority," and these sources typically have diverse and sometimes contradictory expectations for administrative performance. Once having identified to whom and for what administrators will be held accountable, one must consider the questions of how to verify such performance and whether the accountability practices in use are well suited to performance expectations. Civil service reforms have shifted emphases regarding each of these and present challenges to public administrators as they seek to manage under conditions of multiple accountability relationships.

DETERMINING THE MASTER(S): SOURCES OF LEGITIMATE EXPECTATIONS

Accountability, which is understood as answerability for performance, raises an immediate question for the one held to account. Accountable to whom? The answer to this question in the American context is not a simple one. Under our basic constitutional principles, executive branch employees work to implement the law at the direction of political appointees who answer to the president. Laws, of course, represent the collective will of elected officials, who in turn speak for the citizenry as expressed through the will of the voters. Within this system of government, public employees are held accountable for their performance through oversight, monitoring, and executive appointments originating with external democratic institutions, e.g., elected chief executives, courts, and legislatures (Finer 1941; Gruber 1987). But the reality of public management, and the fact that the nature of the work of civil servants affords them many opportunities to exercise discretion in the course of their work (Lipsky 1980), gives rise to expectations and control strategies that derive from internal sources also (Friedrich 1940; Burke 1986).

The pragmatic American approach to public accountability has been to design solutions to accountability problems as they arise, without regard to elegance of design or redundancy. As a management problem or scandal arises, new accountability relationships are instituted to prevent such circumstances from arising in the future. These new accountability arrangements are not substituted for the accountability relationships which were in place at the time of the problem (which in light of the emergent problem are now perceived to be inadequate). Rather they are simply added to accountability relationships already in place. The resulting array of relationships provides numerous opportunities for holding public employees answerable for their performance.

The very structure of federal employment systems represents this incremental and layering approach toward accountability. The infamous mid-19th century spoils system was a reaction to a belief that government had not been sufficiently responsive to changes in electoral will (Mosher 1982). Accountability under spoils emphasized responsiveness to the appointing authority. The merit system, as it developed in reaction to excesses of responsiveness under the spoils system, put in place constraints on appointment and removal authority to insulate employees from external pressures. While the federal government instituted the merit system with the Pendleton Act of 1883, it retained a political appointee system for the highest level positions of government. So while the merit system established new accountability relationships (which emphasized obedience to internal directives), the spoils system and its accountability relationships (which emphasized responsiveness to elected officials) were not discarded entirely. The resulting hybrid system relies on both external and internal sources of control.

This pattern of layering accountability relationships has been repeated time and again. The result is the weaving of a thick web of multiple, overlapping accountability relationships within which public employees work. Different strands of the web of accountability represent different authority relationships with actors or institutions that are legitimate sources of performance expectations and/or control for public employees. These relationships vary in how they hold public employees accountable and what performance standards are used.

Types of Accountability

The resulting web of accountability relationships available in the United States reflects both internal and external sources of expectations and/or control and differing degrees of autonomy regarding administrative actions. These relationships represent four different types: hierarchical, legal, political and professional (Romzek 1998; Romzek and Dubnick 1987). The differences in these types are illustrated in Figure 1 below.

Hierarchical accountability relationships are based on close supervision of individuals who have low work autonomy with efficiency as the operating

Figure 1   Source of Expectations and/or Control: Types of Accountability Relationships

		Internal	External
DEGREE OF AUTONOMY	*Low*	Hierarchical	Legal
	High	Professional	Political

value and obedience as the fundamental behavioral expectation. The stereotype of personnelists acting as rule making *policy police* fit in this category. Rules, regulations, organizational directives, and supervisors are also examples of this type, as are the use of time sheets and annual performance evaluations. Supervisory review of an individual's performance involves an internal actor (one's boss) scrutinizing the employee's behavior in some detail for whether or not performance expectations are met. Traditional "merit" based civil service systems which are organized around position classification schemas are a common example of reliance on low discretion and supervisory control. Executive orders as agency directives, measurement of personnel servicing ratios, administrative program checklists, and management within personnel ceilings also typify this category of accountability.

As every experienced manager knows, hierarchical accountability can have negative consequences when it is overemphasized. In a report on the role of federal supervisors in strategic human resources management, the MSPB (July 1998, 5) found that "procedures and paperwork, implemented to serve as tools to help managers communicate more productively and more frequently with subordinates, seem to have become an end in themselves, and may have left some supervisors with the mistaken impression that this mechanical process is a substitute for performance management." The abolition of the Federal Personnel Manual and the elimination of the standardized federal personnel application, SF-171, represent efforts to break away from an overreliance on rules and standardization. Proposals to reform the position classification system from the 15-level General Schedule to a smaller number of broad bands represent other efforts to break away from rule-bound, low discretion accountability relationships.

Legal accountability relationships involve detailed external oversight of performance for compliance with established mandates under which managers are obliged to work, such as legislative and constitutional strictures. The prevailing value is rule of law. Depending on the nature of the job tasks, there are typically important legal obligations that public employees must meet in performing their jobs, including evaluating the performance of any subordinates. If questions of compliance with external mandates (laws, constitutional principles, court rulings), emerge in the course of an individual's job performance, legal accountability may be invoked. This would manifest itself as detailed external scrutiny for compliance with external expectations through processes such as legislative hearings, audits, grievances, or lawsuits. Legal accountability relationships can be seen in the monitoring undertaken by an Affirmative Action Office, the Equal Employment Opportunity Commission, or the Merit Systems Protection Board when they investigate employee complaints regarding workplace rights.

In American public management, legal accountability relationships are closely, perhaps inextricably, intertwined with hierarchical accountability relationships. When legal accountability is invoked, hierarchical accountability is often quick to follow, e.g., an employee is often placed on administrative leave or suspended during an investigation of serious misconduct. Legal accountability of a supervisor conducting a performance appraisal can be triggered through an appeal for external scrutiny of the appraisal itself on matters of substance or process.

Professional accountability systems are reflected in work arrangements that afford high degrees of autonomy to individuals who base their decision-making on internalized norms of appropriate practice. These norms can derive from professional socialization, personal conviction, organizational training, or work experience. In such accountability relationships, evaluation occurs—but the emphasis is on deferring to the discretion of managers as they work within broad parameters, rather than close scrutiny for compliance with detailed rules and organizational directives. The prevailing value is deference to expertise and employees are evaluated by whether their judgment is consistent with accepted protocols and best practices.

Professional accountability relationships can be seen in programs that decentralize personnel authority and the personnel procurement system into agency-based authority, with an emphasis on results (MSPB July 1998). Programs that allow administrators to manage their workforce under payroll limits rather than with personnel ceilings exemplify this type; they allow administrators considerable discretion in determining the credentials, skills, and pay levels appropriate for their work groups. Self-directed teams and experiments in broad banding of personnel classifications, such as the China Lake federal demonstration project (OPM 1992) are examples of efforts to allow public managers to exercise discretion in accordance with accepted professional practices. The China Lake project allowed greater flexibility and autonomy in assigning, promoting, and rewarding subordinates at the defense lab; it established five broad career paths and correspondingly broad pay (MSPB 1992; Wilson 1994). Another demonstration project, this one within the U.S. Department of Agriculture, the Forestry Service and the Agriculture Research Service, also experimented with a broad three-category grouping system (quality, eligible, ineligible) for hires rather than hierarchical rankings of scores and a "rule of three" (Feller et al. 1995, MSPB 1992).

Political accountability relationships afford managers the discretion (or choice) of being responsive to the concerns of key stakeholders, such as elected officials, clientele groups, the general public, and so on. It is labeled political because the relationship mirrors that of elected officials to constituents with their emphases on responsiveness to the wishes and agenda of the "other." The essential point is that the accountable party anticipates and responds to someone else's agenda or expectations—ones that are beyond the scope of supervisor-subordinate obligations or professional expertise. Managers in this relationship have the discretion to decide whether and how to respond to key stakeholder concerns. Emphasis on customer service orientations and responsiveness to client needs reflect this type of accountability relationship, as does the long-standing system of political appointees intended to insure responsiveness to elected officials. Use of customer or clientele satisfaction surveys are examples of performance measures linked to this value of responsiveness. In the jargon of reinventing government, all public employees, not just top appointees, are encouraged to focus on responsiveness; the key external constituency is the citizen-as-customer (Osborne and Gaebler 1992, Gore 1995). Of course, the challenge for public agencies is identifying all of their "customers" and ascertaining the difference between citizens and customers (Frederickson 1992).

The different values and behavioral expectations emphasized by the various accountability relationships are summarized below in Figure 2. Each of these four types of accountability relationships is used to hold individuals and agencies answerable for their performance. While different authorities may accord different priorities to these various types of accountability, each is legitimate; each promotes a different fundamental value of American government: efficiency, expertise, rule of law and responsiveness.

Dynamics of Accountability

These different types of accountability present dynamics that vary among agencies and within agencies. In theory, any one individual or agency can be

Figure 2   Values and Behavioral Expectations of Different Accountability Types

Type of Accountability	Value Emphasis	Behavioral Expectation
Hierarchical	Efficiency	Obedience to organizational directives
Legal	Rule of law	Compliance with external mandates
Professional	Expertise	Deference to individual judgment & expertise
Political	Responsiveness	Responsive to key external stakeholders

answerable for performance under all four different types of accountability simultaneously. More often, one or two types of accountability relationships are primary, with the others "in place" but underutilized, if not dormant. In times of crises or serious failure, the underutilized types are typically invoked (Romzek and Ingraham 1998; Romzek and Dubnick 1987), often leaving the individual or agency "answerable" under all four behavioral standards.

Each of these four types of accountability relationships can be present within one organization and multiple types may even be used within one office. Furthermore, the same actors can find themselves facing shifts into different accountability relationships as other behavioral expectations become salient. Sometimes sources of expectations (individuals and agencies in a position to hold someone answerable for performance) can switch from invoking one kind of accountability relationship to another, reflecting different behavioral expectations. This results in the same actors being involved in different accountability relationships at different times, sometimes emphasizing obedience, and at other times deference to expertise, rule of law, and/or responsiveness.

For example, a supervisor may issue organizational directives and signal that the employee is expected to answer for his or her performance under a hierarchical accountability relationship. At other times that same boss may delegate discretion to his or her subordinates, signaling that the subordinates will be held to answer for their performance under professional accountability relationships, where they are expected to exercise their best judgment rather than follow rules and directives. In this latter instance, the employees' performance will be judged on whether their decisions were responsible and consistent with accepted practices. At yet other times a subordinate may choose to be responsive to the agenda of his or her boss even though their employment relationship does not require "obedience" on the matter at hand. Examples abound of employees vigorously supporting their superiors' agenda as a politically expedient career move.

A centralized personnel office, such as the Office of Personnel Management, can activate any one of the four types of accountability relationships, depending upon which behavioral expectations and values it seeks to evoke vis-à-vis other agencies or employees. In its earliest incarnation under the CSRA, OPM emphasized a hierarchical accountability between itself and other federal agencies on personnel matters, with OPM in the supervisory role and other agencies in a subordinate role. When OPM established rules or limits for agencies to follow, such as the well-known "rule of three" or position classification schema, it afforded agencies little autonomy and a hierarchical accountability relationship was used.

Over time OPM's role has evolved as it has delegated HR responsibilities to the agencies themselves. When OPM grants discretion to agencies to determine how many staffers they need and what kind of skills mix they need, it establishes a professional accountability mode for those agencies and reserves an oversight role for itself. When OPM's Investigations Service engages in agency oversight, contract management, processing of Freedom of Information and Privacy Act requests, or case adjudication, it is using legal accountability relationships and emphasizing a rule of law orientation. When that centralized personnel office adopts a consultative role and views other federal agencies as "customers" who make use of their services, then OPM is emphasizing responsiveness to customers' needs and is operating in a political accountability mode.

Because agencies and employees work within this web of overlapping accountability relationships, they can find that one type of accountability relationship can be used to trigger another type. For example, when an executive order is issued, the president utilizes his position as chief executive to issue a directive to subordinate agencies. President Clinton's Executive Order 12862, which mandated aggressive pursuit of customer service plans for federal agencies, is an example of one kind of accountability relationship (hierarchical) being used to promote the use of other kinds (professional and political). Executive Order 12862 puts far more discretion into the hands of front-line managers and emphasizes responsiveness to external clientele. It requires agencies to define customer service standards, identify who agency customers are or should be, survey them about satisfaction, post service standards and measure results against them, establish best-in-business benchmarks, survey front-line employees, and make information services and complaint system easily accessible (Kettl 1995:54).

The wide range of potential accountability relationships presents important and complicated questions regarding which one(s) to use. We defer this discussion to later in the chapter while we consider other dimensions of accountability also undergoing change due to administrative reform.

DELEGATING TASKS AND ESTABLISHING EXPECTATIONS

Accountability relationships carry with them a delegation of authority to act on behalf of some legitimate source of authority. Prior to CSRA, legitimate personnel authority was delegated to the U.S. Civil Service Commission. The CSRA and subsequent reforms altered the delegation of authority for federal personnel administration. The Office of Personnel Management (OPM) was charged with management responsibilities and the Merit Systems Protection Board (MSPB) was to oversee merit system appeals. Later reforms included the subsequent delegation of OPM personnel authority to the agencies. Most recently reforms have pushed many personnel duties traditionally performed by agency-based personnel specialists in centralized personnel units down to the level of first level supervisors (MSPB July 1998).

With these authorizations come explicit and implicit expectations for performance. The notion of expectations for performance is a central feature of accountability relationships. Some of these are expectations for commitments to fundamental institutions, such as to uphold the Constitution, to maintain democracy through openness and access to government decisions, and to seek to discover and achieve the public good. Other expectations are more obvious and explicit, such as to obey organizational directives and comply with laws, fulfill agency goals, uphold professional standards, provide clientele services efficiently and effectively, achieve programmatic ends of political leadership, satisfy the demands of active supporters, and achieve one's personal goals and career objectives.

The American political system is complex. And the tasks that the federal government undertakes are often complicated. As a result, public employees typically face multiple expectations that are diverse, changing, and oftentimes contradictory (Dubnick and Romzek, 1991, 1993). This circumstance is in part due to the various stakeholders public employees face, but also due to the nature of the managerial challenges they face in seeking to manage those expectations. Observers of the public management scene describe this context as follows: "As governance becomes increasingly complex and the crossplay of interests more dynamic, the harried public official yearns for refuge from hostile litigators, importunate lobbyists, and investigators from Congress and from the home department's inspector general. The official retreats to some rule to cover for his or her official acts" (Garvey and DiIulio 1994, 23).

If lucky, staff find the multiple expectations they face to be mutually reinforcing and compatible; often they find these multiple expectations to be changing and conflicting. For example, supervisors may be expected by senior management to fill jobs quickly because of budget considerations, such as an impending hiring freeze, while at the same time be expected to cast their nets widely in search of the best candidates to hire. Another commonplace example of this situation in the world of public personnel is the expectation that public managers hire individuals based on merit, make efforts to diversify the work force, protect employees' individual rights, and operate as efficiently as possible (Klingner and Nalbandian, 1998). As anyone who has worked even a short while in the public sector can attest, pursuit of any one of these expectations can sometimes undermine the others.

The main thrust of civil service and government reforms has been to deemphasize performance expectations that are focused on rules and directives from central authorities. Instead they emphasize performance expectations that involve flexibility, initiative, and responsiveness. The currently popular reform approaches of reinvention, reengineering and continuous improvement also embody conflicting expectations. Don Kettl (1995, 47) notes that the "three strategies send contradictory signals, raise different expectations, and often create radically different motivations for the workers who have to do the hard work of reinventing."[4]

VERIFYING PERFORMANCE

Once expectations are established, the accountability question becomes how to verify performance. Much of the impetus behind reform has been to improve or at least clarify accountability and make it more transparent. Consequently a great deal of civil service reform effort has focused on verifying whether individual employees have done the work expected of them.

Prior to CSRA, performance evaluations in the federal government tended to rely on trait based evaluations (Gaertner and Gaertner 1984). CSRA mandated appraisals be based on performance and that those evaluations be linked to merit pay. Experimentation with performance evaluation procedures, in an effort to increase the validity of the evaluations, has been compared to a search for the "Holy Grail"; unfortunately, performance appraisal continues to be the most disliked supervisory task in the federal government today (Schay 1993, 664).[5]

Recent accountability reforms have taken two different but interrelated approaches to verifying performance. Each approach represents an effort to update accountability relationships and better align them with contemporary management practices. One is to broaden the scope of the input used in judging whether the performance of individuals and agencies has met expectations for accountability purposes. The other approach is to shift the standards that are emphasized when individuals and agencies are scrutinized to determine whether they have met the various expectations. Most recent trends focus on measuring performance based on outputs and outcomes rather than following rules and accepted processes. Management reforms such as the use of flex-time and flex-place create challenges for management because it requires performance be evaluated based on outputs or outcomes rather than just physical presence at one's work site.

The Government Performance and Results Act (GPRA) represents the latest effort to strengthen the verification of performance through development of more reliable and valid measures of performance. The challenges in this area are substantial given the multi-tiered nature of performance; one needs to measure performance of an organization as a whole, of individual programs within an organization, of teams within programs, and of individual workers themselves (Kettl et al. 1996, 74). A recent GAO (July 1998, 18) report notes that there has been little progress in the development and usage of performance measures.

Broadening the Scope of Evaluation

Performance appraisals are the primary instrument by which individuals are held accountable for their performance. In government these appraisals typically involve detailed scrutiny (usually annually) of an individual by his or her immediate supervisor according to predetermined expectations and criteria. Experiments with flexible approaches to performance appraisals have found appraisal systems can influence the performance culture and that elimination of performance appraisals creates problems (McNish 1986, Schay 1993).

Experimentation with broadening the scope of the input used for performance appraisals (beyond the judgment of immediate supervisors) takes the form of feedback from coworkers and clientele or "customers." In this kind of reform, known as a *360 degree* performance evaluation, the range of input for determining accountability is broadened considerably (Romzek 1998). Three hundred sixty–degree evaluations continue to encompass supervisory judgment, and hence retain some traditional hierarchical accountability. They also incorporate peer judgments about the individual's performance, including whether the performance was consistent with work group norms of accepted practice. As such, they incorporate a form of professional accountability; coworkers exercise discretion in offering their judgment of coworkers' performance. Measures of clientele or "customer" satisfaction with service represent a form of political accountability, reflecting the extent to which individuals or programs were responsive to clientele expectations. Of course the possibility of legal accountability is ever present, such as when appeals are filed.

Part of the popularity of 360 degree evaluations rests in the fact that input is derived from multiple sources of authority. While this 360 degree approach represents all four kinds of sources of accountability expectations, wider sources of input on evaluations do not necessarily guarantee more accurate evaluations. "The key is to limit the input to areas where the rater has good knowledge and then integrate the information into an accurate measurement of employees' overall performance" (NAPA 1997, 56). While some research has found employees perceive multi-source performance evaluations to be fairer (Deleon and Ewen 1997), MSPB data indicate federal employees in general prefer that their ratings be limited to their first line supervisors (Schay 1993, 659–60).

The next logical step in performance appraisal reform is bringing performance appraisals in line with the team orientation embedded in many of the broader reforms, especially those pursued under the rubric of total quality management or continuous process improvements. This issue has received a great deal of rhetorical attention, especially for its emphasis on shifting from individual to group or team assignments.[6] The accountability challenge in shifting to a team approach to work assignment is developing a team-based performance evaluation system to accompany the team assignments.

Public agencies in general have been slow to adjust to evaluating and rewarding team behavior. The individualistic nature of our public service rules and regulations makes group-based evaluations very difficult. Most agencies that utilize teams evaluate the performance of *individuals* for their contributions to team projects, rather than the team as a whole (NAPA, 1997). The Pacer Share demonstration project, which eliminated individual performance appraisals, did find a substantial proportion of employees (44 percent) recognizing improved teamwork (Schay 1993, 656). Some reinvention labs report experimenting with group based bonus awards but they are quick to note they keep two sets of records—one consistent with individual performance appraisals that headquarters or central agencies want to see, and a second set of records with group performance levels that the reform effort values and seeks to reward.

Changing Standards for Evaluation

Another aspect of reform focuses on changing *how* performance is measured and evaluated rather than *who* is evaluated. Personnel offices have typically been evaluated on the basis of compliance with laws, rules and regulations (MSPB August 1993), reflecting inputs and process orientations. Most contemporary government reforms seek to shift evaluations away from a rules and oversight approach that focuses on inputs and processes toward new emphasis on discretion and responsiveness that focuses on outputs and outcomes. This has manifested itself in efforts to develop more useful (and objective) measurement systems, such as financial measures of cost per employee hired, customer satisfaction measures, workforce capacity measures, employee satisfaction and process effectiveness measures, such as cycle time and productivity. (NAPA 1997, GAO July 1998, 19). Benchmarking, the systematic examination of products, services or work processes against the best practices of similar organizations, reflects this second aspect of reform. It emphasizes developing explicit standards against which performance is evaluated (Ettore 1993, Greengard 1995).

In contrast to inputs and process orientations, a focus on outputs and outcomes emphasizes deliverables of work rather than going through the proper motions. There has been a great deal of activity setting up output measures; outcomes measures have proven much more difficult. Some are qualitative, others are quantitative and yield to statistical analyses. Agencies have control over their outputs; they have much less control over outcomes. OPM recognizes managers are more likely to manage against outputs than outcomes (NAPA 1997, 90). The Government Performance and Results Act (GPRA) is an example of government's aspiration to move toward outcomes and outputs. With GPRA, "Congress recognized that, in exchange for shifting the focus of accountability to outcomes, managers must be given the authority and flexibility to achieve those outcomes" (Bowsher 1996, 11). GPRA requires agencies to develop five-year strategic plans and identify program performance goals and quantifiable measures; and the expectation is that this will help with the development of individual performance measures (Kettl et al. 1996, 69). Use of each of these four orientations is widespread in personnel.

An *inputs* orientation focuses on resources, what an agency or manager has available to carry out the program or activity—such as budget levels, number and skill mix of employees, compensation costs, supervisory ratios, and succession planning programs. Staffing directives in the Federal Workforce Restructuring Act of 1994, which mandated government-wide reductions of 272,900 FTE positions through FY 1999, are an example of an inputs approach to personnel policy. The General Accounting Office reports that several departments are developing performance measures that gauge their personnel servicing ratios. And it notes that while such a ratio "provides a broad measure of efficiency . . . [it] does not indicate how well an agency's personnel office meets the needs of its customers" (GAO July 1998, 19).

A *process* orientation emphasizes proper paper flow and consultation with relevant, appropriate actors and compliance with mandates and regulations (NAPA 1997, 91). In a process orientation, performance measures emphasize compliance, e.g., grievance/appeal/litigation costs, and the question is whether proper procedures are followed and appropriate questions considered, rather than whether the intended result is achieved. In personnel terms an emphasis on process would encompass pursuit of merit principles, conduct of testing and hiring, and management of compensation processes (Kettl et al. 1996). Reductions in force, veterans' preference programs, as well as grievance and disciplinary hearings are personnel activities that reflect a heavily process orientation.

Outputs are the quantity and quality of services delivered or products made. When relying on outputs, there is a tendency to emphasize measures that are easily obtained, for example, the number of candidates interviewed, retirements processed, evaluations conducted. Output measures include standards for *services,* such as timeliness, that clientele can expect when they contact the agency. Employee and customer service satisfaction levels are examples of output measures widely used, such as the employee surveys regularly conducted by the MSPB.

There has been activity in developing performance standards for service throughout the federal government more generally. Examples of output measures include the time callers have to wait to get through by telephone to the Social Security Administration, or the time visitors will have to wait for service at the National Archives and Records Administration, or the time veterans will have to wait to see a benefits counselor. The U.S. Postal Service developed a consumer affairs tracking system that records and reports every customer contact. The Department of Veterans Affairs medical centers have an ongoing complaint tracking system and conduct annual surveys of patients. GAO's research (July 1998, 18) found little progress on the development of performance indicators for service delivery in personnel operations. One instance can be seen in the effort of the Office of Veterans Affairs to develop measures of users' satisfaction with its automated personnel systems (GAO July 1998, 19).

Outcomes reflect the quantity and quality of the *results* achieved by the outputs in satisfying the client, taxpayer, or customer. An outcome in the personnel arena might be levels of retention of expertise when first line supervisors are given intensive training in supervisory skills. Whereas the output measure would be supervisors trained, a potential outcome of such training could be better supervisory practices, resulting in fewer employees with desirable expertise leaving the organization. GAO reports a negative outcome experienced by many federal agencies that experienced the loss of critical expertise due to broadly targeted early retirement opportunities associated with federal downsizing; NASA, for instance, reported losing "centuries of expertise" (GAO March 1998).

Although most reforms aspire to increase the use of outcome measures, success is not assured. There are political, managerial, and methodological challenges associated with developing and using outcome measures for accountability. Political problems lie in the difficulty in getting agreement on definitions of effectiveness and qualitative and subjective measures of outcomes (Kravchuk and Schack, 1996). Managerial problems arise from using outcomes for accountability purposes because of the time lag between administrative action and the desired outcomes—which may be measured in years, the tendency for outcome measures to displace behavior as people seek to maximize the outputs by which they will be measured, and the problem when performance measures do not evolve in tandem with policy changes. Another problem with using outcomes measures is that managers are not always in total control of outcomes, which often depend on other facts besides the programs themselves. For example, GPRA requirements can be difficult for federal agencies when they are accountable for performance that is part of an intergovernmental framework (Risher and Schay, 1994). Methodological problems with outcomes emerge from the difficulty and expense of developing sound measures of outcomes, which tend to be qualitative and subjective. Another challenge is the limit of our knowledge of cause-and-effect relationships.

These distinctions between inputs, process, outputs and outcomes orientations for performance evaluation become important when the focus is on administrative reform. As reforms introduce different managerial strategies and emphases regarding work, accountability practices need to shift accordingly.

ACCOUNTABILITY ALIGNMENTS

The issue of the fit between organizational activities and accountability relationships in use is an important consideration in management reform. In times of reform, there is often a shift in emphasis and priority among the different types of accountability (Romzek, 1998). In fact, frequently calls for "more" accountability are in fact calls for a reliance on a "different kind" of accountability with different expectations for performance, rather than just "more of the same." In seeking to change the operations of agencies and employees, it is essential to have a corresponding shift in accountability relationships to ensure that behavioral expectations are appropriately aligned with managerial emphases. In other words, the new behaviors sought need to be reflected in the administrative measures used to evaluate agency and individual performance.

The decision as to which accountability relationships are appropriate is a function of the organization's institutional environment, managerial strategy, and agency or individual tasks (Romzek and Dubnick, 1987). The institutional environment affects the nature of the assignments agencies and individuals are given and the expectations they face. The American public service's institutional environment has been a turbulent one for the past two decades. For example, the American public service has been subject to a steady stream of severe criticism from elected officials, popularly known as "bureaucrat bashing" (Garvey 1995). And the current institutional environment continues to be highly critical of administrative capacity and effectiveness. This critical stance is in fact the major impetus behind reform. It is also a major reason why the administrative culture continues to emphasize a punitive or "gotcha" approach to accountability.

Managerial strategies which underlie the different reforms are typically multifaceted. Civil service reforms seek to encourage discretion, flexibility, initiative, entrepreneurship, worker empowerment, and customer service orientations. And managerial reforms tend to seek different emphases rather than the complete elimination of any one orientation because managers need to concern themselves with the manner of performance as well as the results (NAPA 1997, 53). The nature of individual core job tasks will

Figure 3   "Ideal" Accountability Alignments: Managerial Strategy and Core Task

		Routine			Nonroutine
	Inputs	HIERARCHICAL			
MANAGERIAL	Process		LEGAL		
STRATEGY	Outputs			POLITICAL	
	Outcomes				PROFESSIONAL

determine whether managerial reforms warrant adjustments in accountability relationships as well. More complex tasks require more discretion.

While the conditions of public administration are rarely ideal, it is possible to discuss "ideal" accountability configurations reflecting a "fit" between reform and accountability practices (Romzek and Dubnick 1994). Figure 3 presents a baseline framework illustrating how current managerial reform strategies and core tasks can be aligned in terms of accountability relationships.

When an agency's managerial focus is on inputs and its tasks are routine, hierarchical accountability, with its emphasis on limited discretion, is an effective alignment. In such instances performance is judged by how well the individual deployed organizational inputs at his or her disposal—e.g., time, effort, workforce (average grade, supervisory ratios) or funds. For example, issuing payroll checks is a relatively routine task that lends itself to administration by organizational direction and application of rules.

When an agency's managerial focus is on processes and its tasks are still relatively routine, legal accountability relationships are typically an effective alignment. Processing veterans' preference claims or bumping rights during a reduction in force requires careful attention to due process and affords limited discretion. In such instances compliance with the rule of law is the important value.

Circumstances where agency tasks are less routine and managerial strategies focus on outputs lend themselves to political accountability relationships, where the emphasis is on responsiveness to some key stakeholders. Customer service programs that emphasize customer satisfaction typify this alignment.

Where the task is very specialized and the managerial strategy is focused on outcomes or results, professional accountability relationships represent the best alignment because it allows for the exercise of discretion and the application of expertise. Proposals to adopt a "block grant" approach to civil service represent an emphasis on discretion at an agency level (Kettl et al. 1996, 71), as does OPM's delegation of HRM authority to federal departments, and those same departments' further delegation of these responsibilities to individual line managers (MSPB June 1998, 9).

This discussion about shifting emphases away from inputs and process toward outcomes and outputs reflects the rhetoric of government reforms. The language of reform is enticing. It is a fairly simple task to repeat the various reform mantras: "cut red tape; empower employees; emphasize results, not rules; delight your customers." These phrases appear on the surface to be obvious and straightforward prescriptions for action: simply tell public managers what outputs and outcomes they are expected to achieve and then give them the flexibility and discretion to do so. The fact of the matter is that following these prescriptions involves difficult shifts "away from the control model and move toward the developmental model, including approaches to motivation and recognition of group performance" (Lane 1994, 39).

This multi-method approach to accountability, where several accountability relationships exist simultaneously, is not a unique situation; it has been the pattern throughout most of the history of American government. In fact, given the presence of multiple expectations, a multi-method approach to accountability may be most appropriate, even if the situation occasionally presents managers with cross pressures. The pattern of multiple, overlapping accountability relationships means that the likelihood of facing at least one less-than-ideal alignment in public management is the norm rather than the exception. For administrators, this circumstance presents a substantial, ongoing management challenge that is critical to successful reform: minimizing the gap between rhetoric and reality.

Gap between Rhetoric and Reality

A troubling dynamic associated with these management reforms is a gap between the rhetoric and expectations of government reform and the reality of the blame-oriented, rule-oriented, litigious American political culture. This gap is characteristic of the accountability environment within which public organizations and public managers operate. While management reforms seek to encourage initiative and sometimes even necessitate entrepreneurial behavior—for example, to continue to provide high levels of service with reduced staff and funding—accountability practices themselves may not change as quickly as the rhetoric suggests.

For management reforms to become thoroughly embedded, widely accepted, and effective, they need to attend to issues of accountability align-

ment. For supervisors, the important managerial implication of accountability alignment is to be sure that performance evaluation criteria match
the managerial emphases and behavioral expectations that management
hopes to elicit from employees. Employees' performance will follow those
aspects of their behavior which are measured and rewarded. If management
reform rhetoric emphasizes employee discretion and autonomy, but performance reviews emphasize rules and processes, then employees will emphasize rules and process in their work efforts.

The accountability landscape for American public administrators is in a
great deal of flux these days as efforts are made to reform administrative
processes, redefine agency missions and values, and adjust reporting relationships. Most of the managerial reforms are intended to break up an
overemphasis on inputs and processes. They emphasize deregulation, increased discretion and flexibility, and greater emphases on outputs and outcomes. Hence the accountability relationships that are best suited to these
reforms are professional and political types which rely on deference to expertise, increased discretion and responsiveness.

Current trends in reform seek a shift toward professional and political
accountability and away from hierarchical and legal types. But this represents only a shift in emphases among accountability relationships rather
than discarding one or another type of accountability relationship altogether. Failure to align government reforms with appropriate accountability practices will seriously undermine the likelihood that the changes will be
successfully implemented. If alignments are less than ideal, a circumstance
that is typical in the multi-method accountability context of public management, then the long term success of management reforms is at risk.

CONCLUSION

Since the passage of the Pendleton Act, the American public service has been
structured with an eye toward eliminating favoritism and constraining
managerial choices. The result has been a large accumulation of administrative rules and regulations concerning human resources management, rendering the personnel function slow and cumbersome (Ingraham and Rosenbloom 1992). Implicitly, those rules and regulations condoned a trade-off
of administrative efficiency for accountability. Pressure for enhanced efficiency in government has forced a re-examination of this trade-off.

Taken as a whole, this twenty-year era of reform has been driven by complex, multifaceted motives, including increasing administrative efficiency, effectiveness, flexibility, fairness, and responsiveness. Administrative changes have included downsizing, decentralization, deregulation, and reengineering with the goal of smaller, more responsive, more entrepreneurial, and more effective public management systems than the old procedure and rule-based approaches allowed. Operationally, these reforms have heightened the visibility and interest in issues of accountability as they encourage more discretion on the part of managers, more flexibility in administrative operations, and greater emphases on outcomes and outputs to enable government to tackle its new challenges better.

The rhetoric of reform usually poses questions of accountability in terms of whether government employees are *more* accountable after the reform than they were before the reform. A more useful line of inquiry reflects the complexity of American public management by focusing on the *kind* of accountability that is appropriate, recognizing that accountability is not a unidimensional, linear concept. De-emphasizing inputs and processes and emphasizing outcomes and outputs does not necessarily mean more or less accountability from government administrators. Rather it means different kinds of accountability relationships should be emphasized.

Government reforms seek to increase the reliance on some kinds of accountability relationships and de-emphasize others, reflecting a "mix and match" approach to accountability practices rather than an all-or-nothing approach. Cutting red tape and speeding up procedures which ensure due process represent efforts to lessen the constraints from hierarchical and legal types of accountability relationships. While hierarchical and legal accountability are never completely abandoned, the success of the current wave of reforms necessitates de-emphasizing obedience to organizational directives and compliance with external mandates. Reforms that seek increased employee discretion, worker empowerment, and flexibility represent professional accountability relationships. Emphases on employees' responsiveness to key clientele and the use of customer satisfaction performance measures reflect political accountability relationships.

Reformers face two implementation questions regarding accountability. One relates to the alignment of accountability practices that are appropriate given the managerial reforms and the behaviors the reforms seek to encourage. It is a truism in management that one needs to measure and evaluate the behaviors one wants to encourage. If reforms seek new managerial strategies and reconfigured tasks, then accountability relationships need to be reconfigured, too. If accountability practices do not reinforce the newer strategies and tasks, then administrative reforms are not likely to become deeply rooted in organizational practices (Schein, 1992). This means that federal government reformers need to measure and evaluate behaviors that are consistent with entrepreneurial management, increased discretion and worker empowerment in daily operations, and greater responsiveness to key stakeholders and customers. The worst situation of all is to have changes in administrative approaches without appropriate shifts in the emphases on accountability relationships.

The other question relates to the design of effective accountability relationships given the behaviors management seeks to elicit from employees. Given an interest in increasing discretion and responsiveness, it is appropriate to rely on output and outcome performance measures for accountability proposals. But the challenge of designing effective accountability measures based on outcomes and outputs is substantial. It requires agreement on outcomes and outputs as well as deference to administrative discretion, standards of acceptable practice, and responsiveness to customers.

There are always questions about the future of any governmental reform effort due to the inevitable ebb and flow of political and administrative support for such changes. Effective civil service reform requires attention to the expectations and interests of three key actors: *political institutions* that represent the body politic, *public agencies* (represented by top management and, in this case, human resource managers) that are charged with implementing public policies, and the *public employees* who staff those agencies and programs. Successful reforms need to accommodate the accountability expectations of each of these key actors. It is unclear whether the American populace, its political institutions, and its managerial culture are ready to afford public agencies and their employees the discretion and flexibility that such reforms entail. The institutional context within which public management operates in the United States has never been very trusting of government and its administrators (Peters and Savoie 1994). And there is no sign that trust is on the upswing; rather it is declining (Ruscio 1996).

Reforms that seek to change administrative practice need to consider also the accountability culture of federal management. Civil service reform must contend with a deep-seated risk averse managerial culture (Light 1994, Ban 1995), which tends to emphasize short term results over long term outcomes (MSPB July 1998, 6). The hope of reform is that public managers and government agencies will shift toward more entrepreneurial and innovative strategies (Osborne and Gaebler 1992, Gore 1995). Reforms have encouraged entrepreneurial management by changing the performance expectations and accountability emphases.

Reformers need to be cognizant of the accountability dynamics that follow logically from reforms and make appropriate adjustments. The challenge is how to shift emphases *away from* a focus on inputs and processes and *toward* outcomes and outputs in light of the fact that some managers may be more comfortable than others with increased discretion and flexibility (Ban 1995). These administrative reforms may be de-emphasizing old, familiar accountability relationships *before* the American polity is comfortable with the heavy reliance on accountability practices that are appropriate for the new reforms. Reformers cannot simultaneously prevent abuse and promote discretion (Kettl et al. 1996, 66). Yet that is what is expected.

These reforms present opportunities and uncertainties for human resource managers. Accountability issues are complex and central to the work of human resource managers, who must concern themselves with the accountability of everyone within their domain as well as themselves. They need to be cognizant of the web of accountability relationships which are legitimate within the American context and how each can be used to hold employees answerable for their performance. Human resource managers who develop and sustain an array of accountability relationships that can be invoked quickly—as warranted by changes in the relevant political context, managerial strategies and core tasks—will find themselves better able to manage accountability for themselves and the employees who work within their domain.

The challenge facing federal employees, whether managers or not, continues to be their age-old one: how to manage the conflicting expectations they face in an institutional environment that relies on an overlapping array of accountability relationships. As a result of reforms, public employees find themselves with fewer detailed directives; they face much less certainty about the accountability consequences of their actions. Yet they must continue to accommodate expectations from several different legitimate sources and be answerable for their behavior under any and all accountability relationships that are relevant. And they must be able to shift the accountability standard under which they answer for their behavior, as needed. Like actors in repertory theater, public employees must be able to play a variety of roles: as obedient subordinate, innovative expert, responsive servant, and principled agent. Successful public employees stand ready to play each role as the performance expectations of the various audiences change.

REFERENCES

Ban, Carolyn. *How Do Public Managers Manage?* San Francisco: Jossey-Bass, 1995.

Ban, Carolyn, and H. C. Reed III. "The State of the Merit System: Perceptions of Abuse in the Federal Civil Service." *Review of Public Personnel Management* 10 (1990): 55–72.

Bowsher, Charles A. "Managing For Results: Achieving GPRA's Objectives Requires Strong Congressional Role." *Testimony (of Comptroller General of the U.S. General Accounting Office) before the Committee on Governmental Affairs,* U.S. Senate, Washington, D.C, GAO/T-GGD-96-79, March 6, 1996.

Burke, John. *Bureaucratic Responsibility.* Baltimore: Johns Hopkins University Press, 1986.

Deleon, Linda, and Ann J. Ewen. "Multi-Source Performance Appraisals: Employee Perceptions of Fairness." *Review of Public Personnel Management* 17 (1997): 22–36.

Dubnick, Melvin J., and Barbara S. Romzek. *American Public Administration: Politics and the Management of Expectations.* New York: Macmillan, 1991.

Dubnick, Melvin J., and Barbara S. Romzek. "Accountability and the Centrality of Expectations," in *Research in Public Administration,* edited by James Perry, v. 2. Stamford, Conn.: AI Press, 1993.

Ettore, Barbara. "Benchmarking: The Next Generation." *Management Review* 82 (June 1993): 10–16.

Federal Quality Institute. *Lessons Learned from the High-performing Organizations in the Federal Government.* Washington D.C.: Office of Personnel Management, Federal Quality Institute, 1994.

Feller, Irwin, Melvin Mark, Jack Stevens, Lance Shotland, Haleh Rastegary, Scott Button, Joe Vasey, and Laurie Hyers. "Decentralization and Deregulation of the Federal Hiring Process." Presented at the Trinity Symposium in conjunction with the meeting of the American Society for Public Administration, San Antonio, 1995.

Finer, Herman. "Administrative Responsibility and Democratic Government." *Public Administration Review* 1(Summer 1941): 335–50.

Frederickson, H. George. "Painting Bull's Eyes around Bullet Holes." *Governing* 6 (December 1992): 13.

Friedrich, Carl J. "Public Policy and the Nature of Administrative Responsibility." In *Public Policy,* ed. Carl J. Friedrich and Edwards S. Mason. Cambridge: Harvard University Press, 1940.

Gaertner, Karen N., and Gregory H. Gaertner. "Performance Evaluation and Merit Pay: Results in the Environmental Protection Agency and the Mine Safety and Health Administration." In *Legislating Bureaucratic Change: The Civil Service Reform Act of 1978,* ed. P. W. Ingraham and C. Ban. Albany: State University of New York Press, 1984.

Garvey, Gerald. "False Promises: The NPR in Historical Perspective." In *Inside the Reinvention Machine: Appraising Governmental Reform*, ed. Donald F. Kettl and John DiIulio, Jr. Washington, D.C.: Brookings Institution Press, 1995.

Garvey, Gerald, and John J. DiIulio, Jr. "Sources of Public Service Overregulation." In *Deregulating the Public Service: Can Government Be Improved?* ed. John J. DiIulio, Jr. Washington, D.C.: Brookings Institution Press, 1994.

General Accounting Office. GAO/GGD-98-46. *Federal Downsizing: Agency Officials' Views on Maintaining Performance during Downsizing at Selected Agencies.* March 1998.

General Accounting Office. (GAO/GGD-98-93). *Management Reform: Agencies' Initial Efforts to Restructure Personnel Operations.* July 1998.

Gore, Albert, Jr. *From Red Tape to Results: Creating a Government That Works Better and Costs Less.* Washington, D.C.: Report of the National Performance Review, 1993.

Gore, Albert, Jr. "The New Job of the Federal Executive." *Public Administration Review* 54 (1994): 317–21.

Gore, Albert, Jr. *Common Sense Government: Works Better and Costs Less.* Washington, D.C.: Third Report of the National Performance Review, 1995.

Greengard, Samuel. "Discover Best Practices through Benchmarking." *Personnel Journal* 74 (November 1995): 62–73.

Gruber, Judith. *Controlling Bureaucracies.* Berkeley: University of California Press, 1987.

Ingraham, Patricia W. "The Civil Service Reform Act of 1978: The Design and Legislative History." In *Legislating Bureaucratic Change: The Civil Service Reform Act of 1978*, ed. P. W. Ingraham and C. Ban. Albany: State University of New York Press, 1984.

Ingraham, Patricia W. *The Foundation of Merit.* Baltimore: Johns Hopkins University Press, 1995.

Ingraham, Patricia W., and Carolyn Ban. *Legislating Bureaucratic Change: The Civil Service Reform Act of 1978.* Albany: State University of New York Press, 1984.

Ingraham, Patricia W., and David H. Rosenbloom, eds. *The Promise and Paradox of Civil Service Reform.* Pittsburgh: University of Pittsburgh Press, 1992.

Kettl, Donald. "Building Lasting Reform: Enduring Questions, Missing Answers." In *Inside the Reinvention Machine: Appraising Governmental Reform*, ed. Donald Kettl and John DiIulio, Jr. Washington, D.C.: Brookings Institution Press, 1995.

Kettl, Donald, Patricia W. Ingraham, Ronald B. Sanders, and Constance Horner. *Civil Service Reform: Building a Government That Works.* Washington, D.C.: Brookings Institution Press, 1996.

Klingner, Donald, and John Nalbandian. *Public Personnel Management: Contexts and Strategies*, 4th ed. Englewood Cliffs, N.J.: Prentice-Hall, 1998.

Kravchuk, Robert S., and Ronald W. Schack. "Designing Effective Performance-Measurement Systems under the Government Performance and Results Act of 1993." *Public Administration Review* 56 (1996): 348–58.

Lane, Larry M. "Old Failures and New Opportunities: Public Sector Performance Management." *Review of Public Personnel Administration* 14 (1994): 26–44.

Light, Paul C. "Watch What We Pass: A Brief History of Civil Service Reform." In P. Ingraham and D. Rosenbloom, eds. *The Promise and Paradox of Civil Service Reform.* Pittsburgh: University of Pittsburgh Press, 1992, 303–25.

Light, Paul. "Creating Government That Encourages Innovation." In *New Paradigms for Government: Issues for the Changing Public Service,* ed. Patricia W. Ingraham and Barbara S. Romzek. San Francisco: Jossey-Bass, 1994.

Lipsky, Michael. *Street Level Bureaucracy.* New York: Russell Sage, 1980.

McNish, Linda. "A Critical Review of Performance Appraisals at the Federal Level: The Experience of the Public Health Services (PHS)." *Review of Public Personnel Management* 6 (1986): 42–56.

Milward, H. Brinton. "Implications of Contracting Out: New Roles for the Hollow State." In *New Paradigms for Government: Issues for the Changing Public Service,* ed. Patricia W. Ingraham and Barbara S. Romzek. San Francisco: Jossey-Bass, 1994.

Moe, Ronald C. "The 'Reinventing Government' Exercise: Misinterpreting the Problem, Misjudging the Consequences." *Public Administration Review* 54 (March/April 1994): 111–22.

Mosher, Frederick. *Democracy in the Public Service,* 2d ed. New York: Oxford University Press, 1982.

MSPB. *Federal Personnel Research Programs and Demonstration Projects: Catalysts for Change.* Washington, D.C.: U.S. Merit Systems Protection Board, December 1992.

MSPB. Office of Policy and Evaluation. *Federal Personnel Officers: Time for a Change?* Washington, D.C.: U.S. Merit Systems Protection Board, August 1993.

MSPB. Office of Policy and Evaluation. *The Rule of Three in Federal Hiring: Boon or Bane?* Washington, D.C.: U.S. Merit Systems Protection Board, December 1995.

MSPB. Office of Policy and Evaluation. *Adherence to the Merit Principles in the Workplace: Federal Employees' Views.* Washington, D.C.: U.S. Merit Systems Protection Board, 1997.

MSPB. Office of Policy and Evaluation. *Federal Supervisors and Strategic Human Resource Management.* Washington, D.C.: U.S. Merit Systems Protection Board, June 1998.

MSPB. Office of Policy and Evaluation. *Civil Service Evaluation: The Evolving Role of the U.S. Office of Personnel Management.* Washington, D.C.: U.S. Merit Systems Protection Board, July 1998.

National Academy of Public Administration. *Leading People in Change: Empowerment, Commitment, and Accountability.* Washington, D.C.: U.S. Department of Health and Human Services, 1993.

National Academy of Public Administration. *Measuring Results: Successful Human Resources Management,* August 1997.

Office of Personnel Management. *Broad Banding in the Federal Government: A Technical Report.* U.S. Office of Personnel Management, December, 1992.

Osborne, David, and Ted Gaebler. *Reinventing Government: How the Entrepreneurial Spirit Is Transforming the Public Sector.* Reading, Mass.: Addison-Wesley, 1992.

Perry, James L. "Strategic Human Resource Management: Transforming the Federal Civil Service." *Review of Public Personnel Review* 13 (1993): 59–71.

Peters, B. Guy, and Donald J. Savoie. "Civil Service Reform: Misdiagnosing the Patient." *Public Administration Review* 54 (1994): 418–25.

Risher, Howard H., and Brigitte W. Schay. "Grade Banding: The Model for Future Salary Programs?" *Public Personnel Management* 23 (1994): 187–99.

Romzek, Barbara S. "Accountability in the Public Sector: Lessons from the *Challenger* Tragedy." *Public Administration Review* 47 (1987): 227–38.

Romzek, Barbara S. "Where the Buck Stops: Accountability in Reformed Public Organizations." In *Transforming Government: Lessons from the Reinvention Laboratories,* ed. Patricia W. Ingraham, James R. Thompson, and Ronald P. Sanders. San Francisco: Jossey-Bass Publishers, 1998.

Romzek, Barbara S., and Melvin J. Dubnick. "Accountability." In *International Encyclopedia of Public Policy and Administration,* vol. 1: A–C, ed. Jay Shafritz. Boulder, Colo.: Westview Press, 1998.

Romzek, Barbara S., and Patricia W. Ingraham. "Cross Pressures of Accountability: Initiative, Command and Failure in the Ron Brown Plane Crash." Presented at the annual meeting of the American Political Science Association, Boston, 1998.

Ruscio, Kenneth P. "Trust, Democracy, and Public Management: A Theoretical Argument." *Journal of Public Administration Research and Theory* 6 (July 1996): 461–78.

Schay, Brigitte W. "In Search of the Holy Grail: Lessons in Performance Management." *Public Personnel Review* 22 (1993): 649–68.

Schein, Edgar. *Organizational Culture and Leadership,* 2d ed. San Francisco: Jossey-Bass, 1992.

Siegel, Gilbert B. "Three Federal Demonstration Projects: Using Monetary Performance Awards." *Public Personnel Management* 23 (1994): 153–64.

Thompson, James R., and Patricia W. Ingraham. "The Reinvention Game." *Public Administration Review* 56 (May/June 1996): 291–8.

Thompson, Paul R. "Laboratories for Change: Lessons from Fifteen Years of Demonstration Projects." *Public Personnel Management* 22 (1993): 675–88.

Wilson, James Q. "Can the Bureaucracy Be Deregulated: Lessons from Government Agencies." In *Deregulating the Public Service: Can Government Be Improved?* ed. John J. DiIulio, Jr. Washington, D.C.: Brookings Institution Press, 1994.

NOTES

1. The author acknowledges the research assistance of Chad Kniss.

2. One widely publicized example of the relevance of these later reforms for the civil service is the "dumping" of the Federal Personnel Manual (FPM). While the 10,000 page FPM was not completely eliminated, reducing it to 1,000 pages represents a substantial streamlining and sends a signal intended to encourage flexibility and initiative. Federal reinvention laboratories also exemplify reform efforts that seek to affect accountability relationships; 44 of the 48 different federal reinvention laboratory innovations identified by Thompson and Ingraham (1996, 294–95) involved loosening of accountability relationships in some fashion. Most sought increased autonomy and waivers of regulations or review rights.

3. These include determining the master(s), delegating tasks and establishing expectations, verifying performance, maintaining responsiveness of agents, assessing blame, sorting out responsibility, and managing under conditions of multiple accountability systems. For a fuller discussion see Romzek and Dubnick 1998.

4. The reinvention movement seeks downsizing and lower expenditures; reengineering seeks efficiency through discontinuous, breakthrough strategies; and continuous improvement reforms seek responsiveness to customers through cooperation. TQM processes imported into government operations represent conflicting expectations in another way. TQM requires the decoupling of individual accountability from performance management—a very difficult challenge in light of the fundamental American principle of individualism.

5. The movement away from trait-based evaluations to performance-based evaluations has been a challenge and demonstration projects have found performance-contingent appraisal systems to be no more or less popular among employees than traditional trait-based systems (Schay 1993, 660).

6. Lane (1994, 33) identifies the opportunities inherent in these new models of work, which "feature replacement of subdivision of labor by the idea of whole tasks, collective instead of individual accountability, formal controls subordinated to shared goals and peer pressure, participation and employee voice, negotiation, employee empowerment, thinning of middle management ranks, flattened hierarchies, and production and quality control as the responsibility of self-directed teams. In summary, supervision becomes less controlling as responsibility and autonomy are pushed downward in organizations."

PART THREE

THE FUTURE
OF MERIT

ONTO THE DARKLING PLAIN: GLOBALIZATION AND THE AMERICAN PUBLIC SERVICE IN THE TWENTY-FIRST CENTURY

MARK W. HUDDLESTON

INTRODUCTION

"Globalization" has perhaps not yet quite achieved the currency of "reinvention," "quality," "performance," or some of the other *mots au courant* in contemporary public administration. It is, however, clearly a term on the move, and one well worth pondering on the occasion of the twentieth anniversary of the Civil Service Reform Act. Most major public administration textbooks now draw students' attention to the growing need to adopt a "global perspective," or to understand the "global environment," especially the "global economy." The 1998 ASPA Conference hosted quite a few papers that dealt with "global" issues, including works on shipping, air transport, ethics, and the environment;[1] and the 1999 ASPA Conference had an entire theme devoted to "international links" in public administration. Although NASPAA has not yet required it for certification purposes, an increasing number of MPA programs seem to be working "globalization" into their curricula.[2] Public officials also now routinely point to the demands of "globalization," especially America's need to remain "globally competitive," to justify any number of policy initiatives, including trade reform, infrastructure improvements, and education reforms.[3]

The emerging consensus in the discipline about globalization seems to be that American public administration—both academic and on-the-ground practice—has been too "parochial."[4] To move away from this parochialism and prepare for the global tomorrow, it is said that the discipline and its members must, among other things:

- Learn from other systems, in part by rediscovering comparative administration and embracing the international component of public administration.[5]
- Abjure traditional management practices rooted in hierarchy, autonomy, representativeness and other passé byproducts of the industrial era in favor of flat, networked, and responsive global styles.[6]
- Recognize interdependence and the fact that no issue will ever again be fully "local."[7]
- Encourage public managers at all levels of government to focus on international economic competitiveness and to remove barriers that inhibit business growth.[8]
- Embrace diversity, avoid ethnocentricity, learn other languages and cultures, and recognize that Americans are increasingly a minority—in every respect—among the world's population.[9]
- Build bridges to partners abroad, sharing ideas and best practices, especially through information technology.[10]

Underlying this consensus is an unspoken assumption that construes globalization as what we might term a manageable challenge.[11] That is to say, globalization is understood to present administrators (and the citizens they serve) with some profound headaches, including—thanks to highly mobile capital, uncontrolled immigration, infectious diseases, pollution, etc.—serious economic dislocation, and overburdened health, education, and social service systems, to name just a few. At the same time, the presumption is that these headaches are, in fact, manageable. We need merely to move aggressively in the directions outlined above—build bridges, learn from other systems, embrace diversity, etc. This roll-up-our-sleeves attitude is not surprising from what has, after all, always been a "can-do" profession.[12] In most treatments of globalization by members of the public administration community there is even a hint—and sometimes more than a hint—of real enthusiasm. Globalization can be seen as "progressive," always a good thing in the field of public administration.[13] And the rest of the world—strange accents, exotic scents and sounds, unusual architecture—is much more interesting than Main Street. The beginning of full engagement with the globe is thus the end of the boring insularity of American public administration.

THE DARKLING PLAIN[14]

Or perhaps not. Perhaps the challenges of globalization may be rather less manageable than public administration has assumed. Indeed, if global political and economic developments unfold in the manner that some serious students of international relations (IR) have foreseen, the future of public administration itself—and of the broader American state—is in doubt. The purpose of this chapter is to explore this darker, more ominous vision of globalization and to consider its implications for the American public service. I do so not in the certainty that the vision will come to pass: The only certainty about the future is that it will differ from the present. Instead, I present this alternative model of globalization because it is at least plausible, and because many in the public administration community appear not to have considered its implications.

Before we begin, however, I want to make it clear that I am not claiming that there is anything like a consensus among IR scholars as to the impact of globalization. In fact, because international relationists look more closely at globalization than the rest of us, one can find in their writings on this subject subtleties, nuances, and fine points that constitute considerable diversity of opinion. A few of them, indeed, believe that forces of globalization may well culminate in a resurgence of state power, a resurgence that would seem to augur well for public administration.[15] What I do claim is that on the subject of globalization the balance of opinion is far bleaker among students of international relations than it is among specialists in public administration. Although this difference in attitude may simply reflect traditional divides of disciplinary temperament—the contemplation of anarchy in IR breeding pessimism, the embrace of order in PA producing optimism—it likely runs deeper than that. We who spend our days hunched in windowless cubicles poring over the day-to-day work of government may simply be oblivious to the gathering storm.

The remainder of the paper is divided into four sections. In the first, I sketch the origins of this storm and its likely track from the perspective of IR theory. The basic argument here is that globalization, fueled by international capitalism and the revolution in telecommunications, poses a fundamental—and perhaps unanswerable—challenge to the nation-state. The second section describes three crises—of accountability, governance, and legitimacy—that globalization will force American public administration to confront. The third section outlines two alternative storm-damage scenarios, each of which is dependent upon how public administration copes with the crises. The final section offers some concluding observations on how the public administration community might want to prepare itself to cope with these crises and their possible aftermath.

THE GLOBALIZATION CHALLENGE

The globalization literature in international relations starts from three related empirical observations:

- Virtually no economic activity is purely local; investment, production, and consumption decisions around the globe are highly interdependent.
- Revolutions in telecommunications and information sciences have radically altered our appreciation of physical space. For all intents and purposes, the globe has become smaller, physical boundaries unimportant.
- Abetted by these revolutions, human social relationships have mirrored economic relationships. For significant groups of people in the world, communities and interests are transnational.

Taken alone, these observations are hardly startling. What makes them interesting from the perspective of IR theory is that they represent three intertwined dynamics that are at fundamental odds with a world of sovereign nation-states. The state has become, in a word, irrelevant.

Looked at in the long view of history, this is not a particularly surprising or unnatural development, globalization theorists point out. The nation-state emerged as the West's preeminent form of political organization only some three and a half centuries ago because it provided a framework of authority that was consistent with the military, economic, and ideological imperatives of the time. Developments in military technology—effective and mobile firearms, in particular—favored the interests of centralizing monarchs against entrenched feudal powers. The growth of market capitalism demanded a structure of law roughly coincident with larger, "national" markets and conducive to capital formation, trade, and enforcement of contract. Liberal trends in political thought, reflecting the age's broader philosophical renaissance, laid the foundations for territorially based sovereignty and ultimately for "national" identity.

These justifications grew even more powerful as the eighteenth and nineteenth centuries unfolded. The forces released by the Industrial Revolution in the West—rapid urban growth, redefined social roles, and democratiza-tion—found ready expression in the institutions of the nation-state. Per-haps most important, the nation-state was able to satisfy two fundamental security concerns. First, it served as a shield against external enemies, pro-viding citizens with "a common defense." Second, it ensured "domestic tranquility," guaranteeing a least a modicum of law and order at home. By the mid-twentieth century, the nation-state had no effective competitors as an organizational form anywhere in the world. For the leaders of the post–World War II decolonialization movements, the creation of a sovereign nation-state was such a *sine qua non* of human freedom and dignity that the number of countries in the world, measured by UN membership, grew from 51 in 1948 to some 185 today.

All these motives and rationales for the nation-state have essentially evaporated. Who now takes seriously the nation-state as a guarantor of se-curity? Missile technology has made territorial defense against other nations problematic at best.[16] The sophistication and ubiquity of terrorists has made territorial defense against bloody-minded individuals almost impos-sible.[17] Despite recent down-ticks in many major crime statistics—fuelled by an aging population and booming economy—government's ability to make citizens feel safe in their homes and on the streets has been declining for years.[18] Anyone who can afford to do so—individuals and corporations alike—now provides for their own security, as the proliferation of gated communities and private security firms attests.

And the nation-state is certainly irrelevant to international business. While government leaders may still feel compelled to *appear* to manage "their" economies, they increasingly seem out of their depth, Chaplinesque figures trying to direct careening traffic that is oblivious to their existence. With over a trillion dollars moving around the globe electronically each day, even the richest nations are subject to the vagaries of international eco-nomic forces, forced to share or even to cede their "sovereign authority" over economic policy to international currency speculators, investors, and bankers. In a parallel development, multinational corporations have been displaced by transnational corporations, entities that have no real national homes, national staff, or national allegiances, and that are nearly impervi-ous to national regulation.

What of the surge of violent "ethno-nationalism" that has racked the world in recent years? Isn't the state-seeking behavior of ethnic entre-preneurs from Quebec to Kurdistan evidence of the state's continuing vi-tality? For most IR theorists, the answer is "no." These movements testify not to the state's continuing strength but to its decline. It has been the growing weakness of central state authorities that has allowed separatism and irredentism to flourish. Bosnian Serbs (and Muslims and Croats), for instance, may think that establishing their own state apparatus—with flag, currency and seat in the United Nations—will accord them some tangible benefits, but they are demonstrably wrong.[19] Sovereignty is an outdated notion. Those that pursue it are chasing the ghost of another century. That won't stop the pursuit, of course, at least not in the short term. As globalization increases, the incidence and virulence of ethnic conflict, civil war, and other forms of violence—domestic, international and transnational— will undoubtedly also increase. But in the absence of what IR theorists term "exogenous territorializing pressures" it is likely that in the middle- to long-term, much of this violence will be unfocused and free-floating, akin more to the strife in the Congo, Somalia and Liberia than to that in Palestine or Northern Ireland.

Ironically but not coincidentally, as state capacity has declined, global policy challenges have multiplied cruelly. Trade in illicit drugs has long since reached epidemic proportions. The number of international refugees has soared from around a million in the early 1960s to nearly 30 million today. The average global temperature has increased by nearly a full degree Celsius in the past 120 years. Rainforests are said to be disappearing at the rate of eighty acres per minute, taking species and our ability to breathe with them.[20] Thus arises a vicious cycle: Globalization undermines the structures of governance that are needed to cope with the challenges of globalization.

THE THREE CRISES

If this synopsis of globalization is correct—and most IR theorists would find its broad outlines unexceptionable—what are the implications for public administration? In this section of the paper, I argue that the dynamics of globalization will generate three inexorable crises—of accountability, governance, and legitimacy. And as I shall argue in a later section, how these crises are resolved—if indeed they are resolvable—will have a determinative impact on the future of the American public service.

The Crisis of Accountability

Although public administration specialists routinely disparage the politics/ administration dichotomy as outdated and simplistic, we cling to its essence—

neutrally competent administrators faithfully executing the will of the people as articulated by elected representatives—as the normative centerpiece of our democracy. We assume that there is a fundamental accountability, flawed though it is in practice, between American public administration and an identifiable American polity.

Globalization undermines this assumption. Much of what American administrators will be asked to do in years to come will reflect the interests and desires of a far less tangible—and less accountable—global political community. In effect, American public administrators will be asked to enforce norms that have been set elsewhere—in the World Trade Organization, G-7 (or 8), International Monetary Fund, an environmental or energy summit, or even in a corporate boardroom. Sometimes the actors in this emerging global political community will have interests and desires that are at least arguably congruent with those of Americans, as may be the case, for instance, with the environmental accords that emerged from Rio and Kyoto. At other times, such congruence will be harder to find. In all such cases, however, transnational agenda-setting and decision-making will raise difficult questions about whose interests are being served in the administrative process.

Although such threats to American sovereignty—if indeed that is what they are—may seem at this point rather contrived, that is only because to date the dominant transnational forces in the globe have been reflections of American hegemony. With the decline of that hegemony, it is likely that the American state will feel the same pressures that every other state, albeit to varying degrees, has felt. The governments of Africa, and, to a lesser extent, Latin America, have long been considered weak, porous and unaccountable. But even Western European states have not been immune to this crisis of accountability, where national administrative systems are constitutionally obligated to implement European Union (EU) directives. Euro-skeptic conservatives in Great Britain vehemently oppose expansion of the powers of the EU because they dislike being ordered about, directly or indirectly, by unaccountable "Eurocrats" in Brussels. Leftists on the Continent are wary of extensions of EU power—especially creation of a single currency—because they feel that a tight central monetary policy will raise unemployment and provoke a neo-fascist backlash that national officials will be unable to combat. Right and left are thus united in the fear that transnationalized, globalized forces will effectively depoliticize decisions, rendering administrators unaccountable and citizens powerless—much as American Buchananite conservatives find common cause with American union activists to oppose NAFTA, GATT, and various other manifestations of globalization.

In principle, even in the face of such externalized agenda-setting there are two ways to maintain accountability. First, global decisions can be made subject to review and approval by existing representative political institutions before administrators begin to take action. If Congress approves an international treaty on greenhouse gases, for instance, then the American administrators who implement the provisions of that treaty are acting in furtherance of what has become legitimately derived American public policy. The second way to maintain accountability is to extend representative institutions beyond national borders. The effort to enhance the power of the Strasburg-based European Parliament is an example of such a strategy in the context of the EU.

Neither of these approaches is likely to stave off the crisis of accountability, however, at least not in the short term. Most of the transnational forces that are fueling the accountability crisis—economic forces especially—do not coincide with any geographic unit short of the globe itself, making organizing representation, at least representation in any traditional sense, a rather tricky business. In fact, the continuing weakness of the European Parliament suggests that even when there is a well-defined super-national geographic unit available it is not easy to develop a transnational political counterweight to transnational economic forces.

Moreover, the processes of globalization are seldom likely to present decisions that are as clearly defined or as subject to a transparent process as a greenhouse gas treaty. Global norms are likely to be imported into domestic administrative contexts in subtler, less obvious ways. How might this happen? First, even when transnational expectations are transmitted formally, in the shape of treaties or agreements, they are often so complex as to be beyond the practical reach of representative institutions. This is especially the case with respect to trade agreements—NAFTA and GATT were notorious for having gone unread on Capitol Hill—which, of course, are closest to the real heart, unfettered international economic activity, of globalization. Second, the professional norms that shape administrative action are likely increasingly to be transmitted by transnational policy communities.[21] Administrators in the Environmental Protection Agency in America routinely consult with counterparts around the globe; they also read the same journals, participate in the same e-mail list-servs, and attend the same professional meetings. This is equally true of officials in the US Treasury, the Public Health Service and any number of other agencies, including those at state and local levels of government. Third, as will be discussed in more detail below, many of the problems that will preoccupy tomorrow's public administrators will be deposited on the desks directly by the global system. The ability of domestic polities to define and control administrative agendas will be sharply limited as a consequence.

The Crisis of Governance

One of the chief effects of globalization, according to many IR scholars, is the "disarticulation of the state." This refers to an "unbundling" or "erosion" of the core functions of government—especially "redistribution, structural regulation . . . and the direct delivery of public services"—in the face of global challenges. [22] Put more simply, globalization means that government is less able to govern.

In some ways, public administration seems already to have faced-up to this problem. Osborne and Gaebler begin their book with the rhetorical question, Is government dead?[23] The answer they—and many observers like them—give is no, but it does in this new age need to be "reinvented," "re-engineered," "performance-based," "entrepreneurial," or "results-oriented."

This response is not unreasonable, and it may even have short-term salutary consequences. But it misses the basic point and is unlikely to produce lasting results. The problem is not *how* we should manage, but *whether* we can manage at all. To pursue Osborne and Gaebler's oft-cited rowing and steering metaphor, public administration has not only lost its oars but has its hand on a broken tiller as well. Although we may for a few years get a bit of steerage from it still, whether it can withstand the heavy seas of the next century is doubtful.

The basic dilemma is that governments increasingly confront problems that have their roots in other jurisdictions, problems that are genuinely global in origin and scope. Although one could argue that crime, for instance, has never been a particularly tractable problem, it was once at least a fairly localized one. The most serious externalities revolved around the legalities of pursuing bad guys across the county line. Today, local police departments must contend with drug-related crimes that have at least part of their origin in the jungles of Colombia or the highlands of Sinaloa, with street gangs that have branches in Moscow, Hong Kong, or San Salvador, and with fraud rings that are networked from Lagos to London. Public health departments still have to worry about sanitary water supplies and controlling outbreaks of infectious diseases; the sources of their worry have increasingly shifted from things like the run-off from Farmer Brown's dairy operation and shutting down the elementary school during a chicken-pox epidemic to emergency preparedness against terrorist attacks and the Ebola virus. In many parts of the country, education and social service administrators are overwhelmed by the problems of immigration, legal and illegal, induced by poverty, repression and civil war in distant lands. Transportation managers are trying to design systems that reflect, at least in part, deforestation in the Amazon basin and a depleted ozone layer. Economic development officials in Kansas and Kentucky seek strategies to counter the fact that people in China and Indonesia will work for a dollar or two a day.

Obviously what all these problems—and many more that might be mentioned—have in common is that their solutions, if they exist at all, are out of the reach of those who must cope with them. Reinventing government is not going to help some city manager shut down international drug trafficking, protect trees in Brazil, or alter the East Asian political economy; he or she simply has no buttons to push, no levers to pull that provide any traction. In fact, the sad truth may be that in the age of globalization problems will inevitably exceed the capacity of administrators to manage. This is not just because the problems of crime, urban decay, poverty, pollution, and so forth are complex and multifaceted—although that is true enough. Instead, it is because cross-border problems require cross-border solutions, which in turn hinge on inter-jurisdictional administrative coordination that is likely to be always at least one beat behind; although agencies may be able to cooperate effectively in discrete cases—FBI coordination with Kenyan and Tanzanian police officials in the wake of the 1998 embassy bombings is one recent example—long term strategic cooperation has fewer examples of success.[24]

Aggravating this problem, some globalization theorists say, is an impending fiscal crisis for government. James Davidson and Lord William Rees-Mogg reason that the Internet, off-shore tax havens, and accounting dodges for "virtual" corporations will make it extraordinarily easy for all but the lowest wage earners to avoid paying most taxes; in fact, they project that tax capacity in OECD nations will fall by 50–70 percent in the next century, despite expected frenzied efforts by the US and other leading nations to capture fleeing wealth.[25] Although this particular vision may seem slightly fevered, we have seen enough squabbling in recent years over taxation of activities on the Web to raise some legitimate questions. Should the state indeed become substantially "defunded," it is hard to see how administrators will be able to shoulder burdens that will surely require even greater, not fewer, resources.

The Crisis of Legitimacy

Taken together, the dynamics of the crises of accountability and governance produce a third crisis for public administration, that of legitimacy. An administrative service that is unaccountable but competent may cause anxiety, but will probably be accepted by those who are well served; some of the bureaucratic-dominant regimes in East Asia come to mind as examples. An administrative service that is incompetent but accountable may well be tolerated if it has some appeal to custom and tradition; many local agencies in the United States—sheriff's departments, small school districts, county courthouses, and so forth—fit this inefficient-but-quaint-and-cozy definition. An administrative service that is both unaccountable and incompetent has no legitimacy, and, absent a special set of circumstances, is unlikely to be able to sustain itself.[26]

Delegitimization pressures on public administration are likely to be felt from two different directions. First, globalization threatens the idea of *res publica*. According to the emerging norms of globalization, that which is private—particularly economic activity—is strengthened and sanctified; that which is public—particularly action that threatens private economic activity—is weakened and reviled. In the future, private contracts between sovereign sub-state entities and individuals—covering everything up to and including collective security—will make current efforts at privatization seem paltry and pathetic.[27] If there is no "public," can there be public administration?

An attack on the logic of administration itself is the second direction from which delegitimization pressures on public administration may emanate. Globalization will engender such philosophical disorder that legal-rationality as a system of thought—the foundation of bureaucracy and of modernity itself, at least in Weber's terms—is at risk. Traditional, neo-patrimonial, and post-modern paradigms will vie with the legal-rational, producing demands for radically different, nonbureaucratic, and perhaps nonadministrative organizational forms. If there is no "administration," can there be public administration? It is to these themes that we next turn.

SCENARIOS

How these crises will be resolved is not at all clear. Nor is it possible to know exactly what the implications would be for public administration of any particular pattern of resolution or non-resolution. Two scenarios, flowing from rough-hewn contrary assumptions, seem at least plausible, however. The first, which I term *global regime management*, assumes that these crises are resolved on reasonably favorable terms, projecting a fairly smooth transition from current understandings of accountability, governance and legitimacy to a new and rather different normative equilibrium. The second scenario, the darker of the two, assumes that these crises are not resolved at all. Normative turmoil, dissensus and fragmentation reign, producing what we might call *neomedieval administration.*[28]

Global Regime Management

The most favorable views of post-hegemonic global society assume that the core remaining functions of the nation state will be exercised by what are often termed "global regimes."[29] A regime is a set of "implicit or explicit principles, norms, rules, and decision-making procedures around which actors' expectations converge in a given area of international relations."[30] A few examples of the hundreds of current international regimes include the Bretton Woods monetary system (and its spin-offs and amendments), various commodity agreements (coffee, oil, tin, rubber, etc.), regional fisheries agreements, and the International Civil Aviation Organization (ICAO)–International Air Transport Association (IATA) system of regulating air transportation. Although some regimes stem from agreements negotiated by sovereign nation-states, what is distinctive about international regimes is their essential "non-stateness." They operate as *social* institutions—networks of interconnected roles and role expectations—that have authoritative political consequences.

Because this system assumes a relatively smooth transition from the Western state system and its embedded ideals, the day-to-day appearance of public administration under global regimes will be similar to what we know today. Administrative edicts will continue to be justified by reference to rational analysis and the rule of law. Indeed, appeals to science as the ultimate authority are likely to be even more persuasive than they are today, owing to the prominence of specialists in regime decision-making. Some sense of a transcendent public interest, albeit ill-defined, will remain in place to provide an orienting ethic for administrators. And reasonably clear functional boundaries will be maintained.

These similarities notwithstanding, global regime management will be a rather different enterprise from traditional public administration. To begin with, it will be substantially "de-territorialized," with a stripped-down, geographically rooted state "body" enforcing norms set by a powerful, non-geographically rooted non-state "head."[31] This will be a form of "virtual" public administration—analogues of which have been present in the private sector for some time—and will constitute a wrenching change for a discipline that has always been substantially defined by its territoriality.[32] Public administration *is* the management of public goods in a geographically fixed place—a city, town, region, state, and so forth. Questions of territory—centralization versus decentralization, field-headquarters relations, interagency coordination in the field, etc.—have always been at the heart of professional debates. Because "local"[33] policy discretion under global regimes—over safety standards, resource use, education, public health, and so forth—will be minimal, administrative entities that have any territorial identification (i.e., responsibility for overseeing activities within fixed geographical boundaries) will be geared simply toward enforcement.

This in turn suggests that to the extent that "national" administrative apparati continue to exist, they will be (a) far smaller than they are today and (b) even less glamorous. The interesting work—research and analysis, norm-setting, evaluation, and so on—in any given functional area will be carried on transnationally, within the institutions of the regime. Although "national" structures may persist for some time either as sources of personnel secondment or as direct participants in regime management, the growth in regime autonomy projected by theorists implies direct transnational recruitment of staff, after the current fashion of the World Bank, as the most stable long term pattern.

Because global regimes are highly differentiated functionally, it is unlikely that the need will arise for a single, even minimally integrated public service. Instead, each regime is likely to define its own needs and to manage its own human resources. In this respect, at least, it may prove easier for (former) American public administrators, used to working in quasi-independent fiefdoms, to adapt to global regime management than for counterparts in nations that have stronger integrative traditions.

I modified the word "American" in the paragraph above with a parenthetical "former" merely to underscore the obvious: Identity in a world of global regimes will be increasingly de-nationalized. Appeals to territorially rooted loyalty, patriotism, and distinct cultural traditions—especially for those involved in the "head" functions of regime management—will be extinguished. In their stead will rise even stronger attachments to non-spatially defined professional communities and, presumably, to the transcendent norms—rule of law, human rights, free markets, etc.—that are said to underlie emergent global society.

Such attachments will be essential to maintain responsiveness in a system that will see the eclipse of traditional methods of administrative accountability. For better or worse, some greater measure of intra-organizational democracy will need to replace what Emmette Redford once termed "overhead democracy."[34] This may manifest itself naturally in the open, non-hierarchical styles of communication said to characterize post-bureaucratic scientific communities.[35] Democratic regime management may also be encouraged by the growth of substantial numbers of transnational interest groups, which have proved quite capable of enforcing a broad view of "stake-holder."

Neomedieval Administration

Global regime management may be an unnerving scenario for those attached to or appreciative of the American public service if for no reason other than it implies the eventual disappearance of the American public service. It is a downright jolly vision, however, compared to that of its primary competitor, neomedieval administration. If the ascendancy of global regimes threatens the operation of traditional liberal democracy, at least it promises peace, prosperity and rationality. Neomedievalism offers none of this. It ushers us instead onto the darkling plain.

The neomedieval scenario is built on the premise that no stable authority structures will emerge from the rubble of the nation-state system once it collapses under the weight of globalization. Chaos, disorder and conflict will reign. Such institutions that persist or develop anew will have neither unchallenged bases of authority nor clearly established boundaries. Regime theorists and other institutionalists who believe that international cooperation will emerge from the ether in the post-state future are, for the neomedievalists, blinkered idealists.

Public administration, following the neomedieval vision, will be constrained, challenged and fragmented. Territorial boundaries will not disappear as regime theorists anticipate, but they will become more fluid. Just as the lords of feudal estates fought with one another (and with rulers higher or lower in the medieval caste hierarchy) for control of contested territories, so too will administrative elites spar, locality against locality, region against locality, region against region, for suzerainty. Although "turf warfare" is already a prominent feature of modern bureaucratic life, the conflict implied by neomedievalism would be far sharper, approaching a modern form of "warlordism." With no courts or overarching authorities to settle disagreements, recourse to violence would not be unexpected, especially if control of important resources—water or arable land, for instance—were at stake. Journalist Robert Kaplan, in a recent book about the American West that eerily echoes his prescient work on the Third World, suggests that this day is not really far off for the United States.[36]

The ability of public administrators to exercise power in a particular domain will be challenged not just by geographic rivals, but also by epistemic competitors. Legal-rationality will no longer be the only authority that justifies action. In a post-modern replay of medieval battles between science and tradition and the sacred and the secular, we can expect ceaseless conflict between fundamentally different *Weltanschauungen*, each with its own orienting values and standards of evidence. Exactly what these will be is hard to predict. Some may be identity-based, some regional, some religious or philosophical. One theorist projects that the "adaptive patrimonial" systems common now in the Southern hemisphere—in which "qualified state systems . . . no longer seek or even need to establish territorial, bureaucratic or consent basic political authority in the traditional sense"—will move North.[37] If so, we may expect the erosion of merit as an operating principle in personnel management, displaced by patron-client links and ties of ethnicity, religion or extended family.[38] The Mexican *camarilla*—a political clique based on kinship, educational ties, institutional loyalty or, less often, ideology that is integral to administrative advancement—may be a model for our neomedieval future.[39] There may, perhaps, be "space" for administration action along modernist, legal-rational, liberal democratic lines in a neomedieval world—but it is likely to be small and uncertain at best.[40]

While authority is fractured in the neomedieval scenario, with a shift of power to local and regional fiefdoms, there is still a strong element of the global in this vision. In fact, one of the neologisms that one hears neomedieval IR theorists use is "glocal," a formulation that is meant to stress the complex interplay of local and global dynamics in the post-state era. Bifurcation of identity is an especially important feature of neomedievalism, at least for the glocal elite: Those at the top of the neomedieval heap are fully plugged in, literally and metaphorically, to a web of global relationships. Race, religion, sex, and ethnicity recede as identifiers, as a new class of cultural *mestizos* arises, a class composed of high-technology knowledge workers, with worldly, sophisticated tastes in music, food, and architecture. At the same time, this elite has intensely local attachments as well, especially to places that offer appropriate "lifestyle" opportunities.[41]

What is lost in this special sense of localism, however, is a sense of *community* that is identified with place; community for the glocal elite becomes a cultural, non-spatial experience. This has enormous implications for public administration, implications not unrelated to our earlier discussion of territory in traditional administrative thought. To an extent even greater than is arguably now the case, administrators in a neomedieval world would work in the service of a narrowly drawn socio-economic class. Appeals to administrators to act in the interests of the broader community—meaning, in our terms, ourselves as well as those folks who live next door or just across the tracks—would be nearly nonsensical. Concern about "social problems" is likely to disappear from the administrative agenda, displaced by concerns for security and property rights. The fracturing of authority systems discussed earlier will reinforce this tendency. The "love thy neighbor" ethic that quietly underpins the modern welfare state—even the modern welfare-*reformed* state—is a fragile thing, anchored in philosophical premises unlikely to be widely distributed in neomedieval systems of thought.[42]

Because globalization is said to widen the gap between haves and have-nots, intensifying socio-economic and political stratification, this is a problem of no small consequence. Exactly what proportion of people will be wine-sipping Web surfers and what proportion will be disenfranchised wretches is impossible to know. If the patterns now characteristic of the Third World are any guide, the news is not good. Substantial populations will be relegated to "gray zones," working in parallel illegal economies at best, living as brigands at worst.[43] Higher walls and stronger gates will be the inevitable—and perhaps even sustainable— response of the elite. Mark Duffield argues that "[c]ontrary to conventional wisdom the main issue in the South is not that of poverty *per se*. It is the wide governance gap which allows elite survival strategies to be pursued regardless of the social cost."[44] Such survival strategies, transplanted to the North, will ultimately change the mix of people who work in "public" administration, emphasizing to an even greater extent than is the case today law, security and criminal justice. They will also wholly transform mechanisms of administrative accountability: Administrators will be responsible only to their immediate masters who, in the absence of even a pretence of liberal democracy, will be responsible to no one at all.

CONCLUSION: FLYING WITH THE OWL OF MINERVA

International relations theorists—social scientists in general, for that matter—have such a poor track record predicting the future that it may not be worth worrying about such dire globalization scenarios. Perhaps IR theory, like philosophy, is best viewed as *Nach-denken*, or afterthought. As Hegel noted in an unusually lucid passage, when it comes "to giving instructions as to what the world ought to be,"

> Philosophy . . . always comes on the scene too late . . . As the thought of the world, it appears only when actuality is already there cut and dried after its process of formation has been completed . . . The owl of Minerva spreads its wings only with the falling of dusk.[45]

Our very awareness of globalization thus may signal its decline. Recent turmoil in global markets and renewed talk of capital controls lend credence to this view. It may be that international *Kulturkampf*, not global interdependence, is in our collective cards, implying a reinvigorated (if militarized) nation-state, and hence reinvigorated (and militarized) public service.[46] In fact, the only thing we know for sure about the public service in the twenty-first century is that it will be substantially different from the one we have today; American administrative institutions have never stood still for more than a generation.

But we should not dismiss the warnings of IR theory too blithely. Even the poorest prophets prove accurate occasionally. And in this particular case we have a lot of prophets from a lot of different perspectives saying substantially the same thing: The state is in long-term decline, thanks in part to the forces of globalization. The main point of this paper has been that public administration in any recognizable form—and perhaps any acceptable form—is incomprehensible absent the framework of the state.

Having identified the dragon, it is traditional at this juncture in a work on public administration to list the steps that we must take in order to slay it: We need to do *x, y,* and *z* to improve budgeting, increase the quality of the workforce, reduce urban poverty, etc. This is not a realistic option given this topic. With globalization, we may well just be along for the ride.

But still, to mix poetic metaphors, we do not want to go gentle onto that darkling plain. Is there anything the public administration community can do to prepare itself for globalization? Probably not—at least not if the question is construed as, How can we safeguard American public administration? More productive will be trying to fashion new administrative institutions that can ride out the storm of globalization without sacrificing accountability, competence, and legitimacy. I do not pretend to know what these might look like. I would guess, though, that the difficulty of forging global representative institutions will give added impetus to privatization, which allows accountability to a nebulous public to be redefined as accountability to distinct customers. For those absolutely core public functions, shriveled though they may be, we have excellent models of what *not* to do in our current leading international organizations, where overstaffing, nationality-based patronage and under-responsiveness have been far too common. The real challenge will be to wed accountability, the traditional essence of public service, to the best characteristics of transnational business—leanness, seamless diversity, and adaptability—to create a new global public administration.

In attempting to meet this challenge, public administration theorists have a unique role to play. The closest historical analogue, perhaps, is the work public administrationists undertook during the New Deal, when, thanks in no small part to their efforts, the tremendous growth in the size and complexity of the American state was managed with far more ease than would otherwise have been the case. Now, in the face of globalization, our colleagues in the rest of political science have again left aside the "mere details" of administration. Can public administration once more rise to the occasion?

NOTES

1. For instance, Homen Boschken, "Strategic Alliances, Mergers, and Combinations in the Global Ocean Shipping Industry"; Scott Tarry, "Global Airlines, Local Airports: The Role of Public Administrators in Developing and Preserving Aviation Links to the Global Economy"; Thomas Lynch and Cynthia Lynch, "Global Ethics and Public Administration: Possible or Foolish"; and Yu-che Chen, "Utilization of Business Self-regulation for Accomplishing Agencies' Missions in the Era of Global Interdependence: The Case of ISO 14000."

2. This admittedly impressionistic observation is based on conversations with colleagues who teach in MPA programs, and a scan of the Web-sites of some of the major schools.

3. One recent example is the Elmer B. Staats lecture ("Reflections on the Role of Regions") given by Energy Secretary Federico Peña at the 1998 National Academy of Public Administration Conference (June 5, 1998, Boulder, Colorado). Quoting Richard Knight and Gary Gappert's (eds.), *Cities in a Global Society* (Newbury Park, Calif.: Sage Publications, 1989), Secretary Peña argued that "[a]s national welfare becomes increasingly tied to the global economy, global linkages that are maintained primarily by cities become more critical. The nation's economy depends on

the competitiveness of its cities, the quality of their relationship with other cities, their global linkages, and their access to knowledge resources." President Clinton and Vice President Gore have also made responding to global economic and environmental challenges central elements of their rhetoric.

4. Although many observers have made this case, Gerald Caiden does so especially thoroughly and directly in his article, "Globalizing the Theory and Practice of Public Administration," in Jean-Claude Garcia-Zamor and Renu Khator, eds., *Public Administration in the Global Village* (Westport, Conn.: Praeger, 1994).

5. This point was made specifically by Renu Khator and Jean-Claude Garcia-Zamor in the "Introduction" to Garcia-Zamor and Khator, *Public Administration in the Global Village*, p. 1. A substantial number of papers devoted to comparative administration in recent issues of *Public Administration Review*, including a symposium in the January/February 1998 issue celebrating the silver jubilee of the Section for International and Comparative Administration (SICA), suggests that this idea has resonance.

6. See Khator, "Managing the Environment in an Interdependent World," in Garcia-Zamor and Khator, *Public Administration in the Global Village*, p. 93.

7. This point, perhaps the essence of the globalist world-view, has been made by virtually everyone who has written about the phenomenon. Examples range from pollution to transportation to public health.

8. Susan Tolchin, "The Globalist from Nowhere: Making Governance Competitive in the International Environment," *Public Administration Review* 56 (January/February 1996): pp. 1–8. Jessica Mathews points out that "nearly all 50 American states have trade offices abroad, up from four in 1970, and all have official standing in the World Trade Organization (WTO)." See Jessica T. Mathews, "Power Shift," *Foreign Affairs* 76 (January/February 1997): 61–2.

9. Phillip J. Cooper et al., *Public Administration for the Twenty-First Century* (Forth Worth: Harcourt Brace, 1998), 16–17. Fred Riggs adds that once we begin to appreciate the depth of our ethnocentrism we might finally learn both "which of our [administrative] practices can be usefully exported and which are relevant only at home" and which "of the reforms we would most like to carry out at home will undermine the viability of our system of government." See Riggs, "Public Administration in America: Why Our Uniqueness Is Exceptional and Important," *Public Administration Review* (January/February 1998): 29–30.

10. The International City/County Management Association (ICMA), for instance, has received substantial funding from USAID to develop an International Resource City program, which involves U.S. municipalities offering direct technical assistance to counterpart cities in the developing world in the areas of solid waste and wastewater management, finance and budgeting, citizen participation, emergency management, transportation, local economic development, and performance measurement. Although the assistance nominally runs only one way, the program is sold to American cities in part as a way to get on board the global bandwagon. The

National League of Cities has been encouraging similar exchanges and has also mounted a series of direct city to city trade missions. Organizations such as the International Union of Local Authorities (IULA) exist in part to encourage "international municipal relations."

11. This is essentially the position that Peter Drucker takes in his essay, "The Global Economy and the Nation-State," *Foreign Affairs* 76 (September/October 1997). "In all probability," he says, "the nation-state [and, by extension, its administrative apparatus] will survive the globalization of the economy and the information revolution that accompanies it" (p. 160).

12. The subtitle of Harlan Cleveland's book on the challenge of globalization, *Birth of a New World*, is "An Open Moment for International Leadership." When he says that the outcome of this exhilarating age "depends on what we—millions of us in diverse cultures in various parts of the world—do to build together a civilization that will, as the United Nations Charter puts it, 'promote social progress and better standards of life in larger freedom,' " Cleveland summons the best of that can-do spirit.

13. See, for instance, Peter G. Brown, "The Legitimacy Crisis and the New Progressivism," *Public Administration Review* 58 (July/August 1998). Although Brown rounds up all the usual transnational suspects—unrestrained capitalism, pollution, urban sprawl, etc.—he suggests that a "regrounded" public administration can advance global progress, human rights and deliberative democracy even as the state "is rapidly losing its power to forces above and below it" (p. 291).

14. From Matthew Arnold's *Dover Beach*:

> The Sea of Faith
> Was once, too, at the full, and round earth's shore
> Lay like the folds of a right girdle furl'd
> But now I only hear
> Its melancholy, long, withdrawing roar,
> Retreating, to the breath
> Of the night-wind, down the vast edges drear
> And naked shingles of the world
> Ah, love, let us be true
> To one another! for the world, which seems
> To lie before us like a land of dreams,
> So various, so beautiful, so new,
> Hath really neither joy, nor love, nor light,
> Nor certitude, or peace, nor help for pain;
> And we are here as on a darkling plain
> Swept with confused alarms of struggle and flight,
> Where ignorant armies clash by night.

15. See, for instance, Daniel Deudney and G. John Ikenberry, "The Logic of the West," *World Policy Journal* 10 (Winter 1994).

16. In the same week that North Korea successfully test fired a medium range ballistic missile, with a trajectory over Japanese territory that unleashed a torrent of protest, the Clinton Administration, in a presumably unrelated story, announced that the costs of continued ABM development were spiraling upwards to such an extent that development may have to be curtailed. See "North Korea Fires Missile over Japanese Territory," *New York Times*, September 1, 1998, p. 1, and "Antimissile Systems' Costs Test U.S. Ability to Pay, General Says," *Washington Post*, September 3, 1998, p. A4.

17. In the wake of the Nairobi and Dar Es Salaam embassy bombings, U.S. officials repeated what has become a Western mantra: Effective defense against terrorists willing to sacrifice their own lives is impossible. This statement, however empirically true, is unlikely to contribute to a renewal of faith in the utility of the nation-state.

18. The Gallup Survey reports that the criminal justice system ranks at the bottom of America's institutional confidence list—alongside Congress and organized labor. *The Gallup Poll Public Opinion 1997* (Wilmington: Scholarly Resources, Inc., 1998), p. 132.

19. Having spent considerable time working in Bosnia in the past three and half years, I can attest that these states are extraordinarily frail, incapable of some of the most basic governmental functions. For more than a few players in the Balkans (and elsewhere in Central and Eastern Europe and the NIS), government has provided a (thin) cover for criminal activities.

20. These and other depressing statistics may be found in *State of the World 1997: A World Watch Institute Report on Progress toward a Sustainable Society* (New York: W.W. Norton, 1997).

21. This is one of the implications of the "new institutionalism" school of sociology. For an example, see Martha Finnemore, *National Interests in International Society* (Ithaca: Cornell University Press, 1996).

22. Philip Cerny, "Globalisation as Durable Disaster," *Civil Wars* 1 (Spring 1998): 43.

23. David Osborne and Ted Gaebler, *Reinventing Government: How the Entrepreneurial Spirit Is Transforming the Public Sector* (Reading, Mass.: Addison-Wesley, 1992), 1.

24. Perhaps the best counter-example here is the difficulty American and British intelligence agencies experienced coordinating activities against the Soviet bloc during the Cold War. Despite a common enemy, common strategic issues, and a very nearly common culture, the "special relationship" was often strained and tense, characterized by nearly as many games played against the respective "cousins" as against the communists.

25. *The Sovereign Individual: How to Survive and Thrive during the Collapse of the Welfare State* (New York: Simon & Schuster, 1997). Davidson is chair of Britain's National Tax Payers' Union, Rees-Mogg is former editor of the *Times* (London).

26. One such set of circumstances is common enough in the developing world: Unaccountable and incompetent administrative agencies retain sufficient power, thanks to moribund civil societies from which they are able to extort taxes and help-ing hands from transnational actors (the IMF, aid agencies, etc.) that provide addi-tional funds, that they are able to stay afloat.

27. See Mark Duffield, "Post-modern Conflict: Warlords, Post-adjustment States and Private Protection," *Civil Wars* 1 (Spring 1998), especially his discussion of the increased acceptability of private armies such as Executive Outcomes and Gurkha Security Guards, 93–4.

28. I borrow this term from Cerny, "Globalisation as Durable Disaster."

29. The creation and persistence of regimes absent (American) hegemony has ac-tually been at issue among regime theorists. I take the view here that regime forma-tion and other forms of international cooperation are not dependent on the exis-tence of a hegemon. For an elaboration of this perspective, see Oran R. Young, *International Cooperation: Building Regimes for Natural Resources and the Environ-ment* (Ithaca: Cornell University Press, 1989).

30. Stephen D. Krasner, "Structural Causes and Regime Consequences: Regimes as Intervening Variables," in Stephen Krasner, ed., *International Regimes* (Ithaca: Cornell University Press, 1983), p. 2.

31. This distinction between "head" and "body" is from Richard Rosecrance, "The Rise of the Virtual State," *Foreign Affairs* 75 (July/August 1996).

32. Rosecrance uses the term "virtual state" to describe the life of government after globalization. He notes, correctly, that many major transnational corporations have long since become virtual, consisting largely of finance, R&D and marketing departments, with all "real" work (i.e., manufacturing) jobbed-out to other entities. See Ibid., 51.

33. Indeed, the very meaning of territorially rooted words such as "local" and "re-gional" will be problematic owing to the globalization of issues.

34. Emmette S. Redford, *Democracy in the Administrative State* (New York: Ox-ford University Press, 1969).

35. See, for instance, "Democracy Is Inevitable," in Warren G. Bennis and Philip E. Slater, *The Temporary Society* (New York: Harper Colophon Books, 1968).

36. Robert D. Kaplan, *An Empire Wilderness: Travels into American's Future* (New York: Random House, 1998). See also Robert D. Kaplan, *The Ends of the Earth: A Journey at the Dawn of the 21st Century* (New York: Vintage, 1997).

37. Duffield, "Post-modern Conflict," 76.

38. A sort of test case of the regime v. neomedieval perspective in personnel ad-ministration now seems to be shaping up around the globe. The World Bank and similar organizations have established a fairly clear international human resources regime, based on Western civil service standards, to which they seek to hold the states that seek their resources. From Africa to Central Asia to Latin America, na-tions are explicitly directed by Bank staff to establish by-the-book merit systems.

This has, in the view of many observers, produced a new wave of what Fred Riggs once called "formalism"—administrative systems that are formally Western, but really either traditional or patrimonial or something else altogether. Whether the Bank and its allies or corrupt local politico-administrative elites will win in the long-term is still an open question.

39. See Roderic Ai Camp, "*Camarillas* in Mexican Politics: The Case of the Salinas Cabinet," *Mexican Studies* 6 (Winter 1990).

40. Cerny makes an argument to this effect. See "Globalisation as Durable Disaster," p. 60.

41. Kaplan, *Empire Wilderness*, is especially evocative on the growth of "glocalism" (although he does not use the term, referring instead to "post-urban pods") in the modern American West.

42. For an elaboration of this argument, see Glenn Tinder, "Can We be Good without God?" *Atlantic Monthly* 264 (December 1989).

43. Cerny, "Globalisation as Durable Disaster," 54–5.

44. Duffield, "Post-modern Conflict," 87.

45. G.W.F. Hegel, *The Philosophy of Right*, trans. T. M. Knox (London: Oxford University Press, 1949), 12–13.

46. It is in this direction that Samuel Huntington's analysis leads. See his *Clash of Civilizations and the Remaking of World Order* (New York: Simon and Schuster, 1996).

CHAPTER NINE

POLITICS OF TRANSITION FROM THE ADMINISTRATIVE TO THE FACILITATIVE STATE

CHESTER A. NEWLAND

The Civil Service Reform Act (CSRA) of 1978 marked a transition from the administrative state to the facilitative state—that is, from an ideal of big, centralized governments that dominate and perform many activities to one of more limited-but-effective governments that facilitate self governance and responsible performance by varied private and public organizations and individuals.

Theories and practices of the administrative state were central to reform politics and later to the American welfare state and the five-decades-long Garrison State of World War II and the Cold War. It was a multigenerational period of increasingly heavy reliance on government as chiefly responsible for economic and social affairs. While oriented to increasingly Big Government, in America it remained mostly anchored in Enlightenment values of constitutional democracy in pursuit of the Good Life and reasonableness—rule of law and human dignity. In many other nations in the twentieth century, faith in governments to solve most if not all problems took more strictly ideological forms, and command economies and authoritarianism kept much of the world fragmented.

In today's emergent era of a facilitative state, global dynamics make insular national economies and closed or narrowly bounded societies dominated by governments increasingly ineffective. By comparison (less than contrast) with the previous era, a facilitative state rests more on three inter-related sets of theories and practices of responsible governance: an increas-ingly global market economy, more open societies with aspirations for re-sponsibly self-governing people and organizations, and limited but effective governments that facilitate constitutionally reasonable conditions for re-sponsible achievement of those aspirations.

These theories were somewhat discernible in CSRA politics in 1977 and 1978. However, while such thinking was important, CSRA efforts focused more on two other levels: the politics of public administration and the pol-itics of civil service. All of these levels of politics—nation-state, public ad-ministration, and civil service—are dealt with here. However, these are too integrally connected to be analyzed discretely.

This chapter first deals briefly with all of these with respect to the ad-ministrative state. Next, it focuses on politics of the CSRA as a development in a continuing transition toward theories and practices of a facilitative state. Finally, without depth of detail about the Office of Personnel Man-agement (OPM) and other topics that are discussed in other chapters of this collection, it deals with political, economic, and social thought and prac-tices of contemporary governance, particularly as they relate to the politics of *The Future of Merit.*

POLITICS AND THE ADMINISTRATIVE STATE

Three aspects of administrative state politics are discussed in this section. First, it is useful to recall that late eighteenth- and early nineteenth-century reforms were not designed as an escape from politics. That came later. Sev-eral other consequences, "intended or not" and both positive and negative, became dominant by the Golden Years when public administration largely defined important dimensions of the American nation state. One of these "consequences" is discussed second here: the emphasis in public adminis-tration theory and in politics on executive aggrandizement of power within a separation of powers theory of the Constitution, rather than shared au-thority and responsibility within a system of checks and balances. Discussed third here are co-joined issues: big bureaucracy and partisanly neutral, de-tached, professional expertise. This last set of issues accounts for concerns about how to reconcile bureaucracy with democracy. A recurrent issue is whether those in public service should be mostly instrumentally employed as agents of partisan politicians and their momentary transactions and/or whether they properly serve a larger role under law in service of constitutional fundamentals.

No Escape from Politics in a Civic Culture

It was Donald Devine, the second director of the Office of Personnel Management, who wrote succinctly in the winter 1982–3 issue of *The Bureaucrat* that, in governmental affairs, escape from politics is a fanciful idea. Principal reformers during the rise of the administrative state would have agreed, except that they rejected partisan spoils in favor of merit staffing. The purpose was not to isolate civil service from politics but to rid governments of incompetence and corruption. Reflecting during the centennial era and following years on civic values of the Enlightenment, long-lost to Robber Barons in the views of agrarian and newly urban reformers, many became vigorously engaged in politics. They did not try to escape civic duty. Most embraced it and public service as connected principles of the essential community of constitutional democracy.

The purpose of early administrative state reforms was to develop a civic-based field, linking citizens, politicians, professionally expert administrators, and relevant academicians in a shared enterprise. The distinction between politics and administration was initially one of different roles, not an ends/means dichotomy that would isolate public service from responsible politics.

Separation often followed, however, especially in later years of the administrative state, as bureaucracy and bigness became joined in American national government during the 1930s and the following decades of the Garrison state that grew to dominance during and after World War II. Public administration as a field also adopted theory and politics that largely separated its academic development from important trends in law. In practice, however, administration did not become entirely trapped in that cul de sac because law is fundamental to American government; thus, the field survived its political mistakes despite major disconnects between theories and realities. But its self-inflicted disabilities would weaken the field of public administration, leading to a loss of autonomy—and failed politics—in the closing years of the administrative state.

Bureaucracy and public-service detachment in later years of the administrative state are touched on after the next section on public administration's sustained support of executive aggrandizement.

Executive Aggrandizement and Disintegrative Politics

America's constitutional framers embraced separation of powers with checks and balances to create a workable small but strong national government while protecting cherished liberties and valued properties. They envisioned shared responsibility to accomplish essential public purposes. However, early in the administrative state era, public administration embraced an ideology of separation of powers in support of ever-expanding presidential powers. In the 1960s, disintegrative politics of elections and of both political parties occurred, followed by demolition politics. That inheritance threatens a facilitative state. It adversely impacts civil service and much else.

In the absence of a shared, transformational ideal of politics in support of a workable system of checks and balances, separation of powers is a formula for gridlock or even disaster. Embraced early on by American public administration in theories of executive-dominated government, it became linked with the notion of a politics and administration dichotomy (in contrast with a distinction between self-serving partisanship and neutral service under law) that became a brief and faulty formula for autonomy of public administration.

Congress has often embraced presidential aggrandizement, as in the CSRA of 1978. But Congress has also struggled often to enlarge shared authority as a principle, as in the Budget and Impoundment Control Act of 1974 (that led to unintended consequences of greatly exacerbated separation and failures to resolve budgetary problems collaboratively), in the Inspectors General Act of 1978 (partially frustrated by President Reagan's Inauguration Day firings), in the Goldwater-Nichols Defense Reorganization Act of 1986 (now presenting "Joint Staff" culture challenges), and in the Government Performance and Results Act of 1993 (oriented to some facilitative state ideals).

Presidential aggrandizement took center stage during the Great Depression and World War II. It remained there during the five decades of the Garrison state, continuing the drama of executive branch empowerment. Added to the examples noted above, Congress sought in the War Powers Act of 1973 to reestablish checks and balances, and provisions were added in 1980 and 1991, to little avail, as this aspect of administrative state politics continued—continues! Impeachment actions against Presidents Nixon and Clinton scarcely altered such institutional basics.

Disintegrative politics of today have roots in the *Powerful Presidency Paradigm* of the closing decades of the administrative state era. Fragmentation into "electoral parties"—*Four Party Politics,* in the terms of James M. Burns[1]—separated presidential and congressional politics during an important window of time. Some fracturing of the old "iron triangle" of interest groups, bureaus, and congressional committees followed. Other forces contributed to a growing system of fragmented, entrepreneurial, demolition politics: media impacts on elections since 1956, including costs of mass marketing of contrived images and issues; development of Political Action Committees (PACs) and various deep-pockets financing mechanisms; and the rise, starting with 1950s pollsters and marketers, of a for-hire political consulting industry as the entrepreneurial successor to former political machines.

Connections of presidential aggrandizement and disintegrative politics to civil service and *The Future of Merit* are evident in growth of a culture of transactional politics (exchanges of narrow partisan and self interests in political markets) at the expense of transformational ideals (civic and market responsibility and facilitative government under law). Nixon's Watergate was a principal example of the administrative state years. Similarly astounding examples from today's facilitative state era, including exotic spoils staffing of the Department of Defense under Clinton, are noted later.

Big Bureaucracy and Neutral Public Service

An image of detachment of U.S. civil service from civic community, not simply from politics, grew into a problem by the 1960s. A challenge became not simply one of distance of civil servants from the people served but also that the civil service culture increasingly became oriented to bureaucratic organizations served.

Partisan neutrality was an issue in the Eisenhower years, following the Republican takeover of the executive branch after a twenty-year absence. That led to creation of Schedule Cs and other efforts to facilitate political responsiveness. Following elections of both Eisenhower and Kennedy, transition task forces relied on external policy advisors, significantly reducing dependence on career leadership of the Bureau of Budget. Special assistants in the Executive Office of the President (EOP) assumed increasing roles under Kennedy and Johnson, leading to creation of the Domestic Council in the Nixon Administration, along with restructuring in July 1970 of the Bureau of Budget into the Office of Management and Budget.

Although struggles to reconcile big bureaucracy with democracy and responsiveness under law to political leadership came to a head during the

Kennedy and Johnson years, that period continued what had become considered, under Truman and Eisenhower, more-or-less Golden Years for the professional practice of public administration. John W. Macy, Jr., a careerist, became not only chair of the U.S. Civil Service Commission but personnel adviser in the EOP under Kennedy, continuing under Johnson, who favored reliance on professional expertise of civil servants. Macy enjoyed strong presidential support under Johnson for "merit system principles": democracy (open competition and equal opportunity); job ability (expertise and performance); and "freedom from political influence or tribute"[2] (neutrality for civil service stability and continuity). Macy also routinely stressed administrative priorities of Presidents Kennedy and Johnson: "efficiency, responsiveness to the public, flexibility of administration, and adaptability to change."[3]

The greatest civil service change was Kennedy's Executive Order 10988, authorizing a modified form of collective bargaining—a political payback for AFL-CIO support in Kennedy's narrow 1960 election victory—one-half percent and Chicago, in political punsters' terms.

President Johnson's politics produced a less visible change that was a closer fit to traditional merit-system ideals: policies designed to attract talented professional experts to top government jobs. Actions included establishment of the Federal Executive Institute (FEI) in 1968 to facilitate development of a "supergrade cadre" of civil service leadership to deal with growing challenges of big government. That vision included deconstructing bureaucracy to create a responsible culture in the upper reaches of civil service despite inevitable bigness of "modern" government (reaching back to Graham Wallace's Great Society ideals instilled in Johnson during his youth).

Despite such presidential support for the idealized merit model, how to reconcile burgeoning bureaucracy with the increasingly turbulent politics of the 1960s continued as an alarming question. Professor Frederick C. Mosher of the University of Virginia probed for answers in *Democracy and the Public Service*, first published in the year that the FEI started. That analysis quickly became a modern classic, revised in 1982, during the transition period to a new era. It helped to define civil service preoccupation with "responsiveness" throughout the Nixon administration and then, after Mosher chaired the National Academy of Public Administration's (NAPA's) Watergate study for Congress, into Reagan's presidency. In the late 1990s, this same fundamental political issue recurred, but with a reverse concern about civil service "instrumentalism" in the facilitative state.

THE TRANSITION STRUGGLE AND THE CSRA

Responsiveness to the president and Congress became a conflicted mantra of the U.S. Civil Service Commission during the Nixon years, while leaders struggled to reconcile it with growing concerns about preservation of government under law. Presidential control of the civil service became the theme of the Carter administration, and Congress approved that policy under the CSRA. Together, those developments are the first of four subjects in this section on the transition to today's struggling version of facilitative government. The other three topics are performance and productivity, reorganization politics of 1977–8, and interest groups involved in CSRA politics.

Responsiveness to the President! . . . and to Congress and the Law?

Robert Hampton, Civil Service Commission chair during the Nixon administration, observed at an Interagency Advisory Group (IAG) conference that the president and top officials often complained about lack of employee responsiveness. Hampton noted that, at a cabinet meeting, he responded with a question: Have you told them what you want done? Purpose and responsiveness thus became combined themes of civil service politics.

Nixon's OMB directors, George Shultz and Roy Ash, were both sympathetic with Hampton's question. They heard complaints by civil service professionals that enhanced clarity of purposes and structures was needed. A barrier to that was the complicated and expensive Planning, Programming, Budgeting System (PPBS) imposed with ideological uniformity government-wide in August 1965 by President Johnson on advice of RAND Corporation consultants. In June 1971, PPBS was dropped as a one-best-way, government-wide requirement (but it continued in the Department of Defense). Ash later urged agencies to manage flexibly in terms of results, but career civil servants, trained in the culture of big, centralized bureaucracy, insisted on a more definitive, uniform prescription. In April 1973, a requirement for management by objectives responded to those wishes.

However, despite such positive Nixon-era management developments, responsiveness of the personnel administration apparatus continued as an issue that became politically explosive. The U.S. Civil Service Commission (CSC) continued trends started under John Macy toward decentralization of authority and responsibilities to agencies, with some flexibilities to be responsive to agencies' differences. Ralph Nader's Public Interest Research Group took umbrage at that. In the summer of 1971, it undertook a study of the CSC, and in June 1972 it issued two reports, *The Spoiled System* on civil service and *Behind the Promises* on equal employment opportunity. A version of the Nader studies was published in 1975 as a book by Robert G. Vaughn, with a subtitle, *A Call for Civil Service Reform*. It was particularly critical of adoption by the CSC of a consultative role, responsive to organizations: "The agencies themselves, or the President, come more and more to be seen as the Commission's clientele, a situation well illustrated in the case of John Macy."[4] Criticisms of CSC's facilitative posture continued: "A part of the Commission's rationale for its present role and perspective is that the vast federal establishment requires decentralization of efforts. . . . Functionally, the Commission has become a purveyor of technical services to the management of the federal agencies. Politically, it has become a servant of the administration in power at the moment, defining itself as the 'President's Personnel Office.' "[5] By contrast with the 1990s, that was not a compliment.

One year after the Nader group's initial criticisms, the CSC began an investigation that "disclosed the existence of politically-oriented employment practices intended to bypass and evade merit system requirements."[6] It found that "special referral units" to get appointments for specified individuals operated in the General Services Administration, the Department of Housing and Urban Development, and the Small Business Administration that "were distinguished by the degree to which they were organized and systematized—and by the extent to which they were successful in evading merit system requirements."[7] The CSC ordered termination of these units and practices. Then, in 1974, in an unprecedented move, CSC issued disciplinary charges against 19 officials. In 1975, the CSC lost in an Administrative Law Judge's (ALJ) decision on its first action, and then it lost on appeal. A second case resulted in another ALJ rejection, and the CSC gave up on all nineteen cases.

More damaging to the CSC were counter charges against it by those accused. Charges were that CSC Commissioners and others had made referrals and that CSC officials had prior knowledge of politically oriented employment systems in agencies and did nothing to stop them. These allegations became the subject of hearings before the House Post Office and Civil Service Committee in March and April 1975. In October, CSC's Executive Director Bernard Rosen appointed a Merit Staffing Review Team to investigate CSC's operations. Retired Philadelphia Regional CSC Director Milton I. Sharon was appointed as director. On May 7, 1976, the *Sharon Report* was submitted to the CSC. It documented several "special referrals" and other merit system violations. To put it mildly, these findings gave responsiveness a bad name—temporarily.

But that was not all. During these years, Senate Watergate hearings and other sources revealed a Nixon administration manual (written by Alan May and others, but usually called *The Malek Manual*, named after OMB's deputy director) that explained how to use civil service "selective certification" to further partisan presidential aims. This "secret" document was published in January 1976 by *The Bureaucrat*, which had already sponsored a Washington conference in 1975 on "the civil service crisis." Also, Nixon appointee Professor Richard Nathan published an unapologetic book, *The Plot That Failed*,[8] explaining a deliberate strategy to facilitate direct responsiveness to presidential interests by filling positions with Nixon partisans.

Following Watergate, the Ford administration collaborated with the House Committee on Post Office and Civil Service to pave the way for civil service reforms to follow the 1976 elections. Also, CSC Chairman Hampton met at the FEI to consider a statutory basis for labor-management relations for consideration after November 1976, irrespective of the election outcome. Alternative reforms of the appeals apparatus were likewise considered.

Also, the EEOC charged CSC with inadequacies, and the CSC found deficiencies in the EEOC, as each agency conducted recriminating audits of the other. At one point, the politics took the physical form of a fight on stage at a plenary session of the International Personnel Management Association conference in St. Louis. The American combatants were separated by Canadian attendees.

In short, the Golden Era of the administrative state was on its last leg if not long-gone, and struggles toward a successor political regime in the system of civil service were more-or-less forcefully underway. Two connected questions took on growing political importance: Responsiveness to what . . . and/or to whom? What constitutes merit?

Performance and Productivity

Performance and productivity became central as partial answers to these questions. Annual productivity increases averaged 3 percent during four decades before the late 1960s. A first-time negative productivity change and a trade deficit confronted Nixon's administration in its first year. In 1970, the president appointed a National Commission on Productivity to deal with causes and solutions. The following year, a Joint CSC/GAO/OMB Project on Measuring and Enhancing Productivity in the federal sector was created, with strong leadership by Comptroller General Elmer Staats, along with Bob Hampton. Earlier, with Staats's involvement, a five-agency study of productivity measurement in the federal government had been initiated by President Kennedy in 1962, and a major study was published in 1964. However, PPBS soon pushed that project aside by consuming all available resources. The 1971–3 Joint Project resurrected performance measurement and results evaluation, along with related civil service programs, as ways to improve productivity.

These policies were in much the same vein as the GPRA in the 1990s. However, they were not in legislation, and they were largely terminated by the Carter administration. Carter's appointees were initially preoccupied with other priorities, including Zero-Based Budgeting and related "policy analysis" under leadership of OMB Director Bert Lance; Equal Employment Opportunity Commission (EEOC) reform (including removal of CSC authority over such appeals), promised personally by Carter to Coretta Scott King and other New South supporters; and civil service reform, the centerpiece in Carter's campaign against "the Washington establishment."

As noted earlier, nonperformance became a theme in a campaign to subject the federal civil service to presidential control. Negative politics prevailed. Carter's critics charged, as the nation's economy soured, that the Administration lacked understanding to deal with larger conditions of national performance and productivity, as it became bogged down in internal details of government. Short-term interest rates reached over 30 percent, and even ordinary certificates of deposit were in the 16 percent range. In those respects, by the time that CSRA became law, the nation's political judgment was that the Carter administration was Jello that would not set.

Irrespective of that political context, performance continued as a major theme in civil service affairs. But it is important to recall that successful CSRA enactment, while matched with major successes in EEOC and in some social affairs, was largely overtaken by failed performance of the Carter presidency on broader measures of the economy and in international affairs. CSRA implementation would pay a high price for those major political failures.

Reorganization Politics and CSRA

Reorganization authority to carry out Carter's plan did not exist when he entered office. As a result of Watergate, that authority of every president from Franklin Roosevelt to Nixon was not renewed. When Carter sought its restoration, the Congress controlled by his own party had reservations about again granting that tool of presidential aggrandizement. Congressman Jack Brooks of Texas (House Governmental Affairs chair), who had supported extensive authority for President Johnson, surmised that it would be unconstitutional to grant it to Carter. However, as a result of Johnson's Civil Rights Act of 1964, Brooks's Beaumont–Port Arthur district was becoming New South, and he had to yield—a bit.

The Reorganization Act of 1977 (P.L. 95-17; 5 USC 901) was signed into law on April 6, 1977, less than three months after Carter entered office. However, the president had to settle for relatively few bare bones: authority only for sub-cabinet levels and for no more than one reorganization proposal before Congress at the same time, with constraints that made more than three a year impossible and over two quite difficult.

Carter kept his campaign promise and submitted his EEOC Reform as Reorganization Plan 1 under the 1977 authorization, and it became law in 1978. Only after that could the President submit his Reorganization Plan 2 on May 23, 1978. On March 2, however, Carter had already informally sent to Congress the broad outlines of his civil service proposals. Long before then, principal proposals had been developed with both expert analysis and broad political participation.

That process was facilitated by a Personnel Management Project, established in 1977 with Dwight Ink as executive director and with nine task forces to deal with proposals. Transparency was a key strategy. Its offices at Buzzard's Point, on an isolated but colorfully well known Washington waterfront, were wide-open, and task force professionals were "all over town" to consult on and formulate proposals. This relatively open, highly participatory process was in sharp contrast to the secrecy of the generally closed strategy of the administrative state's Brownlow Committee.

CSC Chair Scotty Campbell moved quickly to secure support for civil service reform among members of the National Academy of Public Administration, working especially with those with Hill respect, like Elmer Staats, comptroller general. Dwight Ink was both a NAPA leader and the national president elect of the American Society for Public Administration for 1978–9. These and many others who became associated with CSRA politics were familiar with the 1930s Brownlow Committee proposal to replace the bipartisan CSC with a personnel agency headed by a professionally qualified, fixed-term presidential appointee. That became the essence of the proposed CSRA, but without the Brownlow provision for professional qualifications.

Many experienced personnel-community leaders in 1977 opposed replacement of the bipartisan CSC by an Office of Personnel Management

(OPM) to be headed by a presidential partisan. They recalled that Congress had earlier rejected President Roosevelt's Brownlow proposals to terminate bipartisanship, even when combined with strict requirements, like those in GAO, for professional qualifications and insulation against presidential control. Bernard Rosen, former CSC executive director, for example, struggled diligently for alternatives. However, David Henderson, former House Post Office and Civil Service Committee chair who had worked in 1975–6 on other designs for reform, did not seek reelection in 1976. Coherency in congressional committee politics was fast evaporating before Henderson's departure, and a free-for-all culture helped CSRA supporters to open doors for change and to close others. "Obstructionists" of the professional personnel community, including the IAG, could be and were largely shunted aside.

Scotty Campbell observed after leaving office that, in part, he was taught politics in support of CSRA by congressman Mo Udall. Early in the 1977 political game, Campbell followed his professorial habit of highlighting distinctions and probing solutions. He said later, "One day after a hearing, Mo Udall motioned me to follow him to his office. When we got into his office, he pointed to a chair and said, 'Professor, sit down.' [Which I did.] I must teach you something. Up here we don't try to sharpen differences, we fuzz them.' "[9] Besides learning to create political fuzz, Campbell accepted the reality that CSRA politics was to consist largely of negative attacks on the federal civil service: demolition. Campbell explained that negative statements were "a reflection of what the politicians believe is public opinion."[10] Undermining public service, without much regard for long-term damage to government, was a successful means in 1977–8 to secure adoption of CSRA. The aim was to enhance presidential power, and that succeeded in the fashioning of the OPM.

It succeeded in large part because Republicans shared that aim. Congressman Edward Derwinski, a key Republican in both committee and floor deliberations, observed during negotiations that future Republican presidents would benefit from responsiveness of the civil service—without need to resort to a *May-Malek Manual*.

However, one provision *fuzzed* by professionals into the final CSRA as adopted went largely unnoticed. While a Brownlow Committee–type term limit remained low-key in proposals, a fixed-term limit was in fact adopted: an incumbent OPM director could not continue in office beyond the term of appointment without reappointment and Senate confirmation. That provision was invoked when the term of OPM's second director ended. Political complications surrounding his continued exercise of authority at OPM then led to withdrawal of his nomination for a second term.

The most crucial change in the CSRA process was accomplished by Reorganization Plan 2. Once Congress allowed that, it had to adopt the Civil Service Reform Act of 1978 to revise Title V and to empower the OPM and other new agencies. The Plan 2 structural changes technically reorganized the CSC into the new, relatively tiny Merit Systems Protection Board (MSPB) to serve as an adjudicatory body. Some observers, recalling civil service scandals of the 1970s, initially saw the MSPB as an intentionally down-bred toothless chihuahua—all the watchdog that presidential partisans would ever want. However, a legally empowered Office of Special Counsel was attached to (while separate from) the MSPB, rather like the NLRB structure (and the Federal Labor Relations Authority [FLRA] structure, to be noted next below, from which the design was derived). During early CSRA implementation, concerns of skeptics seemed to be confirmed. As a result of inability to win Senate confirmation of Carter's partisan nominee for Special Counsel (and his failure to send up another name) and because of quite visible conflicts between MSPB's able chairperson and the acting counsel, MSPB's image was damaged from the outset. When the Reagan administration entered office, that situation continued, but with more grace. A young Republican who was a top graduate of UCLA's law school became special counsel, but he lacked knowledge, experience, and specialized interest needed for the position. The new board chair, while capable interpersonally, held views that were in conflict with both long-settled jurisprudence and substantive constitutional law. These were inconsistent with success in highly technical public personnel law and key agency leadership. Only MSPB's research arm gained early respect, while its more visible units had much to overcome to earn regard in later years.

Before CSRA, a Federal Labor Relations Council (FLRC) created by executive order and chaired by the CSC chair was the adjudicatory body for the limited version of collective bargaining. It was converted in 1978 into the FLRA, with three presidentially appointed members and with continuation of a pre-existing Office of General Counsel similar to the NLRB's structure. The word *authority* (not board or council) in the agency's name was by design to indicate the importance of respect by all parties for the *rule of law*. For unions in 1977–8, that was politically attractive, since their bottom-line issue was for a statutory provision for labor-management relations. Unions opposed CSRA without such a provision. And the Carter administration blundered politically and lost much by refusing to include such a provision in their initial CSRA submission to Congress.

Task Force Six of the Personnel Management Project had completed work well in advance of time needed to submit a proposal, and unions, agencies, and congressional offices all had that. It basically called for including in the CSRA a modestly refined version of existing executive order provisions. Except that they wanted judicial review of FLRA decisions added as a minimum, unions were willing to accept that proposal.

However, Scotty Campbell decided, against expert advice, not to include anything on labor-management relations in the CSRA until union leaders first agreed to support other provisions, including those on performance pay and SES. Union leaders were generally supportive of CSRA, but they could not have survived internal union politics had they publicly supported the performance-pay provisions (such as those for GM 13–15 levels that proved unworkable when later implemented). Thus, unions wrote their own version of Title VII, using the Task Force Report and working with congressional staffers. Having lost the initiative, the Carter administration submitted a Title VII proposal to Congress on May 12 (two months after submission of other provisions). When Title VII finally reached the Committee of the Whole in August, it contained extensive language drafted by unions that the administration could not support—including an expanded scope of bargaining to include management functions such as job classification, promotion standards, and Reduction-in-Force (RIF) standards and processes. The administration's bungling had created too much antagonism among usual Democratic Party supporters to permit them to do much. Republican Congressman Derwinski handled the matter, signaling to unions GOP willingness to adopt statutory LMR language, but: "I suggest to those who are interested in true reform that it is important to correct Title VII so that it essentially conforms with the Executive Order, as originally proposed [by the Task Force], and supported by the administration."[11] Thus, the original Task Force provisions were adopted, but with the addition of judicial review of FLRA orders, except those involving arbitration awards and unit determination. When initially implemented by mostly marginally qualified and unqualified political appointees, judicial review became a crucial provision, since FLRA determinations earned little respect and more reversals than affirmations in appeals to circuit court.

Other Interest Groups' Issues and Politics

Besides the labor management relations issues just discussed, Hatch Act repeal was a major union issue. Veterans' preference and EEO were also large political issues for external interest groups. Among civil servants as "internal interest groups," performance pay, SES provisions, and merit protection and employee rights were highly political issues.

Hatch Act repeal was a nonstarter in combination with CSRA. The reason was simple: Republicans and many Democrats opposed it, and they had votes to defeat the CSRA if it included Hatch Act repeal. Thus, Carter and Campbell promised that, after passage of CSRA, they would sponsor separate Hatch Act repeal. Once they got Title VII, unions agreed to defer on the Hatch Act.

Veterans' preference was both a gender and a generational issue during the transition years away from the administrative state. But in 1978, it remained politically sacred on the Hill. Early on, Congressman Jack Brooks directed the LMR Task Force manager to inform others that CSRA as a whole would get nowhere if officials dared challenge the essence of veterans' preference.

EEO, on the other hand, was sacred downtown: as noted earlier, Carter had run on that issue and would not swerve from it. Besides EEOC reform, a bottom-line commitment was inclusion of EEO as a "critical performance standard" for supervisors, managers, and executives. Failure to meet that requirement in individual performance reviews was to result in mandatory exit. John Macy's earlier emphasis on "democracy in staffing" included EEO, and some changes occurred, but not enough to impress authors of the Nader Report or many others. Merit was clearly defined by Senator Ed Muskie to include EEO in the 1971 Intergovernmental Personnel Act, but changes at upper levels remained slow. By contrast, the CSRA provisions soon produced a "quota-like response," facilitating something of a diversity revolution. Merit was, in practice, redefined by CSRA for a new era.

Performance pay and executive bonuses were Scotty Campbell's issues. As an economist, he *believed*. Crafted into the CSRA were assumptions that economic incentives, much more than civic and public service values, are *the* basic motivators for performance. That set of issues has been researched and elaborated upon too extensively for repetition here.[12]

SES provisions and developments are dealt with in other chapters. Only political dynamics related to the transition from the administrative to the facilitative state era are touched on here. Those include a failed Nixon administration proposal in 1971 of a Federal Executive Service (FES) to be 25 percent noncareer. To compel civil service responsiveness, Nixon's White House sought a provision for one-year term appointments of careerists; the CSC proposed five-year terms; the final proposal to Congress was for a fixed three-year, renewable contract; Congress rejected subjecting career executives to presidential control by the fixed-term proposal. In 1977–8, the ratio of non-career to career SES members again became an issue, settled at maximums of 10 percent noncareer and 5 percent limited-term. Fixed contracts were considered but rejected in favor of annual performance reviews with "critical performance factors" and other requirements for continuation or exit.

The most fundamental theory issue in SES provisions was the old one of the administrative state era: executives as generalists and/or specialists. Generalist theories in support of "an elite corps" had been around since the 1920s, but realities of the administrative state were that top careerists were mostly highly specialized scientists, engineers, lawyers, and security affairs professionals. Those experts commonly had "iron-triangle links" with Congress and associations of leaders in their specialties. Congress was not about to give up those essential connections for government oversight and lawmaking to support presidentially controlled generalists. That issue surfaced again in OPM's April 6, 1998, draft *Framework for Improving the Senior Executive Service*. Since the SES is the topic of a separate chapter, that development and others are not discussed here.

In terms of CSRA as a transition marker to a facilitative state, the most important merit change was adoption of provisions already noted that accelerated movement toward gender and racial diversity. With respect to employee rights, two sets of political policies were crucial: 1960s–70s Supreme Court decisions against the doctrine of employment at will and supporting property rights in the job were accepted almost without challenge (although a brief effort to reverse was mounted in the first Reagan term); negotiated grievance procedures and union representation in protection of employee rights became remedies of choice, but in a redress system of multiple venues and appeals. These administrative redress provisions were departures from past theories and practices, and politically intended jurisdictional overlaps have presented major problems ever since.

TODAY'S FACILITATIVE STATE

The administrative state era stressed the predominant importance of government and "rational principles" of bureaucracy for its administration. From the mid-1970s through the 1980s, reaction produced a period in which government was devalued. Thatcherism and Reaganism even connoted hostility toward government generally. Reagan's first inaugural address expressed definitive disillusionment: "Government is not the solution to our problem; government is the problem."[13] That period of reaction against government is briefly discussed as the first topic here. Then facilitative roles of government are noted.

Laissez-Faire Reaction against the Administrative State

Letting people do as they choose came as a reaction in the 1970s–80s against big, bureaucratic government of the welfare/Garrison state eras. In the United States, while the reaction was partially against big government, it was mostly positive in support of social self governance and a responsible market economy. However, extremism against government briefly matched earlier excesses that had elevated it to dominance. Two examples outside of civil service illustrate this: (1) international developments leading to and following the collapse of the former Soviet Union and (2) domestic cutbacks on external economic and internal administrative regulatory functions. These are noted here both to illustrate the political theory that impacted the period of initial CSRA implementation and to stress the importance of facilitative government, including effective civil service.

Fiscal crises of the welfare state hit most established industrial countries by the end of the 1960s. Causes were associated with impacts of globalization on national economies—movement toward a world-level economy and global communications. In constitutionally democratic socialist countries of Europe, reaction that became most familiar was led by Britain's Prime Minister Thatcher. While similar American reaction against big nation-state government was basic to President Carter's campaign against Washington, it was Reagan who best typified the changed political culture.

The collapse of command-and-control economies of authoritarian states of the former Soviet Union and its colonially controlled countries of Central and Eastern Europe resulted in part from similar developments. Soviet problems mounted from Reagan's strategic "Star Wars" and related policies designed to destroy the communist system. It collapsed. In the wake, caught in a period that more-or-less discounted the importance of governments, the West largely applied politics of laissez faire to the former Soviet Bloc. That failed. Foundations for market economics, such as laws and a culture of lawfulness did not exist, and they were initially almost beyond comprehension. Foundations for social self governance, such as civicness, industriousness, and saving and self reliance were often absent. Capable and honest civil service systems did not exist. It became clear that hostility toward government was not an answer, any more than the wrong-headed theory of the total state and big government had been. Governance became the preferred design internationally by the mid-1990s, stressing three components: social self governance, more-or-less global market economy, and facilitative government, particularly including professionally expert and law-abiding civil service.

Domestically within the United States, examples of similar transition struggles were numerous in the 1980s. America's banking deregulation (a result of transactional politics) and the later $400+ billion bailout jarred faith in ideological laissez faire. Illicit drug commerce and culture since the 1960s have provided daily lessons about both the necessity of government and limitations in what it can accomplish. These examples from many sources illustrate realities that have moved America toward general embrace of *three-dimensional governance*, including facilitative government that is limited but strong.

Reaction against government of the administrative state explains in part the CSRA. Initial implementation under Scotty Campbell was characterized by imposition of partisan control over OPM, an increase in partisan appointees from 3 to 30, more-or-less, and some talk of "flexibilities" for agencies. Major cut-backs in OPM budgets and staffing followed in the first Reagan Administration and continued into Clinton's National Performance Review (NPR)/National Partnership for Reinventing Government (NPRG), with repeated reductions and market-oriented restructuring, including staffing and investigations and, especially, load-shedding in training. Policies set in 1993 called for agencies to cut costs of administrative positions, including personnel, by half by 1999. Between 1993 and 1997, "the number of civilian personnelists across government decreased by about 8,900 employees (or about 21 percent)."[14]

Roles of the Facilitative State

Facilitation of collective actions, rather than determining and doing most of them and dominating society and markets in the process, is today's dominant theory of the role of the state. For example, it is the view set forth by the World Bank in its *World Development Report, 1997: The State in a Changing World*.[15] That theory is much like an Enlightenment-era vision of limited but empowered government. In short, it is a contemporary theory of transformational polity in which the state serves mediating roles among social and economic institutions, facilitating values creation.

The idealized image of the streamlined state in that theory is of government serving as a catalyst for private creativity and helping people and organizations to balance forces of change and stability. Both internationally and domestically within America, experience of the past two transitional decades has demonstrated several basic roles and institutional features of such facilitative government. Among others, these include facilitation of integrity; real-time, trustworthy information; market discipline; and social and physical infrastructures.

CIVIL SERVICE AND POLITICS OF A FACILITATIVE STATE

The two decades following passage of the CSRA have been characterized by a stark contrast: an increasingly rapid pace of social, economic, and technological changes which streamlined, facilitative government is expected to mediate—and sometimes snail-like, limited use of the 1978 Act to make responsive changes in human resources management (HRM) beyond reductions of OPM's capacities and enlarged partisan politicization and control of civil service.

Small but strong is an ideal of facilitative government. Strong central, facilitative leadership of the institution of civil service is essential to such government. Under CSRA, such leadership has been limited, while more has been done under such programs as Total Quality Management under OPM Director Newman in the Bush administration and, more recently, through the GPRA. Limited innovation under CSRA is first discussed in this section. Next, deficient theory and politics—false dichotomies—that partially account for deficient facilitative leadership are discussed.

Strong Central Facilitation for Decentralized HRM Responsibility

Three examples of failure to provide strong central leadership under CSRA for responsive, merit-based, and efficient and effective civil service are (1) deficient use of demonstration project authority, (2) deficient merit oversight and thickening political layering, and (3) deficient policy leadership for needed reforms, as in redress procedures. It must be noted, however, that innovations, such as 1998 proposals on the SES and consultative OPM services have been developed.

Demonstration Project Authority and Agencies' Needs
A most glaring example of failure to meet facilitative requirements of the past two decades is the extremely limited use of personnel demonstration

project authority. CSRA specifies that no more than ten such projects may be underway at one time; no more than five thousand employees can be covered by a project; and that five years is the maximum time of a project. The original purpose of that provision was facilitation of HRM innovations, with prospects of transfers to other agencies or to civil service generally.

However, from the outset in the Carter administration, OPM failed to provide facilitative leadership provided for by CSRA. The first Demo Project had to be pushed by the China Lake "Nav Air" advocates and University of Southern California researchers to secure Navy action and to budge OPM's inaction. According to June and September 1998 GAO Reports,[16] that situation has continued for twenty years at departmental levels and OPM. Only eight Demo Projects have been implemented in two decades, and only four have been completed. Congress has made special authorizations. More important today are Pilot Projects authorized by the Government Performance and Results Act of 1993 and flexibilities encouraged through the Clinton/Gore NPR/NPRG.

Merit Oversight and Thickening Political Layers

Special referral units that became 1970s storm centers now facilitate political appointment by name referral in Washington without much apparent criticism or oversight by OPM, MSPB, or GAO. Paul Light's 1995 book, *Thickening Government*, documents how partisan layering also now extends deeply into the field service.

With respect to public service merit, the most significant facts reported in the 1998 *Starr Report* may be these: "White House officials arranged for Ms. Lewinsky to get another job in the Administration. 'Our direction is to make sure she has a job in an Agency,' Patsy Thomasson wrote in an email message on April 9, 1996. Ms. Thomasson's office (Presidential Personnel) sent Ms. Lewinsky's resume to Charles Duncan, Special Assistant to the Secretary of Defense and White House Liaison, and asked him to find a Pentagon opening for her. Mr. Duncan was told that, though Ms. Lewinsky had performed her duties capably, she was being dismissed for hanging around the Oval Office too much. According to Mr. Duncan—who had received as many as 40 job referrals per day from the White House—the White House had never given such an explanation for a transfer."[17] In the uproar that followed release of *The Starr Report*, nothing was heard from OPM or MSPB about the Lewinsky name referral or others at DOD reported by Mr. Duncan, and little was mentioned by others about the nonmerit means by which she earlier got her White House internship.

A decade earlier, ten years after CSRA, concerns about growing failures under the Act led to creation of the National Commission on the Public Service—the Volcker Commission. That group criticized "the growth in recent years in the number of presidential appointees,"[18] and it made twelve proposals, including reduction by at least one-third in numbers of partisan presidential appointees.

Instead of reductions, increases have continued. Paul Light's 1995 book, subtitled *Federal Hierarchy and the Diffusion of Accountability*, shows that vertical and horizontal increases in numbers of partisan appointees have been inexorable products of the presidency.

Needed Policy and Implementation Leadership

Facilitation of HRM innovations was a major purpose of the CSRA. As noted earlier, Demonstration Projects were authorized as key means to accomplish that. However, OPM has been relatively limited in its capacity to provide facilitative leadership, in part because it has been increasingly crippled in size and influence since 1981.

Although OPM has often provided useful technical leadership, including on employees health insurance, retirement, SES, and training, it has not been able, in politically sensitive areas, to provide much policy leadership. One glaring example is the administrative redress system. In 1977–8, unions, EEO advocates, agencies, and traditional personnelists all had favored methods to protect federal employees against adverse agency actions and prohibited personnel practices. Most employee advocates also favored inclusion of all sorts of redress venues into CSRA to provide "multiple bites of the apple." Although the visible and noisy politics of CSRA focused on making it easier to get rid of poor performers, the real politics of drafting resulted in creation of four independent adjudicatory agencies to handle employee complaints and appeals, plus judicial review, including *de novo* trials in discrimination cases.[19] Despite congressional concerns in the late 1990s, partisan politics continued to be against much real reform, just as in 1978.

Damaging Dichotomies versus Diversity

Damaging dichotomies account for many difficulties in transitioning the federal civil service from the administrative state to a new facilitative state era. Two false dichotomies that are most troublesome politically are briefly discussed below: (1) markets versus a legal system framework, and (2) instrumentalist versus constitutive, professional civil service. A third dichotomy is then considered in conclusion: transactional versus transformational politics.

The False Dichotomy of Markets versus Legal System

Struggles to escape from the negatives connoted by Big Bureaucracy of the administrative state era have included embrace of a false dichotomy: public-sector uses of entrepreneurial, flexible, and competitive market mechanisms versus a reasonable rule of law. In practice, the two are not irreconcilable. However, failures to reconcile them are especially evident in some Reinvention-in-Government efforts, including political aspects of the NPR/NPRG that frame issues in terms of laissez faire responsiveness to the customer or the presidency versus legal authority and responsibility. That false dichotomy is understandable, given distortions of law-based bureaucracy in constitutional government through legal technicalities and parsing of words (President Clinton's, *it depends on what the meaning of is is?*). Law as a search for reasonableness, as defined in Western jurisprudence and in most American public administration, is entirely consistent with essential flexibilities, under law, for effective government.

Reasonably interpreted and applied, law is essential to all three dimensions of today's governance: market economics, social self governance, and facilitative government. Contemporary rejection of some arcane legal systems and processes of civil service (such as today's redress system) in Big Bureaucracy does not require throwing out the baby of reasonable, law-based civil service or faithful execution of the laws with the dirty bathwater of legal nitpicking gone amok.

The False Dichotomy of Instrumentalist versus Professional Civil Service

Responsiveness of civil service to elected political officials versus adherence to the Constitution and authoritative law is another false but often-practiced dichotomy. On one side, it assumes that elected politicians generally do not share respect for legal frameworks of constitutional government. Too often, a few do not. On another side, it assumes that career civil servants do not share respect for responsibilities and authority of elected officials. Too often, a few do not. This old conflict reaches back before famous exchanges from 1935 and 1941 between Herman Finer and Carl Friedrich on administrative responsibility.[20]

At a deeper level than undisciplined assumptions, civil service serves both instrumental and constitutive roles. Responsiveness to elected officials under a rule of law is fundamental. Tensions in balancing responsiveness to partisan officials with faithful execution of the law are challenging. That is one reason why civil service is called work. But it is doable. An either/or dichotomy between the two is not. As noted earlier, there is "no escape from politics." So long as the Constitution prevails, there must also be "no escape from law" for politicians and military and civil servants.

MERIT IN PUBLIC SERVICE AND TRANSACTIONAL AND TRANSFORMATIONAL POLITICS

Dichotomous separatism has plagued both theory and practice of American public affairs since the beginning of the administrative state, when a highly useful distinction was made between political and administrative roles in shared civic enterprise.[21] In practice, that analysis of roles was not intended to separate the inseparable responsibility of public servants—political or career—to both popular sovereignty and constitutionally based law. Extremism soon followed, however, and politics and administration were often made a false dichotomy until the 1950s, when a reverse academic extremism even rejected essential distinctions in political and administrative roles. That resurrected the earlier, somewhat settled dispute over instrumental versus constitutive civil service responsibility. It also undermined foundations of autonomy of public administration as a field, as some partisans concluded that, if it is all political with no role distinctions, then it should all be the responsibility of political officials. As noted above, a false dichotomy was reborn, leading some to reject constitutive civil service responsibilities under law. That problem continues in struggles to create a responsible facilitative state.

Underlying extremist dichotomies that have damaged civil service and other public institutions are similarly distorted theories and practices of *transactional* and *transformational politics.* Transactional, instrumental politics came to prominence as *the theory* in the 1950s, as Harold Lasswell and others defined politics in terms of who gets what, when, where, and how; political industries arose in polling, marketing of candidates, and financing of commercialized election campaigns, lobbying, and law suits. While it is easy to portray with accuracy much that is faulty in such politics of the moment, transactional politics has also produced many transformational results, particularly in helping to move American society toward multicultural inclusiveness and creativity of more diverse social and economic values and means to produce and enjoy them. In today's facilitative state, refined transactional tools of law, political science, economics, and other social sciences are used domestically and internationally in public values creation and accomplishment. That is what transformational politics is also about when shared values sustain enriched civic, social, and economic conditions of civilization. In short, a separatist dichotomy of these concepts is false.

In politics of CSRA and its implementation, some bad results of extremist and harmful transactions are easy to identify: the complex redress system produced and sustained by self-interested civil service groups; the initial performance pay system, with assumptions as adopted that flew in the face of research findings; special referral systems of appointment, as between the Clinton White House and DOD; and fragmented, weak central institutions for HRM leadership. Yet, when reinforced by shared responsibility of both Congress and the executive branch, as in the GPRA, flexibilities under law to accomplish desirable results are achievable.

Many problems blamed on transactional politics are due to marginally qualified political officials below top agency heads who are appointed to positions with highly knowledge-based responsibilities for which some are woefully inadequate. That was a major error in CSRA: elimination of legally enforced qualifications standards for political appointees to crucial technical positions that do not require Senate confirmation. Transactional politics does not have to be characterized by incompetence, corruption, and sleazy immorality and commonly is not, as much of American history and some contemporary practices demonstrate. Prior to CSRA of 1978, qualified experts with responsible partisan credentials were available and passed qualifications reviews. But, without a supportive legal framework that facilitates excellence in politics, it is difficult for elected leaders to follow quality transactional standards that are likely to produce transformational results. In short, consideration of *The Future of Merit* needs to make meritorious politics, not escape from politics, a highest priority. If that can be accomplished, merit in career civil service will easily follow. For such merit in both political leadership and career civil service, respect for a Rule of Law and faithful execution of the laws is essential.

Globally, trends define the present era in terms of three dimensions of nation-state governance that make it clear that the dominating Big Government ideal of the decades of the administrative state has nearly passed—for the moment, at least. Social self governance and market economics are today's parallel ideals, but experience has demonstrated that, without facilitative government, those are impossible. Such government is ideally limited but strong. It must especially exercise legal authority to implement constitutionally framed standards of integrity, trusted access to basic indicators/information, market disciplines, and social and physical infrastructures, including security affairs. Effective civil service institutions—including competitive merit, devotion to the public good, and adherence to fundamental law—are vital to such facilitative government. Erosion of effectiveness of such central administrative institutions threatens the dispersed authority ideal of limited but strong government to help facilitate societal self governance to sustain America's fundamental constitutional values of human dignity and a rule of law.

NOTES

1. James M. Burns, *The Deadlock of Democracy: Four Party Politics in America* (Englewood Cliffs, N.J.: Prentice Hall, 1963).

2. John W. Macy, Jr., *Public Service: The Human Side of Government* (New York: Harper & Row, 1971), 17.

3. Ibid.

4. Robert G. Vaughn, *The Spoiled System: A Call for Civil Service Reform* (New York: Charterhouse, 1975), 3.

5. Ibid., 4–5.

6. Milton I. Sharon, Director, Merit Staffing Review Team, *A Self Inquiry into Merit Staffing* (Washington, D.C.: U.S. Civil Service Commission, May, 7, 1976), 1.

7. Ibid.

8. Richard P. Nathan, *The Plot That Failed: Nixon and the Administrative Presidency* (New York: Wiley, 1975).

9. Alan K. Campbell, "The Institution and Its Problems," *Public Administration Review* 42 (July/August 1982): 305–8, 306.

10. Ibid., 307.

11. Edward Derwinski, "Remarks on the House Floor, *Congressional Record* 124 (1978): H8460-75, H8463.

12. Edward E. Lawler, *Pay and Organizational Effectiveness: A Psychological View* (New York: McGraw Hill, 1971). For early critiques of merit pay under CSRA, see Phil Godwin and John Needham, "Reframing Reform—Challenging the Assumptions for Improving Public Employees' Performance," *Public Personnel Management* 10 (Summer 1981): 233–43. Also see Jone L. Pearce and James L. Perry, "Federal Merit Pay: A Longitudinal Analysis," *Public Administration Review* 43 (July/August 1983): 315–25.

13. "Inaugural Address of President Ronald Reagan," *Weekly Compilation of Presidential Documents* (Washington, D.C.: U.S. Government Printing Office, Week ending January 23, 1981): 1–5, 2.

14. U. S. General Accounting Office, *Management Reform: Agencies' Initial Efforts to Restructure Personnel Operations* (Washington, D.C.: GAO/GGD-98-93, July 1998), 1–2.

15. World Bank, *The State in a Changing World* (Oxford: Oxford University Press; and Washington, D.C.: The World Bank, 1997).

16. U.S. General Accounting Office, *Civil Service Reform: Observations on Demonstration Authority, the Use of Official Time, and the Administrative Redress System* (Washington, D.C.: GAO/GGD-98-162, June, 24, 1998); and GAO, *Performance Management: Aligning Performance with Agency Goals at Six Results Act Pilots* (Washington, D.C.: GAO/GGD-98-162, September 1998).

17. Kenneth Starr, *The Starr Report: The Independent Counsel's Complete Report to Congress on the Investigation of President Clinton* (New York: Simon & Schuster Pocket Books, 1998), 92–3.

18. National Commission on the Public Service, Paul A. Volcker, Chair, *Leadership for America: Rebuilding the Public Service* (Washington, D.C.: National Commission on the Public Service, 1989), 7.

19. GAO/GGD-98-160.

21. Carl J. Friedrich, "Responsible Government Service under the American Constitution," in Friedrich et al., *Problems of the American Public Service* (New York: McGraw-Hill, 1935). Herman Finer, "Administrative Responsibility in Democratic Government," *Public Administration Review* 1 (Summer 1941): 335–50. For 1990s perspectives, see a splendid review of four books: Douglas F. Morgan, "Bureaucracy and the American Constitution: Can the Triumph of Instrumentalism Be Reversed?" *Public Administration Review* 58 (September/October 1998): 453–63.

22. For more detailed analysis on the administrative state era and on CSRA politics, see Chester A. Newland, *Public Administration and Community: Realism in the Practice of Ideals* (McLean, Va., 1984); and Newland, "The Politics of Civil Service Reform," in Patricia W. Ingraham and David H. Rosenbloom, *The Promise and Paradox of Civil Service Reform* (Pittsburgh: University of Pittsburgh Press, 1992), 63–89.

CHAPTER TEN

THE FUTURE OF MERIT

HUGH HECLO

Earlier chapters have provided grounds for drawing a number of conclusions about the merit system for high level civilian employees in the federal
government. Before drawing any conclusions, however, we would do well
to recall that this is only one piece of a larger picture. Little has been said in
this volume about military personnel, the most rigorously organized and
disciplined portion of the nation's workforce. Instinctively, every reader
knows that "merit" is meant to characterize the system for managing military personnel, though from the outside it is often difficult to gain a realistic sense of how that particular merit system works. Our chapters have also
not dealt very much with the middle and lower levels of the federal workforce or with the growing number of indirectly employed, contract employees. And we have had nothing to say about the state and local levels of
public service. Obviously there is much more territory to explore if one
wants a rounded picture of the merit concept in the government workforce.

THREE SIGNPOSTS FROM THE RECENT PAST

Nonetheless, the area surveyed by the prior nine chapters does cover an aspect of the federal workforce that is crucial for our system of government.
Civilian employees who hold top administrative management positions are

in a vital linkage position between the big ideas and aspirations of political figures on the one hand and the nitty-gritty work of organizations on the other. In not only domestic but also international and defense agencies, this is tough, demanding territory where governance is given operational definition. Typically it is where the desirable runs up against the doable, where new blood encounters concern for precedent, where politics meets the rule of law.

The preceding chapters make three preliminary points quite clear. Although they may seem obvious, each one carries an important message in pointing toward the future of merit.

In the first place, the federal higher civil service is inextricably bound up with broader play of political power. It is power contested quadrilaterally—between the Republican and Democratic parties, between presidential appointees and permanent officials, between the executive and legislative branches, and between the politicians and public opinion.

For example, in chapter one James Pfiffner describes how the parties' battle over the role of government during the past generation has set the context for delegitimizing and fragmenting the civil service. Later in chapter four, Aberbach and Rockman show the one clear success of the 1978 reform has been political—providing political appointees with a tool to promote responsiveness from top civil servants; the two authors aptly entitle their larger Brookings study (of which this chapter is a part) "In the Web of Politics." Chapter three by Carolyn Ban highlights an account of how a multiyear, multimillion dollar effort for government to learn by evaluating the effects of its reform was abruptly ended by a change in political leadership. Likewise it appears that in the 1990s, the Clinton administration's National Performance Review shunned any effort to monitor the effects of its own reforms and reported in the vein of "good news boosterism" out of a straightforward political desire to pump up public support. What all these examples point to is the idea that internal civil service controversies—issues that seem rather narrow concerns for personnel specialists—provide channels through which broader, external political pressures are variously absorbed.

Second, it seems reasonable to conclude that there is nothing that might be termed institutional leadership of the higher civil service. In using the term institutional leadership we are not simply speaking about organized ways for some people to tell other people what to do. "Institutional leadership" refers to certain participants' committed ability to infuse processes and organizations with value beyond the technical requirements of the task at hand.[1] Institutional leadership seeks to promote and keep faith with long-term goals of a going concern, to instill a sense of the larger worthiness of what is being done in day-to-day operations. By contrast, the preceding chapters tell a story of developments in America's higher civil service that have been largely a form of collateral damage produced by the quadrilateral political contests sketched under point one above. One listens in vain for any sustained voice championing the values of the higher civil service as such beyond the immediate task of responding to political demands for reforming the bureaucracy. Cycles of reform do not represent a struggle with the institutional leadership of the civil service because there is no such presence at the table. Let us consider some examples of what existentialist philosophers would call the nonbeing of institutional leadership.

In chapter two, Dwight Ink emphasizes that the creators of the 1978 reform clearly recognized that without strong leaders, people who understood how to administer the new law with a long-term commitment to developing a professional career service, the reforms would accomplish little. But that is more or less exactly what has not been in evidence over the succeeding twenty years. Executive development and workforce planning appear to have been no one's priority. A corps of broadly experienced managers has not been created. Mobility has not increased as means of nurturing future executives. Instead, the reassignment process has gotten a bad name as a form of punishment

The closer look provided by chapters three through five reaffirms what Dwight Ink suggests: a tendency toward the very opposite of institutional leadership for the higher civil service. In chapter five, Ingraham and Moynihan point out that the idea of individual performance appraisal was the cornerstone of the 1978 reform of the civil service. But mismanagement made the cornerstone more of a stumbling block. Top careerists in the SES and their political superiors failed to provide coherent guidance, and the SES in general did not supply any reliable institutional linkage between individual performance appraisals in the ranks below them and organizational objectives set by political executives above them. The same authors describe the high expectations and dismal fate of the Office of Personnel Management. Created in 1978 with the hope of providing the presidential counterpart in personnel management to OMB's budget management, OPM has found its staff shrunk by almost half and largely bypassed in subsequent personnel reform efforts. Instead of an overall institutional intelligence embodying civil service values, one finds "a vacuum for a central body that can provide leadership in promoting the use of human resources management." Far from institutional leadership infusing civil service values into the task at hand, it is the task at hand—promoting short-term political responsiveness—that has infused the definition and evidence of successful performance (Ingraham and Moynihan; Aberbach and Rockman).

In chapter three, Carolyn Ban suggests something similar with regard to the Clinton administration's National Performance Review in the 1990s. In reporting on human resources, the NPR posits that SES members will be the drivers of the change in organizational culture that will make the "reinvention of government" a reality. Simultaneously, the OPM is to provide the corporate vision and policies supporting governmentwide "culture change." But as Ban points out, the main NPR report passes by the SES in silence as if having nothing to do with the reinvention of government effort. Buried away in other portions of the NPR's work are findings about the often poor relationships between career SES and political executives, about agency weaknesses in managing the SES itself, and about the dearth of generalist SES managers to carry out any government-wide change, cultural or otherwise. And as Ban politely observes, it is a questionable assumption to think that OPM has the knowledge, strength or respect to plausibly project any corporate vision for the higher civil service. To put it more bluntly, when it comes to NPR's view of institutional leadership, there seems to be a lot of hot air and bubble-blowing.

The closer one looks into the preceding chapters, the clearer becomes this common theme of absence in institutional leadership. Thus the continuing dismal record of such leadership for the civil service—from excesses of the administrative redress system to the blatant jobbery illustrated by Monica Lewinsky's government career—is one highlight of Chester Newland's chapter nine. In chapter six, Hal Rainey and J. Edward Kellough describe how the reformed civil service's incentives were too narrowly drawn as a "pay for performance" approach to the bureaucratic task at hand, an approach that according to Ingraham and Moynihan constituted a giant pilot experiment in transferring private business techniques into the public service while being ill-informed about how well such appraisal actually worked in the private sector (chapter five). Rainey and Kellough urge a broader incentive structure that would relate to matters of leadership and career development, overall organizational mission, public service motives, and public image of the civil service. But consider. In saying these are the things needful that are being neglected, one is also pointing to exactly those features that are of long-term significance for the viability of the higher civil service as such and not simply its short-term responsiveness to the bureaucratic tasks at hand. In other words one is talking about the pervasive lack of institutional leadership in the administration of the nation's business.

The matter of public image brings us to a third preliminary conclusion. It has to do with the American public more generally. In the background of all these chapters is a public that is disengaged from anything having to do with issues of the civil service. This may not be an entirely bad sign. In one sense it is subtle testimony to a basic level of success achieved during the 100-year development of the merit system in Washington. If the spoils system were rampant, rather than being largely held in check as it is against natural human avarice, we would probably see a good deal more public engagement in civil service reform and "good government" issues. Favoritism and other kinds of spoils in government employment are easy to understand. The more complex problem of sustaining a higher civil service fit for the ongoing management of truly imponderable program and policy issues is not so easy to dramatize for public attention.

However the American public does figure in the preceding accounts of civil service reform and operations. It appears off-stage, rather like a crazy uncle whose fits the various actors are trying to both exploit and placate. Typically we see this occurring as politicians have fanned the flames of the public's anti-bureaucratic sentiments. More recently reformers have cajoled people to think of themselves as customers being served by bureaucracy, rather than as citizens who invest power in government to do their public business.

In either case, it often seems from the preceding chapters as if the main role of the public is to be pandered to. And as Barbara Romzek points out in chapter seven, by the end of the 1900s this has led to a curious paradox. Repeatedly, the energy behind civil service reform has come from exploiting public dissatisfactions and distrust of government. But to produce outcomes satisfying to customer-client-stakeholders, bureaucratic discretion is to be freed from familiar forms of legal and hierarchical accountability. It is a situation resembling the spouse who claims he can dispel his wife's charges of adultery if only she will trust him more.

Romzek's description of four types of accountability makes clear that the higher civil service falls in between two stools as it inevitably deals with nonroutine as its daily workload (chapter seven). Either it can accept the trope of short-term political responsiveness or it can claim a specialized expertise that Romzek terms professional accountability. And as earlier chapters indicate, both are exactly how the postreform SES experiences have been portrayed. What the public is not prepared to accept, indeed what it has been persistently educated to reject in a political culture of bureaucrat bashing, is the idea that the civil service itself could be a high professional calling. Though never quite put this way, it appears unbelievably naïve to imagine there could be civil service professionals as such—that is to say, career people whose "internalized norms of appropriate practice" would have to do with respect for precedents inherited and in the making, with the long-term mission integrity of organizations, with keeping the machinery of government in good working order regardless of who wins the last or next election. In short, there does not seem to be so much as a wrinkled niche in the public mind for affirming the institutional values of high-level civil service work.

TWO CONCEPTIONS OF MERIT

If the arguments of the foregoing section are roughly accurate, then the "future of merit" is signposted in certain ways. We can expect that future will be more a byproduct of other political contests than an expression of concern for the merit system itself. We can expect there will be a lack of what we have been calling institutional leadership. This is no call to pessimism but simply an acknowledgment of the reality of the situation, for institutional leadership is not something that can be called into being simply because it is needful. As Dwight Ink observes (one suspects from many years of painful experience), poor leadership can destroy in months what it takes years for good leadership to build (chapter two). Finally, we can expect a large dose of public indifference and exploitable misunderstanding when it comes to bureaucrats in the higher civil service.

What then about the actual shape of that future? Several authors are fairly explicit about what they see on the horizon. Thus the one thing that Mark Huddleston's and Chester Newland's chapters agree on is that we are entering into a quite new stage for the federal civil service.

For Huddleston, globalization is drawing us into a threefold crisis of accountability, governance, and legitimacy. Looming ahead are de-nationalized forms of government. Huddleston argues these forms will likely veer into one, or even both, of two directions. The first foresees real governing as something that will be done by specialized, legal-rational elites who serve distinct international regimes and privatized customer-publics. The second, which may occur at the same time, is what the author calls "neomedievalism." This pattern of governance will resemble premodern forms of identity politics, a scramble for resources and cultural values among global fief-doms of patron-client tribes, high-tech Mexican *camarilla* writ large (chapter eight). In either case, one is given the strong impression that in this new world the ultimate duty of the federal civil service will be to turn out the lights on the American nation-state and close the door behind it as reformers seek to create a new global public administration to combat the new "warlordism." Perhaps it is time to take a few deep breaths of the depleting ozone layer.

For Chester Newland the new stage for public management is summed up in the term "facilitative state." Rather than itself determining and administering the collective actions of society, the emerging facilitative state will be a lean but strong mediator among economic and society institutions. A much tighter, focused intelligence in America's higher civil service will be called on to facilitate integrity in the rule of law, trustworthiness in the information all participants depend on, and strong regulations in the sustaining of effective global markets. What at first seems a contradiction in trends toward globalization and decentralization, Newland projects as a future opportunity for meritorious politics. In the new facilitative state, political appointees will be held to high qualifying standards, and civil service institutions will be central trustees for the norms of competitive merit, devotion to the public good, and adherence to fundamental law (chapter nine).

One has to read a little more closely, but spread across several other chapters in this volume is a third view of the future of merit. It is one that sees no breakthrough transition into a new stage of administration in public affairs but instead previews a story of recurrence. Thus whatever else happens, we are told to expect wavelike cycles of reform for correcting the excesses of the last round of good intentions. In chapter one James Pfiffner approvingly cites George Frederickson's projection of another reform wave to correct the conditions for fraud and corruption created by recent cutbacks in bureaucratic rules and controls. At the same time Pfiffner hopes we have reached at least a temporary equilibrium point in the rounds of debate over big government. With that one could expect restoration of the more traditional, ironic view of administration and politics whereby "the public service can return to its mission of faithfully executing the laws" (chapter one). Likewise in chapters three and five, the authors anticipate another turn in the life-cycles of administrative reform to correct the overemphasis on decentralization, or to cycle back and forth between individual-based and organization-based assessments of performance, between private and public scrutiny (chapter three; chapter five). Often, it seems, to reform is to toggle.

What then of the future of merit? In looking forward we may be sure that the future of merit will be written more by people's actions than by the words of academics. Two conceptions are vying, unequally it seems, for dominance. They have been doing so since the constitutional founding of the nation, even though buried during the twentieth century with ever deeper layers of political science and public administration jargon. The two conceptions might be called instrumental merit and substantive merit.

Let it be immediately said that Chester Newland offers a valuable warning (chapter nine) to the effect that we need to be careful not to suppose these are two absolutely disconnected conceptions. As theologians like to say about the three Persons of the Trinity, *distinctio non separatio*—distinct but not separate. But it is a distinction worth drawing as we try to think seriously about the future. In its un-disaggregated form, who can be against merit? Would one then be for unmerit? Could anyone dare to argue that merit does not have a bright future in a nation that celebrates personal effort and achievement?

The picture changes to become intellectually richer when we draw a distinction between merit instrumentally and substantively understood. The essence of instrumental merit is an evaluation process for job competence. The essence of substantive merit is attention to the constitutive standards for judging worthiness. Instrumental merit is means-oriented, seeking right skills for doing something. Substantive merit is ends oriented, seeking right character for being something. The idea of instrumental merit is a more modern development. It goes back to the nineteenth century and the invention of jobs as tools for organizing the rational technical means of bureaucratic effectiveness (in private business no less than the public sector). The idea of substantive merit is much older, traceable to ecclesiastical offices and clerics serving the great medieval monarchies.

Indeed much of the distinction between the two conceptions of merit could be encompassed in a more extended discussion of job versus office. Suffice it here to say that jobholding implies no larger vision beyond the working self and the task at hand. In a deep sense the concept of office subordinates self to larger normative responsibilities that cannot be captured by a list of job tasks to be performed. The skills package of a job are not the same thing as the duties of an office. A job is discharged by performing in accordance with assigned specifications. An office is discharged by understanding its customary and proper function. There is therefore a fiduciary quality in office-holding that is missing from job-holding. One is expected to understand what is expected of an office in light of the purposes of a larger scheme of things. It is something qualitatively different from "only doing my job."

In thinking about the historical record covered not only by this book but the various cycles that started with the 1883 Pendleton Act, there seems to have always been something slightly schizophrenic hovering around civil service reform. In reformers' heart of hearts it often appears to be the statesmanship of substantive merit that they yearn for. This is the result they sense will help the nation rise to its challenges, whether these be demands of a brash industrializing nation of a century ago or the globalizing superpower of the new millennium. But for purposes of pursuing both what is politically acceptable as well as what one actually knows how to do in designing personnel systems, it is instrumental merit that is reformers' preoccupation.

By now it is conventional wisdom to observe that Americans have never had a strong, European-style concept of the "State" and thus the odds have always been stacked against any substantive idea of a higher civil service. If anything is remembered about the *Federalist Papers* it is usually the idea of interest set against interest, of men not being angels and thus the desirability of the Constitution's institutional arrangements to correct for the defects of men's better nature. Such is indeed our country's urtext for the longstanding commitment to instrumental merit. But this leaves out half of the story in our founding schizophrenia. The other half is that the new constitutional arrangements were to serve as a "sieve of talent" for bringing forward men of republican character and virtue.[2] As the Constitution-makers saw it, poor institutional design had left republican government too directly dependent on the people and open to demagoguery. The new Constitution machinery would encourage the cream rather than the scum to rise to the top, not just good job performers but men worthy of approbation and thus worthy of office. Thus we would do well to recall that when pushed on precisely this issue of substantive merit versus clever procedural machinery (i.e., instrumental merit), Madison in the crucial 1788 Virginia ratification debate returned to bedrock civic virtue for his defense of the draft Constitution.

> I have observed, that gentlemen suppose, that the general legislature will do every mischief they possibly can, and that they will omit to do every thing good which they are authorized to do. If this were a reasonable supposition, their objections would be good. I consider it reasonable to conclude, that they will as readily do their duty, as deviate from it; Nor do I go on the grounds mentioned by gentlemen on the other side—that we are to place unlimited confidence in them, and expect nothing but the most exalted integrity

and sublime virtue. But I go on this great republican principle, that the people will have virtue and intelligence to select men of virtue and wisdom. Is there no virtue among us? If there be not, we are in a wretched situation. No theoretical checks—no form of government can render us secure. To suppose that any form of government will secure liberty or happiness without any virtue in the people, is a chimerical idea. If there be sufficient virtue and intelligence in the community, it will be exercised in the selection of these men. So that we do not depend on their virtue, or put confidence in our rulers, but in the people who are to choose them.[3]

Since Madison was speaking of relations between voters and their representatives, what one might ask does this have to do with unelected officials and substantive conceptions of merit? Quite a bit, because in essence Madison was speaking of citizenship as an office, indeed the highest office bestowed in the new republican form of government. Madison's comments are fully in line with the effort of George Washington and a few other leaders who persistently and unsuccessfully urged creation of a national university as the seedbed for substantive merit in many future generations of republican officials.

But the ratification debates were a long time ago, and the idea of a national university eventually languished amid the anti-elitist sentiments of popular democracy. Instrumental merit will most likely continue holding the privileged position into the future because it fits well not only with the demands of practical politics among an indifferent public but also with the predispositions of contemporary American culture. Instrumental merit of job performance rests comfortably with a procedural liberalism that focuses on right process, lest one be thought intolerant and judgmental about the worthiness of other people's life projects. When it comes right down to it, the substantive conception of merit *is* in an important sense intolerant. It discriminates. It is prejudiced in that it prejudges based on certain preexisting standards of meritoriousness.

If one asks what stands at the center of the professional code of a substantively conceived higher civil service, I think the answer is clear. It is the idea of the nation. On this crucial point I think Chester Newland leaves too much aside in contrasting the new facilitative state with the alleged pro-executive bias of the traditional civil service in the administrative state (chapter nine). The heart of the civil service idea is not so much pro-executive as pro-nation. The nineteenth century anti-spoils reformers came out of Unionist commitments, their civil service out of their Civil War sensibilities. The Garfields, Carl Schutzes, John Wesley Powells, and the like were nation-preservers who sought to press forward as nation-builders. The same perspective explains the particular spirit and elan of civil service idealism in the New Deal struggle with the Depression and then World War II. National emergencies and national challenges were seen to require national responses and national perspectives. Obviously being pro-nation and pro-executive could often amount to the same thing. But it could also mean telling a chief executive that an action would harm *the* (not "your") presidency, or that ill-considered aggrandizement of executive power would harm rather than help the management of public affairs in the long-run.

As a desideratum of government there is much to be said for rehabilitating the concept of substantive merit in the nation's higher civil service. This is especially true given all the other forces arrayed and pressing in the other direction of instrumentalism. There has been more than two hundred years of painful sacrifice in the American experiment to create a self-governing nation of the people—a people that stretches through time as the dead, the living, and the not yet born. Such a history is obligating. A long-term, institutionalist perspective on the nation is not something that ought to be lightly cast aside as an outdated notion. If it is only a simultaneous globalization and decentralization that lies ahead, then the American nation, as a nation, is in big trouble. Not only the hearts but also the heads of reformers are in the right place when they seek after the substantive statecraft of a "higher" civil service, higher in the calling to office and not merely responsive jobbers. Such a civil service voice is not something that can be provided by customer satisfiers. It is not something that can be provided by interest representatives, people with international ties and other loyalties that may have little regard for the American people. At the same time this is not necessarily a voice brought to the table by the nation's thousands of elected politicians. Those voices are inherently and inescapably localist. And in the general course of events they should be. A "de-territorialized" Congress or statehouse is no Congress or statehouse at all.

So should we then count on the one voice of the chief executive and his or her placemen as speaking from the national perspective? The track record of modern media presidents from Kennedy to Clinton should not reassure us that this is the place to look for an institutionalist perspective on national affairs. Nor can we count on occupants of the Oval Office to realize this is one of the voices they need most regularly to ask to hear. Few seem to have had the wisdom of Elizabeth I when she instructed her great advisor William Cecil in 1588:

This judgement I have of you, that you will not be corrupted by any manner of gift and that you will be faithful to the State, and that without respect of my private will, you will give me that counsel that you think best.[4]

On a superficial reading it might be thought the queen was simply identifying a set of job skills. That would be to miss the point. Any skills were mere derivatives from what such a person would have to be—incorruptible in faithfulness to the whole nation and unintimidated in confronting power with one's best knowledge of the truth of a given situation. In short, the four hundred-year-old injunction spoke to the weightiness of substantive merit we have been trying to highlight. But realistically speaking, from the preceding chapters this does not appear to be what is wanted in our higher civil service, not now and apparently not in the future. This much seems sure. Since Americans remain a largely self-governing people, any history the future writes about the present will not leave much room for making excuses. In the long run of things, the people will get exactly the government and form of merit that they deserve.

NOTES

1. Philip Selznick, *Leadership in Administration* (Berkeley: University of California Press, 1984), 17, 28.

2. Gordon S. Wood, *The Creation of the American Republic, 1776–1787* (New York: Norton, 1993), 506ff.

3. Quoted in James T. Kloppenberg, "The Virtues of Liberalism: Christianity, Republicanism, and Ethics in Early American Discourse," *The Journal of American History* 74 (June 1987): 9–33.

4. Quoted in Peter Hennessy, *Whitehall* (New York: Free Press, 1989), 345.

SELECT BIBLIOGRAPHY

BOOKS

Aberbach, Joel D., and Bert Rockman. *In the Web of Politics: Three Decades of the U.S. Federal Executive.* Washington, D.C.: Brookings Institution Press, 2000.

Aberbach, Joel D., Bert Rockman, and Robert D. Putnam. *Bureaucrats and Politicians in Western Democracies.* Cambridge, Mass.: Harvard University Press, 1981.

Ban, Carolyn. *How Do Public Managers Manage? Bureaucratic Constraints, Organizational Culture, and the Potential for Reform.* San Francisco: Jossey-Bass, 1995.

Bennis, Warren G., and Philip E. Slater. *The Temporary Society.* New York: Harper Colophon Books, 1968.

Burke, John. *Bureaucratic Responsibility.* Baltimore: Johns Hopkins University Press, 1986.

Burns, James M. *The Deadlock of Democracy: Four Party Politics in America.* Englewood Cliffs, N.J.: Prentice-Hall, 1963.

Caiden, Gerald E., and Heinrich Siedentopf, eds. *Strategies for Administrative Reform.* Lexington, Mass.: Lexington Books, 1982.

Cleveland, Harlan; foreword by Robert S. McNamara. *Birth of a New World.* San Francisco: Jossey-Bass, 1993.

Cooper, Phillip J., et al. *Public Administration for the Twenty-First Century.* Fort Worth: Harcourt Brace, 1998.

Denhardt, Robert B. *The Pursuit of Significance.* Belmont, Calif.: Wadsworth, 1993.

Dubnick, Melvin J., and Barbara S. Romzek. *American Public Administration: Politics and the Management of Expectations.* New York: Macmillan, 1991.

Finnemore, Martha. *National Interests in International Society.* Ithaca: Cornell University Press, 1998.

Garcia-Zamor, Jean-Claude, and Renu Khator, eds. *Public Administration in the Global Village.* Westport, Conn.: Praeger, 1994.

Gruber, Judith. *Controlling Bureaucracies.* Berkeley: University of California Press, 1987.

Hegel, G.W.F. *The Philosophy of Right.* Trans. T. M. Knox. London: Oxford University Press, 1949.

Holzer, Marc, and Kathe Callahan. *Government at Work.* Beverly Hills, Calif.: Sage, 1998.

Huddleston, Mark W., and William W. Boyer. *The Higher Civil Service in the United States: Quest for Reform.* Pittsburgh: University of Pittsburgh Press, 1996.

Huntington, Samuel. *Clash of Civilizations and the Remaking of World Order.* New York: Simon and Schuster, 1996.

Ingraham, Patricia W. *The Foundation of Merit.* Baltimore: Johns Hopkins University Press, 1995.

Ingraham, Patricia W., and Carolyn Ban. *Legislating Bureaucratic Change: The Civil Service Reform Act of 1978.* Albany: State University of New York Press, 1984.

Ingraham, Patricia W., and Barbara Romzek, eds. *New Paradigms for Government: Issues for the Changing Public Service.* San Francisco: Jossey-Bass, 1994.

Ingraham, Patricia W., and David H. Rosenbloom, eds. *The Promise and Paradox of Civil Service Reform.* Pittsburgh: University of Pittsburgh Press, 1992.

Kaplan, Robert D. *An Empire Wilderness: Travels into America's Future.* New York: Random House, 1998.

_____. *The Ends of the Earth: A Journey at the Dawn of the 21st Century.* New York: Vintage, 1997.

Kettl, Donald, and John J. DiIulio, Jr., eds. *Inside the Reinvention Machine: Appraising Governmental Reform.* Washington, D.C.: Brookings Institution Press, 1995.

Kettl, Donald, Patricia W. Ingraham, Ronald B. Sanders, and Constance Horner. *Civil Service Reform: Building a Government That Works.* Washington, D.C.: Brookings Institution Press, 1996.

Klinger, Donald, and John Nalbandian. *Public Personnel Management: Contexts and Strategies.* 4th ed. Englewood Cliffs, N.J.: Prentice-Hall, 1998.

Klitgaard, Robert. *Controlling Corruption.* Berkeley: University of California Press, 1988.

Knight, Richard, and Gary Gappert, eds. *Cities in a Global Society.* Newbury Park, Calif.: Sage, 1989.

Krasner, Stephen, ed. *International Regimes.* Ithaca: Cornell University Press, 1983.

Lawler, Edward E. *Pay and Organizational Effectiveness: A Psychological View.* New York: McGraw Hill, 1971.

Lipsky, Michael. *Street Level Bureaucracy.* New York: Russell Sage, 1980.

Macy, John W., Jr. *Public Service: The Human Side of Government.* New York: Harper and Row, 1971.

Meir, Kenneth J. *Politics and the Bureaucracy.* Pacific Grove, Calif.: Brooks/Cole, 1993.

Milkovich, George T., and Alexandra K. Wigdor. *Pay for Performance: Evaluating Performance Appraisal and Merit Pay.* Washington, D.C.: National Academy Press, 1991.

Mosher, Frederick. *Democracy in the Public Service.* 2nd ed. New York: Oxford University Press, 1982.

Nachmias, David, ed. *The Practice of Policy Evaluation.* New York: St. Martin's Press, 1980.

Nathan, Richard P. *The Administrative Presidency.* New York: Wiley, 1983.

_____. *The Plot That Failed: Nixon and the Administrative Presidency.* New York: Wiley, 1975.

Osborne, David, and Ted Gaebler. *Reinventing Government: How the Entrepreneurial Spirit Is Transforming the Public Sector.* Reading, Mass.: Addison-Wesley, 1992.

Peters, Thomas J., and Richard Waterman. *In Search of Excellence: Lessons from America's Best-Run Companies.* New York: Harper Collins, 1982.

Pfiffner, James P., ed. *The Modern Presidency,* 2d ed. College Station, Texas: Texas A&M University Press, 1998.

_____. *The Strategic Presidency: Hitting the Ground Running,* 2d ed. Lawrence: University Press of Kansas, 1996.

Redford, Emmette S. *Democracy in the Administrative State.* New York: Oxford University Press, 1969.

Risher, Howard, and Charles Fay, eds. *New Strategies for Public Pay: Rethinking Government Compensation Programs.* San Francisco: Jossey-Bass, 1997.

Rosenbloom, David H., and Patricia W. Ingraham, eds. *The Civil Service Reform of 1978: A Retrospective Evaluation.* Pittsburgh: University of Pittsburgh Press, 1992.

Schein, Edgar. *Organizational Culture and Leadership.* 2nd ed. San Francisco: Jossey-Bass, 1992.

Shafritz, Jay, ed. *Classics of Public Administration.* New York: Harcourt Brace College Publishers, 1969.

The Sovereign Individual: How to Survive and Thrive during the Collapse of the Welfare State. New York: Simon and Schuster, 1997.

Vaughn, Robert G. *The Spoiled System: A Call for Civil Service Reform.* New York: Charterhouse, 1975.

Weiss, Carol H., and Allen H. Barton, eds. *Making Bureaucracies Work.* Beverly Hills, Calif.: Sage, 1980.

Wilson, James Q. *Bureaucracy.* New York: Basic Books, 1989.

Young, Oran R. *International Cooperation: Building Regimes for Natural Resources and the Environment.* Ithaca: Cornell University Press, 1989.

ARTICLES AND BOOK CHAPTERS

Aberbach, Joel D., and Bert A. Rockman. "Clashing Beliefs within the Executive Branch: The Nixon Administration Bureaucracy." *American Political Science Review* 70 (June 1976).

_____. "The Political Views of the U.S. Senior Federal Executives, 1970–92." *Journal of Politics* 57 (August 1995).

Abramson, Mark, Richard Schmidt, and Sandra Baxter. "Evaluating the Civil Service Reform Act of 1978: The Experience of the U.S. Department of Health and Human Services." In *Legislating Bureaucratic Change: The Civil Service Reform Act of 1978,* ed. Patricia W. Ingraham and Carolyn Ban. New York: State University of New York Press, 1984.

"Antimissile Systems' Cost Test U.S. Ability to Pay, General Says." *Washington Post* (September 3, 1998): A4.

Ban, Carolyn. "The Crisis of Morale and Federal Senior Executives." *Public Productivity Review* 43 (Fall 1987): 31–49.

_____. "Q.E.D.: The Research and Demonstration Provisions of CSRA." *Policy Studies Journal* (Winter 1988–9): 420–34.

_____. "Research and Demonstration under CSRA: Is Innovation Possible?" In *The Civil Service Reform of 1978: A Retrospective Evaluation,* ed.

David Rosenbloom and Patricia W. Ingraham. Pittsburgh: University of Pittsburgh Press, 1992.

———. "Unions, Management, and the NPR." In *Inside the Reinvention Machine: Appraising Governmental Reform*, ed. Donald F. Kettl and John J. DiIulio, Jr. Washington, D.C.: Brookings Institution Press, 1995.

Ban, Carolyn, Edie Goldenberg, and Toni Marzotto. "Controlling the U.S. Federal Bureaucracy: Will SES Make a Difference?" In *Strategies for Administrative Reform*, ed. Gerald E. Caiden and Heinrich Siedentopf. Lexington, Mass.: Lexington Books, 1982.

Ban, Carolyn, Edie N. Goldenberg, and Toni Marzotto. "Firing the Unproductive Employee: Will Civil Service Reform Make a Difference?" *Review of Public Personnel Administration* 2 (Spring 1982): 87–100.

Ban, Carolyn, and Patricia W. Ingraham. "Retaining Quality Employees: Life after PACE." *Public Administration Review* 48 (May/June 1988): 708–18.

Ban, Carolyn, and Toni Marzotto. "Delegations of Examining: Objectives and Implementation." In *Legislating Bureaucratic Change: The Civil Service Act of 1978*, ed. Patricia W. Ingraham and Carolyn Ban. Albany: State University of New York Press, 1984.

Ban, Carolyn, and Harry C. Reed III. "The State of the Merit System: Perceptions of Abuse in the Federal Civil Service." *Review of Public Personnel Management* 10 (1990): 55–72.

Brown, Peter G. "The Legitimacy Crisis and the New Progressivism." *Public Administration Review* 58 (July/August 1998).

Brown, Robert W. "Performance Appraisal: A Policy Implementation Analysis." *Review of Public Personnel Administration* 2 (Spring 1982): 69–86.

Buchanan, Bruce. "The Senior Executive Service: How We Can Tell If It Works." *Public Administration Review* 41 (1981): 349–58.

Camp, Roderic Ai. "Camarillas in Mexican Politics: The Case of the Salinas Cabinet." *Mexican Studies* 6 (Winter 1990).

Campbell, Alan K. "Civil Service Reform as a Remedy of Bureaucratic Ills." In *Making Bureaucracies Work*, ed. Carol H. Weiss and Allen H. Barton. Beverly Hills, Calif.: Sage, 1980.

———. "The Institution and Its Problems." *Public Administration Review* 42 (July/ August 1982): 305–8.

———. "Reflections on CSRA's First Decade." *The GAO Journal* (Spring 1989): 9–13.

Cerny, Philip. "Globalisation as Durable Disaster." *Civil Wars* 1 (Spring 1998): 43.

Colby, Peter, and Patricia W. Ingraham. "Civil Service Reform: The Views of the Senior Executive Service." *Review of Public Personnel Administration* 1 (1981): 75–9.

Deleon, Linda, and Ann J. Ewen. "Multi-Source Performance Appraisals: Employee Perceptions of Fairness." *Review of Public Personnel Management* 17 (1997): 22–36.

"Democracy Is Inevitable." In *The Temporary Society,* Warren G. Bennis and Philip E. Slater. New York: Harper Colophon Books, 1968.

Deudney, David, and G. John Ikenberry. "The Logic of the West." *World Policy Journal* 10 (Winter 1994).

Drucker, Peter. "The Global Economy and the Nation-State." *Foreign Affairs* 76 (September/October 1997).

Dubnick, Melvin J., and Barbara S. Romzek. "Accountability and the Centrality of Expectations." In *Research in Public Administration,* ed. James Perry, vol. 2. Stamford, Conn.: AI Press, 1993.

Duffield, Mark. "Postmodern Conflict: Warlords, Post-adjustment States, and Private Protection." *Civil Wars* 1 (Spring 1998).

Ettore, Barbara. "Benchmarking: The Next Generation." *Management Review* 82 (June 1993): 10–16.

Finer, Herman. "Administrative Responsibility and Democratic Government." *Public Administration Review* 1 (Summer 1941): 335–50.

Fox, Charles J., and Kurt A. Shirkey. "Employee Performance Appraisal: The Keystone Made of Clay." In *Public Personnel Management: Current Concerns, Future Challenges,* ed. Carolyn Ban and Norma M. Riccuci. New York: Longman Press, 1991.

Frederickson, H. George. "Painting Bull's Eyes around Bullet Holes." *Governing* 6 (December 1992).

Friedrich, Carl J. "Public Policy and the Nature of Administrative Responsibility." In *Public Policy,* ed. Carl J. Friedrich and Edward S. Mason. Cambridge, Mass.: Harvard University Press, 1940.

_____. "Responsible Government Service under the American Constitution." In *Problems of the American Public Service,* Carl J. Friedrich, William Carl Beyer, Sterling Denhard Spero, John Francis Miller, and George Adams Graham. New York: McGraw Hill Book Company, 1935.

Gaertner, Karen N., and Gregory H. Gaertner. "Performance Evaluation and Merit Pay: Results in the Environmental Protection Agency and the Mine Safety and Health Administration." In *Legislating Bureaucratic Change: The Civil Service Reform Act of 1978,* ed. P. W. Ingraham and C. Ban. Albany: State University of New York Press, 1984.

Garvey, Gerald. "False Promises: The NPR in Historical Perspective." In *Inside the Reinvention Machine: Appraising Governmental Reform*, ed. Donald F. Kettl and John J. DiIulio, Jr. Washington, D.C.: Brookings Institution Press, 1995.

Garvey, Gerald, and John J. DiIulio, Jr. "Sources of Public Service Overregulation." In *Deregulating the Public Service: Can Government Be Improved?* ed. John J. DiIulio, Jr. Washington, D.C.: Brookings Institution Press, 1994.

Godwin, Phil, and John Needham. "Reframing Reform—Challenging the Assumptions for Improving Public Employees' Performance." *Public Personnel Management* 10 (Summer 1981): 233–43.

Gold, K. A. "Managing for Success: A Comparison of the Public and Private Sectors." *Public Administration Review* 42 (1982): 568–75.

Gore, Albert, Jr. "The New Job of the Federal Executive." *Public Administration Review* 54 (1994): 317–21.

Greengald, Samuel. "Discover Best Practices through Benchmarking." *Personnel Journal* 74 (November 1995): 62–73.

Greiner, Larry E. "Patterns of Organizational Change." *Harvard Business Review* 45 (1967): 119–28.

Hale, Sandra J. "Achieving High Performance in Public Organizations." In *Handbook of Public Administration*, 2nd ed., ed. James L. Perry. San Francisco: Jossey-Bass, 1996.

Harper, Kirke. "The Senior Executive Service after One Decade." In *The Promise and Paradox of Civil Service Reform*, ed. Patricia W. Ingraham and David H. Rosenbloom. Pittsburgh: University of Pittsburgh Press, 1992.

Hays, Steven W., and Richard C. Kearney. "Riding the Crest of a Wave: The National Performance Review and Public Management Reform." *International Journal of Public Administration* 20 (1997): 11–40.

Huddleston, Mark W. "Background Paper." In *The Government's Managers*. New York: The Twentieth Century Fund and Priority Press, 1987.

———. "To the Threshold of Reform: The Senior Executive Service and America's Search for a Higher Civil Service." In *The Promise and Paradox of Civil Service Reform*, ed. Patricia W. Ingraham, and David H. Rosenbloom. Pittsburgh: University of Pittsburgh Press, 1992.

Ingraham, Patricia W. "The Civil Service Reform Act of 1978: The Design and Legislative History." In *Legislating Bureaucratic Change: The Civil Service Reform Act of 1978*, ed. Patricia W. Ingraham and Carolyn Ban. Albany: State University of New York Press, 1984.

_____. "Of Pigs in Pokes and Policy Diffusion: Another Look at Pay-for-Performance." *Public Administration Review* 53 (1993): 348–56.

Ingraham, Patricia W., James R. Thompson, and E. F. Eisenberg. "Political Management Strategies and Political/Career Relationships: Where Are We Now in the Federal Government?" *Public Administration Review* 55 (1995): 263–72.

Kaufman, H. "Administrative Decentralization and Political Power." In *Classics of Public Administration,* ed. Jay M. Shafritz. New York: Harcourt Brace College Publishers, 1969.

Kellough, J. Edward, and Haoran Lu. "The Paradox of Merit Pay in the Public Sector: Persistence of a Problematic Procedure." *Review of Public Personnel Administration* 13 (Spring 1993): 45–64.

Kershaw, David N. "A Negative Income-Tax Experiment." In *The Practice of Policy Evaluation,* ed. David Nachmias. New York: St. Martin's Press, 1980.

Kettl, Donald. "Building Lasting Reform: Enduring Questions, Missing Answers." In *Inside the Reinvention Machine: Appraising Governmental Reform,* ed. Donald Kettl and John DiIulio, Jr. Washington, D.C.: Brookings Institution Press, 1995.

Kline, Ray. "Let the Cultures Grow." *Government Executive* (October 1998): 52–3.

Knotter, John P. "Leading Change: Why Transformation Efforts Fail." *Harvard Business Review* 53 (March/April 1995): 59–65.

Krasner, Stephen D. "Structural Causes and Regime Consequences: Regimes as Intervening Variables." In *International Regimes,* ed. Stephen Krasner. Ithaca: Cornell University Press, 1983.

Kravchuk, Robert S., and Ronald W. Schack. "Designing Effective Performance-Measurement Systems under the Government Performance and Results Act of 1993." *Public Administration Review* 56 (1996): 348–58.

Lane, Larry M. "Old Failures and New Opportunities: Public Sector Performance Management." *Review of Public Personnel Administration* 14 (1994): 26–44.

Light, Paul C. "Creating Government That Encourages Innovation." In *New Paradigms for Government: Issues for the Changing Public Service,* ed. Patricia W. Ingraham and Barbara S. Romzek. San Francisco: Jossey-Bass, 1994.

_____. "Watch What We Pass: 'A Brief History of Civil Service Reform.'" In *The Promise and Paradox of Civil Service Reform,* ed. Patricia W. Ingraham and David H. Rosenbloom, 303–25. Pittsburgh: University of Pittsburgh Press, 1992.

Lynn, L. E. "The New Public Management: How to Transform a Theme into a Legacy." *Public Administration Review* 58 (1998): 231–8.

Lynn, Naomi, and Richard Vaden. "Federal Executives: Initial Reactions to Change." *Administration and Society* 12 (1980): 101–20.

McNish, Linda. "A Critical Review of Performance Appraisals at the Federal Level: The Experience of the Public Heath Services (PHS)." *Review of Public Personnel Management* 6 (1986): 42–56.

Marshall, G. S. "Whither (or Wither) OPM?" *Public Administration Review* 58 (1998): 280–2.

Matthews, Jessica T. "Power Shift." *Foreign Affairs* 76 (January/February 1997): 61–2.

Milward, H. Brinton. "Implications of Contracting Out: New Roles for the Hollow State." In *New Paradigms for Government: Issues for the Changing Public Service,* ed. Patricia W. Ingraham and Barbara Romzek. San Francisco: Jossey-Bass, 1994.

Moe, Ronald C. "The 'Reinventing Government' Exercise: Misinterpreting the Problem, Misjudging the Consequences." *Public Administration Review* 54 (March/April 1994): 111–22.

Morgan, Douglas F. "Bureaucracy and the American Constitution: Can the Triumph of Instrumentalism Be Reversed?" *Public Administration Review* 58 (September/October 1998): 453–63.

Newland, Chester A. "The Politics of Civil Service Reform." In *The Promise and Paradox of Civil Service Reform,* ed. Patricia W. Ingraham and David H. Rosenbloom. Pittsburgh: University of Pittsburgh Press, 1992.

"North Korea Fires Missile over Japanese Territory." *New York Times* (September 1, 1998): A1.

Pearce, Jone L. "Rewarding Successful Performance." In *Handbook of Public Administration,* ed. James L. Perry. San Francisco: Jossey-Bass, 1989.

Pearce, Jone L., and James L. Perry. "Federal Merit Pay: A Longitudinal Analysis." *Public Administration Review* 43 (1983): 315–25.

Perry, James L. "Making Policy by Trial and Error: Merit Pay in the Federal Service." *Policy Studies Journal* 17 (1988–9): 389–405.

_____. "Merit Pay in the Public Sector: The Case for a Failure of Theory." *Review of Public Personnel Administration* 7 (1986): 57–69.

_____. "Strategic Human Resource Management:Transforming the Federal Civil Service." *Review of Public Personnel Review* 13 (1993): 59–71.

Perry, James L., B. A. Petrakis, and T. K. Miller. "Federal Merit Pay, Round II: An Analysis of the Performance Management and Recognition System." *Public Administration Review* 49 (1989): 29–37.

Peters, B. Guy, and Donald J. Savoie. "Civil Service Reform: Misdiagnosing the Patient." *Public Administration Review* 54 (1994): 418–25.

Pfiffner, James P. "The National Performance Review in Perspective." *International Journal of Public Administration* 20 (1997): 41–70.

_____. "The Public Service Ethic in the New Public Personnel Systems," *Public Personnel Management* (Winter 1999): 541–55.

Radin, Beryl A. "The Government Performance and Results Act (GPRA): Hydra-Headed Monster or Flexible Management Tool?" *Public Administration Review* 58 (1998): 307–15.

_____. "Varieties of Innovation: Six NPR 'Success Stories.' " In *Inside the Reinvention Machine: Appraising Governmental Reform*, ed. Donald F. Kettl and John J. DiIulio, Jr. Washington, D.C.: Brookings Institution Press, 1995.

Rainey, Hal G. "Assessing Past and Current Personnel Reforms: The Pursuit of Flexibility, Pay-for-Performance, and the Management of Reform Initiatives." In *Governance in a Changing Environment*, ed. B. Guy Peters and Donald Savoie. Montreal, Canada: McGill-Queen's University Press, 1998.

_____. "Perceptions of Incentives in Business and Government: Implications for Civil Service Reform." *Public Administration Review* 39 (September/October 1979): 440–8.

Riggs, Fred. "Public Administration in America: Why Our Uniqueness Is Exceptional and Important." *Public Administration Review* 58 (January/February 1998): 29–30.

Risher, Howard H., and Brigitte W. Schay. "Grade Bending: The Model for Future Salary Programs?" *Public Personnel Management* 23 (1994): 187–99.

Robisch, Thomas G. "The Reluctance of Federal Managers to Utilize Formal Procedures for Poorly Performing Employees: A Case Study." *Review of Public Personnel Administration* 16, 2 (Spring 1996): 73–85.

Romzek, Barbara S. "Accountability in the Public Sector: Lessons from the *Challenger* Tragedy." *Public Administration Review* 47 (1987): 227–38.

_____. "Where the Buck Stops: Accountability in Reformed Public Organizations." In *Transforming Government: Lessons from the Reinvention Laboratories*, ed. Patricia W. Ingraham, James R. Thompson, and Ronald P. Sanders. San Francisco: Jossey-Bass, 1998.

Romzek, Barbara S., and Melvin J. Dubnick. "Accountability." In *International Encyclopedia of Public Policy and Administration*, ed. Jay Shafritz. Vol. 1: A–C. Boulder, Colo.: Westview Press, 1998.

Rosecrance, Richard. "The Rise of the Virtual State." *Foreign Affairs* 75 (July/August 1996).

Rosenbloom, David H. "The Context of Management Reforms." *The Public Manager* 24 (1995): 3–6.

Ruscio, Kenneth P. "Trust, Democracy, and Public Management: A Theoretical Argument." *Journal of Public Administration Research and Theory* 6 (July 1996): 461–78.

Sanders, Ronald P. "Reinventing the Senior Executive Service." In *New Paradigms for Government: Issues for the Changing Public Service,* ed. Patricia W. Ingraham and Barbara S. Romzek. San Francisco: Jossey-Bass, 1994.

Schay, Brigitte W. "In Search of the Holy Grail: Lessons in Performance Management." *Public Personnel Review* 22 (1993): 649–68.

Siegel, Gilbert B. "The Jury Is Still Out on Merit Pay in Government." *Review of Public Personnel Administration* 7 (1987): 3–15.

———. "Three Federal Demonstration Projects: Using Monetary Performance Awards." *Public Personnel Management* 23 (1994): 153–64.

Tanner, Lucretia Dewey. "Fragmentation: A Quick Fix for a Failed Policy." *Government Executive* (October 1998): 53–4.

Thayer, Frederick. "The President's Management 'Reform': Theory X Triumphant." *Public Administration Review* (July/August 1978).

Thompson, James R., and Patricia W. Ingraham. "The Reinvention Game." *Public Administration Review* 56 (May/June 1996): 291–8.

Thompson, James R., and Ronald Sanders. "Reinventing Public Agencies: Bottom-Up Versus Top-Down Strategies." In *Transforming Government: Lessons from the Reinvention Laboratories,* ed. Patricia W. Ingraham. San Francisco: Jossey-Bass, 1998.

Thompson, Paul R. "Laboratories for Change: Lessons from Fifteen Years of Demonstration Projects." *Public Personnel Management* 22 (1993): 675–88.

Tinder, Glenn. "Can We Be Good without God?" *Atlantic Monthly* 264 (December 1989).

Tolchin, Susan. "The Globalist from Nowhere: Making Governance Competitive in the International Environment." *Public Administration Review* 56 (January/February 1996): 1–8.

Wilson, James Q. "Can the Bureaucracy Be Deregulated? Lessons from Government Agencies." In *Deregulating the Public Service: Can Government Be Improved?* ed. John J. DiIulio, Jr. Washington, D.C.: Brookings Institution Press, 1994.

Wolf, Patrick J. "A Case Study of Bureaucratic Effectiveness in U.S. Cabinet Agencies: Preliminary Results." *Journal of Public Administration Research and Theory* (April 1993): 161–81.

_____. "Why Must We Reinvent the Federal Government? Putting Historical Developmental Claims to the Test." *Journal of Public Administration Research and Theory* 7 (1997): 353–88.

DOCUMENTS AND REPORTS

Bowsher, Charles A. "Managing for Results: Achieving GPRA's Objectives Requires Strong Congressional Role." *Testimony [of Comptroller General of the U.S. General Accounting Office] before the Committee on Governmental Affairs,* GAO/GGD-96-79. Washington, D.C: March 6, 1996.

Derwinski, Edward. "Remarks on the House Floor." *Congressional Record,* H8460-75, H8463. 1978.

Clinton, William Jefferson, and Albert Gore. *Blair House Papers: The National Performance Review.* Washington, D.C.: GPO, 1997.

Federal Quality Institute. *Lessons Learned from the High-Performing Organizations in the Federal Government.* Washington, D.C.: OPM, Federal Quality Institute, 1994.

The Gallop Poll Public Opinion 1997. Wilmington, Del.: Scholarly Resources, 1998.

Gore, Albert. *Common Sense Government: Works Better and Costs Less.* Washington, D.C.: Third Report of the National Performance Review, 1995.

_____. *From Red Tape to Results: Creating a Government That Works Better and Costs Less.* Washington, D.C.: Report of the National Performance Review, 1993.

National Academy of Public Administration. *Leading People in Change: Empowerment, Commitment, and Accountability.* Washington, D.C.: U.S. Department of Health and Human Services, 1993.

_____. *Measuring Results: Successful Human Resources Management.* Washington, D.C: U.S. Department of Health and Human Services, August 1997.

_____. *Modernizing Federal Classification: An Opportunity for Excellence.* Washington, D.C.: National Academy of Public Administration, 1991.

National Performance Review. *The Best Kept Secrets in Government.* Washington, D.C.: U.S. Government Printing Office, 1996.

_____. *Reinventing Human Resources Management.* Washington, D.C.: U.S. Government Printing Office, 1993.

National Research Council. *Pay for Performance: Evaluating Performance Appraisal and Merit Pay*. Washington, D.C.: National Academy Press.

Reagan, Ronald. "Inaugural Address of President Ronald Reagan." *Weekly Compilation of Presidential Documents*. Washington, D.C.: GPO, Week ending January 23, 1981.

Report to the Congress by the Comptroller General of the United States. *Civil Service Reform—Where It Stands Today*. Report FPCD-80-38. Washington, D.C.: Government Printing Office, May 13, 1980.

Schay, Brigitte W., Craig Simmons, Evelyn Guerra, and Jacqueline Caldwell. *Broad-Banding in the Federal Government: Technical Report*. Washington, D.C.: Government Printing Office, 1992.

Sharon, Milton I., Director, Merit Staffing Review Team. *A Self Inquiry into Merit Staffing*. Washington, D.C.: U.S. Civil Service Commission, May 7, 1976.

Starr, Kenneth. *The Starr Report: The Independent Counsel's Complete Report to Congress on the Investigation of President Clinton*. New York: Simon and Schuster Pocket Books, 1998.

State of the World 1997: A World Watch Institute Report on Progress toward a Sustainable Society. New York: W. W. Norton, 1997.

U.S. General Accounting Office. *Agencies' Strategic Plans under GPRA: Key Questions to Facilitate Congressional Review*, GAO/GGD-10.1.16. Washington, D.C.: GAO, 1997.

_____. *Civil Service Reform: Observations on Demonstration Authority, the Use of Official Time, and the Administrative Redress System*, GAO/GGD-98-162. Washington, D.C.: GAO, September 1998.

_____. *Federal Downsizing: Agency Officials' Views on Maintaining Performance during Downsizing at Selected Agencies*, GAO/GGD-98-46. Washington, D.C.: GAO, March 1998.

_____. *Management Reform: Agencies' Initial Efforts to Restructure Personnel Operations*, GAO/GGD-98-93. Washington, D.C.: GAO, July 1998.

_____. *Management Reform Status of Agency Reinvention Lab Efforts*, GAO/GGD-96-69. Washington, D.C.: GAO, 1996.

_____. *Managing for Results: Enhancing the Usefulness of GPRA Consultations between the Executive and Congress*, GAO/T-GGD-97-56. Washington, D.C.: GAO, 1997.

_____. *Managing for Results: The Statutory Framework for Performance Based Management and Accountability*, GAO/GGD/AIMD-98-52. Washington, D.C.: GAO, 1998.

_____. *Performance Management: How Well is the Government Dealing with Poor Performers?* GGD-91-7. Washington, D.C: GAO, 1990.

_____. *The Results Act: An Evaluator's Guide to Assessing Agency Annual Performance Plans,* GAO/GGD-10.0.20. Washington, D.C.: GAO, 1998.

_____. *A 2-Year Appraisal of Merit Pay in Three Agencies.* Washington, D.C.: U.S. General Accounting Office, 1984.

U.S. Merit Systems Protection Board. *Federal Personnel Research Programs and Demonstration Projects: Catalysts for Change.* Washington, D.C.: U.S. MSPB, December 1992.

U.S. Merit Systems Protection Board. Office of Policy and Evaluation. *Adherence to the Merit Principles in the Workplace: Federal Employees' Views.* Washington, D.C.: MSPB, 1997.

_____. *Civil Service Evaluation: The Evolving Role of the U.S. Office of Personnel Management.* Washington, D.C.: MSPB, July 1998.

_____. *Federal Personnel Officers: Time for a Change?* Washington, D.C.: MSPB, August 1993.

_____. *Federal Supervisors and Strategic Human Resource Management.* Washington, D.C.: MSPB, June 1998.

_____. *The Rule of Three in Federal Hiring: Boon or Bane?* Washington, D.C.: MSPB, December 1995.

U.S. Office of Personnel Management. *Representing the Agency before the United States Merit Systems Protection Board: A Handbook on MSPB Practice and Procedure.* Washington, D.C.: OPM, 1984.

_____. *Results of Title VI Demonstration Projects: Implications for Performance Management and Pay-for-Performance.* Washington, D.C.: OPM, 1991.

_____. *A Strategy for Evaluation: The Civil Service Reform Act of 1978,* 134-06-6. Washington, D.C.: OPM, 1981.

U.S. Office of Personnel Management. Office of Workforce Information. *Monthly Report of Federal Civilian Employment,* SF113-A. Washington, D.C.: OPM.

U.S. President's Reorganization Report Project. Personnel Management Project, v.1. *Final Staff Report.* Washington, D.C.: Government Printing Office.

Volcker, Paul, Chair. National Commission on the Public Service. *Leadership for America, Rebuilding the Public Service.* Washington, D.C.: National Commission on the Public Service, 1989.

World Bank. *The State in a Changing World.* Oxford: Oxford University Press; Washington, D.C.: The World Bank, 1997.

CONTRIBUTORS

Joel D. Aberbach is professor of political science and policy studies and director of the Center for American Politics and Public Policy at the University of California, Los Angeles. He studies executive and legislative politics in the United States and abroad. He is co-chair of the International Political Science Association's research committee on structure and organization of government. He has been a fellow at the Swedish Collegium for Advanced Study in the Social Sciences, and he has been a senior fellow at the Brookings Institution and a fellow at the Advanced Study in the Behavioral Sciences. He is the author or editor of five books and fifty articles and book chapters.

Carolyn Ban is dean of the Graduate School of Public and International Affairs at the University of Pittsburgh. She was previously a member of the faculty in the Rockefeller College of Public Administration and Policy, State University of New York at Albany, where she directed the MPA program. She has also served as division chief of a research division at the U.S. Office of Personnel Management, and as a manager at Arthur Young & Company. She has served as a consultant to the World Bank and to several federal and state agencies. Ban has published broadly in the areas of public management and personnel policy, with a focus on civil service reform and reinventing government.

Douglas A. Brook is vice president, government affairs, for the LTV Corporation where he manages all aspects of the company's federal, state, and local government relations activities. Prior to joining LTV, Brook was acting director of the Office of Personnel Management and before that he was Assistant Secretary of the Army for Financial Management. Both appointments were made by President Bush. Prior to his government service Brook worked for several private sector organizations and served as an active duty officer in the U.S. Navy and retired from the Naval Reserve with the rank of captain. He is currently pursuing a Ph.D. in Public Policy at George Mason University.

Hugh Heclo is Robinson Professor of Public Affairs at George Mason University and former professor of government at Harvard University. He has also taught at the University of Essex in England and the Massachusetts Institute of Technology. He has worked in the Office of the Vice President and has been a consultant to the British Department of Health and Social Security, the National Research Council, the Office of Management and Budget, the General Accounting Office, and the Office of Personnel Management. He has written many books and articles on comparative government and social policy; his books have won the Woodrow Wilson Award and the Gladys Kammerer Award from the American Political Science Association. His *Government of Strangers* won the Brownlow Award of the National Academy of Public Administration.

Mark W. Huddleston is chair and professor of political science and international relations at the University of Delaware. He also has an appointment in the Institute for Public Administration of the University of Delaware's School of Urban Affairs and Public Policy and serves as a fellow in the International Union of Local Authorities Office of Research and Training. Huddleston is the author of several books and articles on the Senior Executive Service and related issues, including most recently, *The Higher Civil Service in the United States: Quest for Reform* (with W. W. Boyer). Huddleston's interest in globalization has been piqued in recent years by consulting adventures in Bosnia, Mexico, South Africa, Botswana, Zimbabwe, and Kazakhstan.

Dwight Ink was director of President Carter's Personnel Management Project, which designed the Civil Service Reform Act of 1978. His final report was based on recommendations of nine interagency task forces that he managed and included 120 recommendations. Most of those requiring legislation were included in the Act. Beginning his government career as a GS-9, Ink served in a series of positions in different federal agencies during which he progressed to an agency head at Executive Level II. He also served as vice president of two government corporations and chaired several projects. Over the years, Ink served in policy level assignments under seven presidents.

Patricia W. Ingraham is professor of public administration and political science at the Maxwell School of Citizenship and Public Affairs and director of the Alan K. Campbell Public Affairs Institute, Syracuse University. A former career civil servant, she has spent much of her academic career examining the issues related to reform of public management systems and structures. She is the author or editor of a number of books and articles related to these issues. Her most recent books are *The Foundation of Merit: Public Service in American Democracy* and *Civil Service Reform: Making Government Work.* She served as a staff member of the National Commission on the Public Service (the Volcker Commission). She is a fellow of the National Academy of Public Administration, and International fellow of the Canadian Centre for Management Development, and past president of the national association of the schools of public affairs and administration. She has won a number of awards for teaching and scholarship excellence.

J. Edward Kellough is associate professor in the Department of Political Science at the University of Georgia. His areas of expertise are in the fields of public administration, public policy analysis, and American politics. His principal research interests are in the area of public personnel management. He has published in a number of scholarly journals including *Public Administration Review, American Journal of Political Science,* and others. He has also published a book entitled *Federal Equal Employment Opportunity Policy and Numerical Goals and Timetables.* Presently, he is completing work on a second book that takes a broad look at affirmative action policy and is to be published by Georgetown University Press.

Donald P. Moynihan is a doctoral student in public administration at the Maxwell School of Citizenship and Public Affairs, Syracuse University. He is a Syracuse University Fellow, a John F. Kennedy Scholar, and a research associate with the Alan K. Campbell Public Affairs Institute. His research interests lie in civil service systems and developing a comparative international perspective on public sector reform. He received his M.P.A. from the Maxwell School, and B.A. from the University of Limerick in Ireland. Upon graduation from Limerick he received the Silver Medal for Humanities, the highest academic award from graduates of the College of Humanities. He has experience working in the Irish Civil Service and Shannon Development, an economic development company in the mid-west region of Ireland.

Chester A. Newland is the Duggan Distinguished Professor of Public Administration at the University of Southern California. He is a fellow and past trustee of the National Academy of Public Administration. He is a past national president of the American Society for Public Administration and an honorary member of the International City/County Management Association. He was editor in chief of the *Public Administration Review*, 1984–90. Newland was the initial director of the Lyndon Baines Johnson Presidential Library, and he served twice as director of the Federal Executive Institute. He was manager of the Labor-Management Relations Task Force in the Personnel Management Project that worked on the Civil Service Reform Act of 1978.

James P. Pfiffner is professor of government and public policy at George Mason University. He has taught at the University of California, Riverside, and California State University, Fullerton. He has written or edited seven books on the presidency and has published about fifty articles on public management, the presidency, and American national government. He worked as a staff member of the National Commission on the Public Service (the Volcker Commission) and is a member of the National Academy of Public Administration. In 1980 and 1981 he was special assistant to Jule M. Sugarman who was deputy director and later acting director of the Office of Personnel Management.

Hal G. Rainey is professor of political science at the University of Georgia. He has published books and professional journal articles on management in the public sector, with emphasis on leadership, incentives, organizational change, organizational culture and performance, and the comparison of organizations and management in the public and private sectors. His book *Understanding and Managing Public Organizations* won the Best Book Award of the Public and Nonprofit Division of the Academy of Management. His most recent book is *Advancing Public Management* (co-edited with Jeffrey Brudney and Laurence O'Toole).

Bert A. Rockman is the University Professor of Political Science at the University of Pittsburgh and is co-editor of *Government: An International Journal of Policy and Administration*. He has received from the American Political Science Association the Pi Sigma Alpha Prize for the best paper presented at the annual APSA meeting (1980) and the Richard E. Neustadt Prize for the best book published on the U.S. presidency (1985). He is a past president of the APSA's Organized Section on the Presidency and is presently on the executive board of the APSA's Organized Section on Public Administration. He is co-author with Joel D. Aberbach on *In the Web of Politics: Three Decades of the U.S. Federal Executive.*

Barbara S. Romzek is professor of public administration at the University of Kansas where she has served a five-year term as department chair. She is a member of the National Academy of Public Administration and is recognized for her publications on public management and accountability, which have focused on both civil servants and public employees directly appointed by elected officials. She has analyzed employment dynamics in a variety of work settings, from NASA, Congress, and the U.S. Air Force, to state social service agencies and local governments around the nation. Her most recent books include *New Governance for Rural America: Creating Intergovernmental Partnerships* (with Beryl Radin and Associates) and *New Paradigms for Government: Issues for the Changing Public Service* (with Patricia Ingraham).

INDEX

NOTE: Page numbers in *italics* refer to tables and figures.